SCOTLAND

AZ VISITORS' ATLAS and GUIDE

D0334229

CONTENTS

Glenfinnan Monument, Loch Shiel, Glenfinnan

Geographers' A-Z Map Company Ltd.
Fairfield Road, Borough Green,
Sevenoaks, Kent TN15 8PP
01732 781000 (Enquiries & Trade Sales)
01732 783422 (Retail Sales)

www.az.co.uk

Edition 5 2014
Copyright © Geographers' A-Z Map Company Ltd.

MOTORWAY	**M9**
MOTORWAY UNDER CONSTRUCTION	
MOTORWAY PROPOSED	
MOTORWAY JUNCTIONS WITH NUMBERS	**6**
Unlimited interchange	**6**
Limited interchange	**7**
MAJOR ROAD SERVICE AREA (with 24 hour Facilities)	DREGHORN **(S)**
MOTORWAY SERVICE AREA	HARTHILL **(S)**
with access from one carriageway only	**(S)**
PRIMARY ROUTE	A82
PRIMARY ROUTE DESTINATION	**PERTH**
DUAL CARRIAGEWAYS (A & B Roads)	
CLASS A ROAD	**A701**
CLASS B ROAD	**B7009**
NARROW MAJOR ROAD (Passing Places)	
MAJOR ROADS UNDER CONSTRUCTION	
MAJOR ROADS PROPOSED	
SAFETY CAMERAS WITH SPEED LIMITS	
Single Camera	30
Multiple Cameras located along road	50
Single & Multiple Variable Speed Cameras	V V

FUEL STATION	
GRADIENT 1:5 (20%) & STEEPER (Ascent in direction of arrow)	«
TOLL	*TOLL*
MILEAGE BETWEEN MARKERS	8
RAILWAY AND STATION	
LEVEL CROSSING AND TUNNEL	
RIVER OR CANAL	
COUNTY OR UNITARY AUTHORITY BOUNDARY	
NATIONAL BOUNDARY	+
BUILT-UP AREA	
VILLAGE OR HAMLET	
WOODED AREA	
SPOT HEIGHT IN FEET	• 813
RELIEF OVER 400' (122M)	
NATIONAL GRID REFERENCE (Kilometres)	100
PAGE CONTINUATION	48
AREAS COVERED BY TOWN AND HOLIDAY RESORT PLANS	

TOURIST INFORMATION

AIRPORT	✈
AIRFIELD	+
HELIPORT	
BATTLE SITE AND DATE	⚔ *1066*
CASTLE (Open to Public)	
CASTLE WITH GARDEN (Open to Public)	
CATHEDRAL, ABBEY, CHURCH, FRIARY, PRIORY	✝
COUNTRY PARK	
FERRY (Vehicular)	
Please contact ferry operator for crossing times (Foot only)	
GARDEN (Open to Public)	❀
GOLF COURSE 9 HOLE 18 HOLE	
HISTORIC BUILDING (Open to Public)	
HISTORIC BUILDING WITH GARDEN (Open to Public)	
HORSE RACECOURSE	
LIGHTHOUSE	
MOTOR RACING CIRCUIT	

MUSEUM, ART GALLERY	
NATIONAL PARK	
NATIONAL TRUST PROPERTY (Always Open)	*NT*
(Restricted Opening)	*NT*
(National Trust for Scotland)	*NTS* *NTS*
NATURE RESERVE OR BIRD SANCTUARY	
NATURE TRAIL OR FOREST WALK	
PLACE OF INTEREST	*Monument* •
PICNIC SITE	
RAILWAY, STEAM OR NARROW GAUGE	
THEME PARK	
TOURIST / VISIT SCOTLAND INFORMATION CENTRE	ℹ
VIEWPOINT	
VISITOR INFORMATION CENTRE	V
WILDLIFE PARK	
WINDMILL	
ZOO OR SAFARI PARK	

SCALE

1: 200,000   3.156 Miles to 1 inch (2.54 cm) / 2 Km (1.243 Miles) to 1 cm

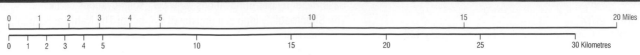

0 1 2 3 4 5   10   15   20 Miles

0 1 2 3 4 5   10   15   20   25   30 Kilometres

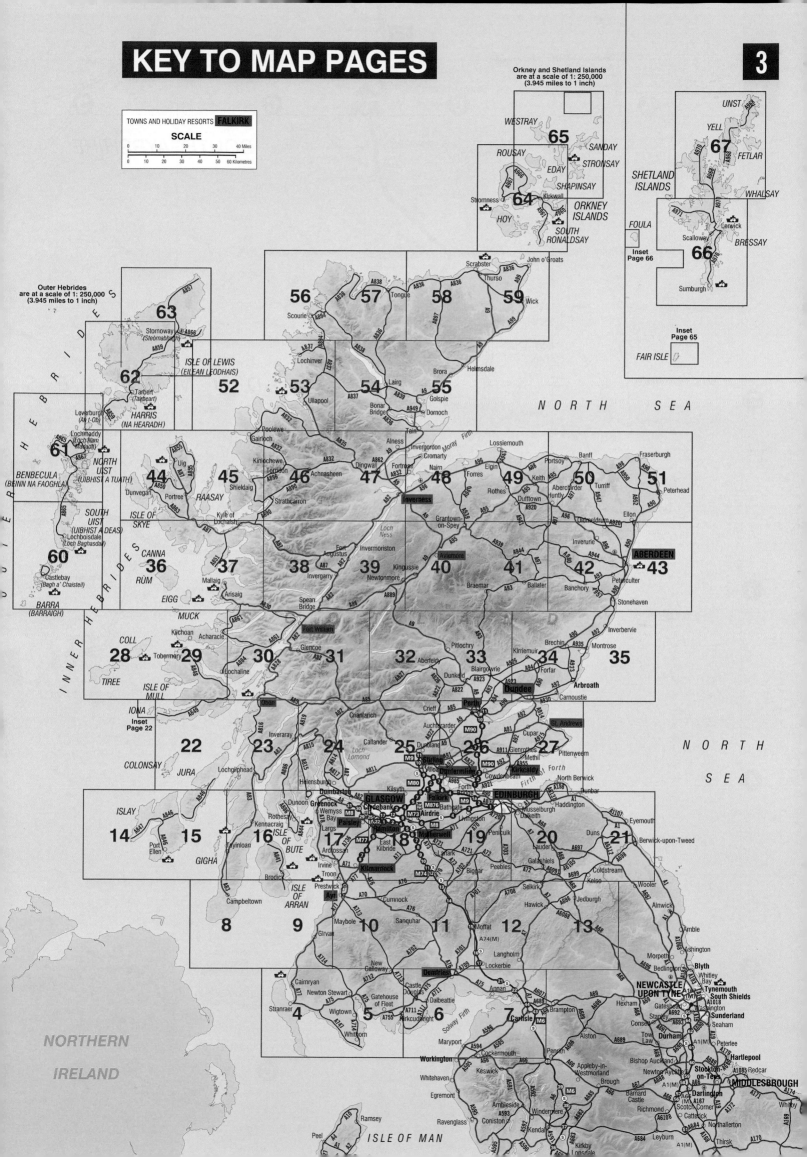

KEY TO MAP PAGES

TOWNS AND HOLIDAY RESORTS **FALKIRK**

SCALE

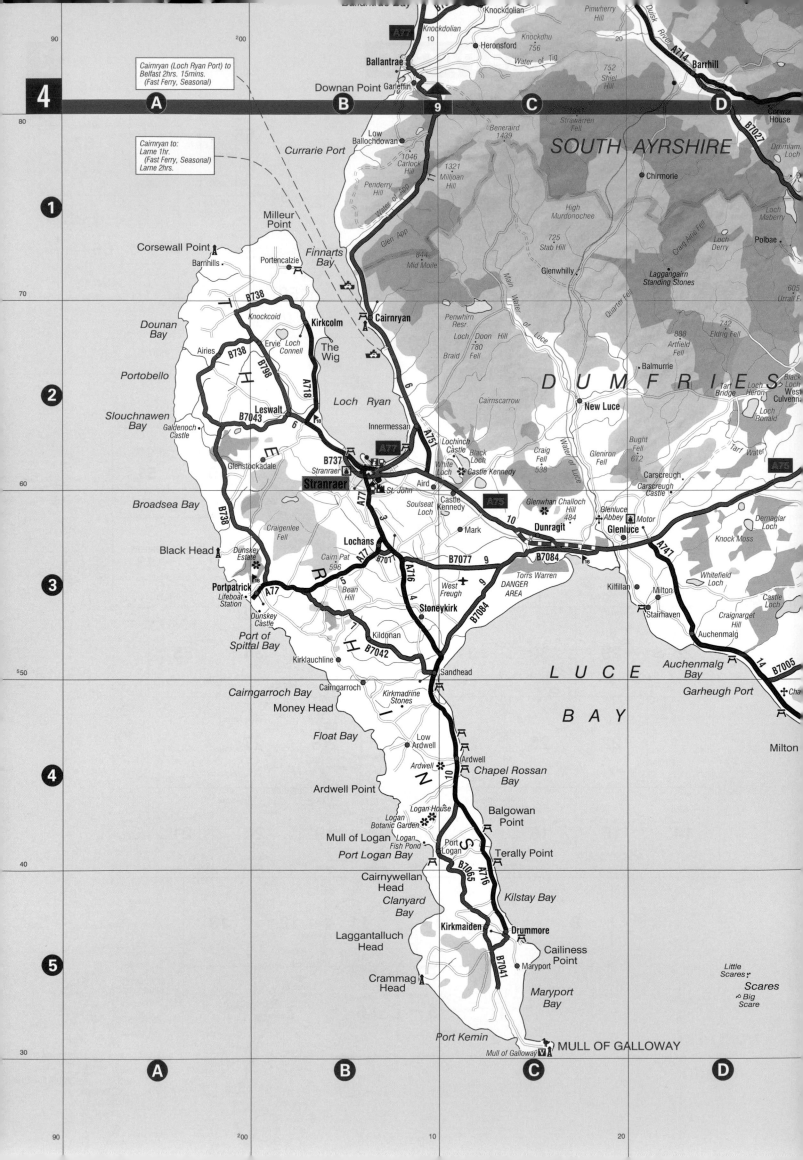

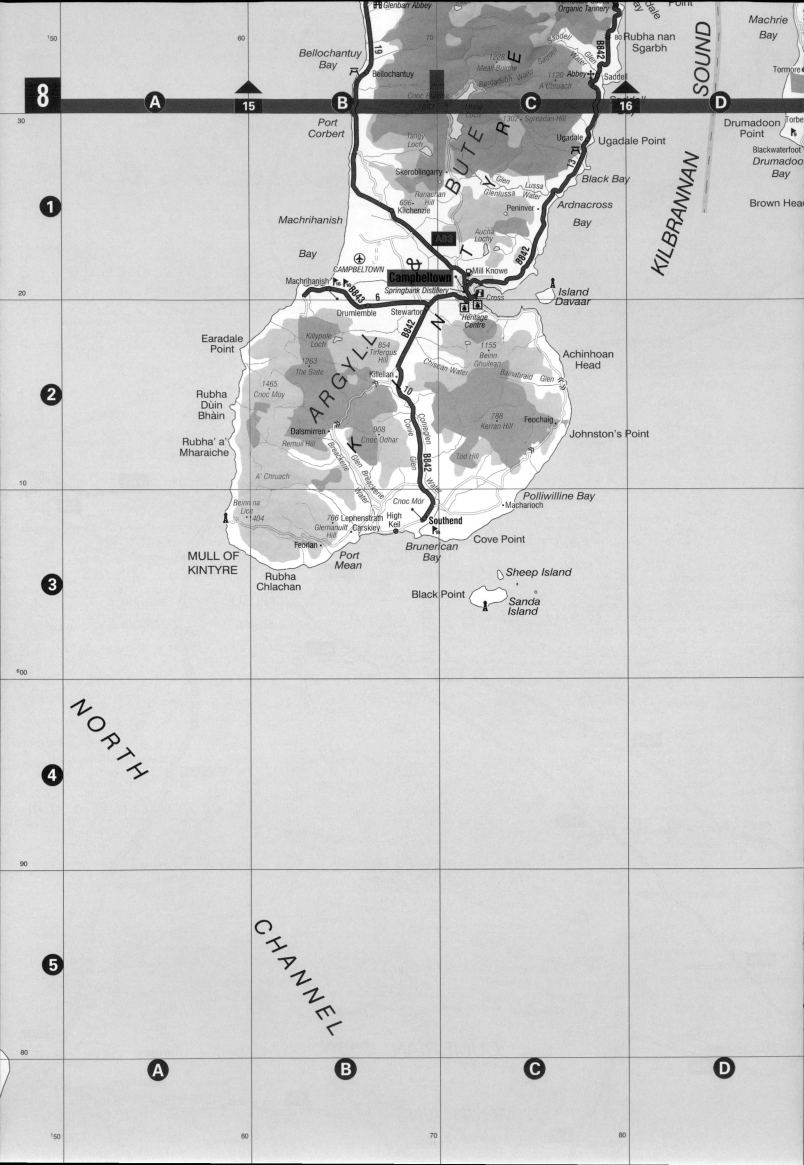

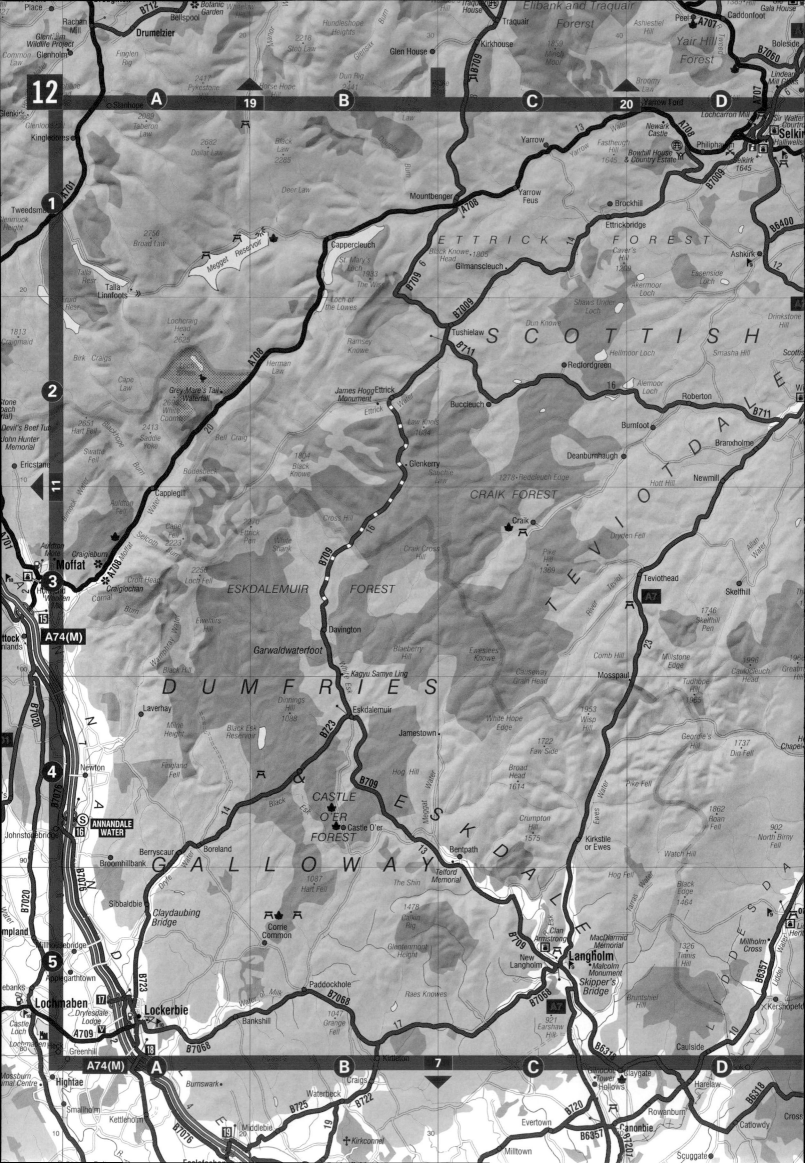

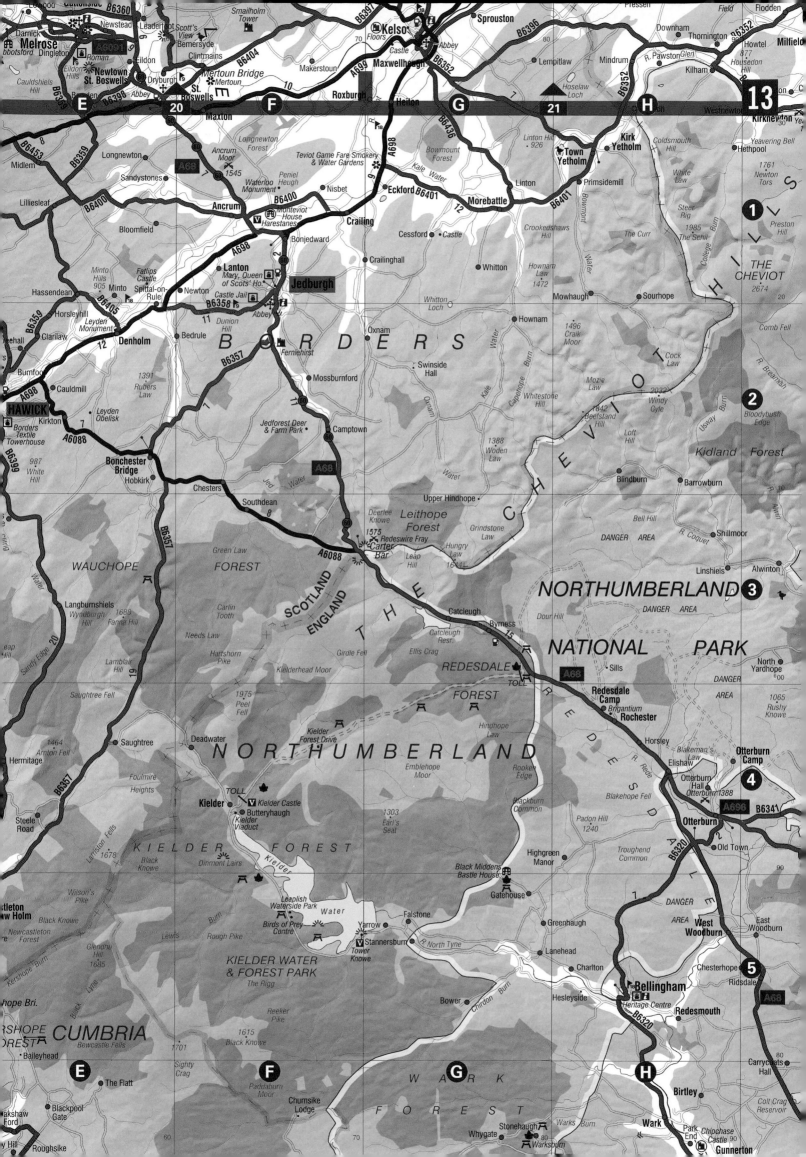

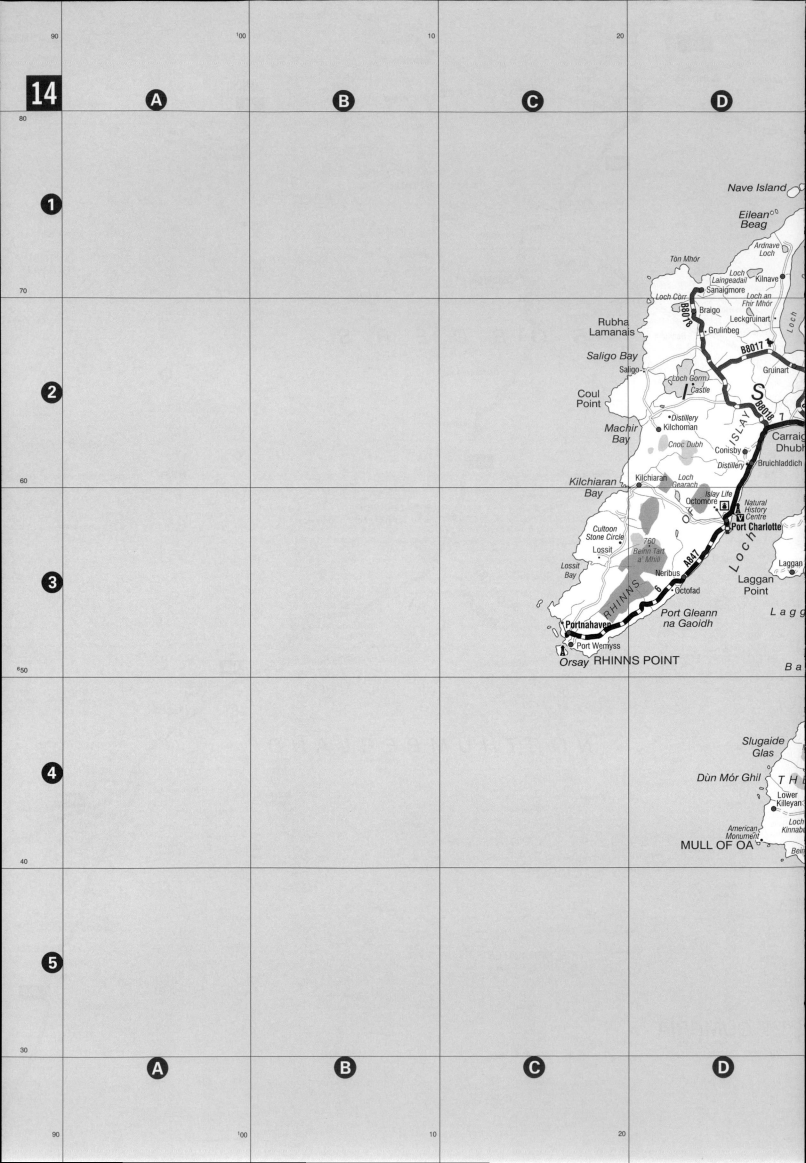

Nave Island

Eilean Beag

Ardnave Loch

Tòn Mhór

Loch Laingeadail   Kilnave

Loch Còrr   Sanaigmore   Loch an Fhir Mhór

Braigo   Leckgruinart   Loch

B8018

Rubha Lamanais

Grulinbeg

B8017

Saligo Bay

Saligo   Loch Gorm   Gruinart

Coul Point   Castle

ISLAY

Distillery   B8018

Machir Bay   Kilchoman   S

Cnoc Dubh   Conisby   Carraig Dhubh

Distillery   Bruichladdich

Kilchiaran   Kilchiaran   Loch Gearach

Bay   Islay Life   Natural History Centre

Octomore   Port Charlotte

Cultoon Stone Circle   760 Beinn Tart a' Mhill   Loch

Lossit   Laggan

Lossit Bay   Neribus   A847   Laggan Point   Lagg

RHINNS   Octofad

Portnahaven   Port Gleann na Gaoidh

Port Wemyss

Orsay   RHINNS POINT   Ba

Slugaide Glas

Dùn Mór Ghil   TH

Lower Killeyan

American Monument   Loch Kinnab

MULL OF OA   Bei

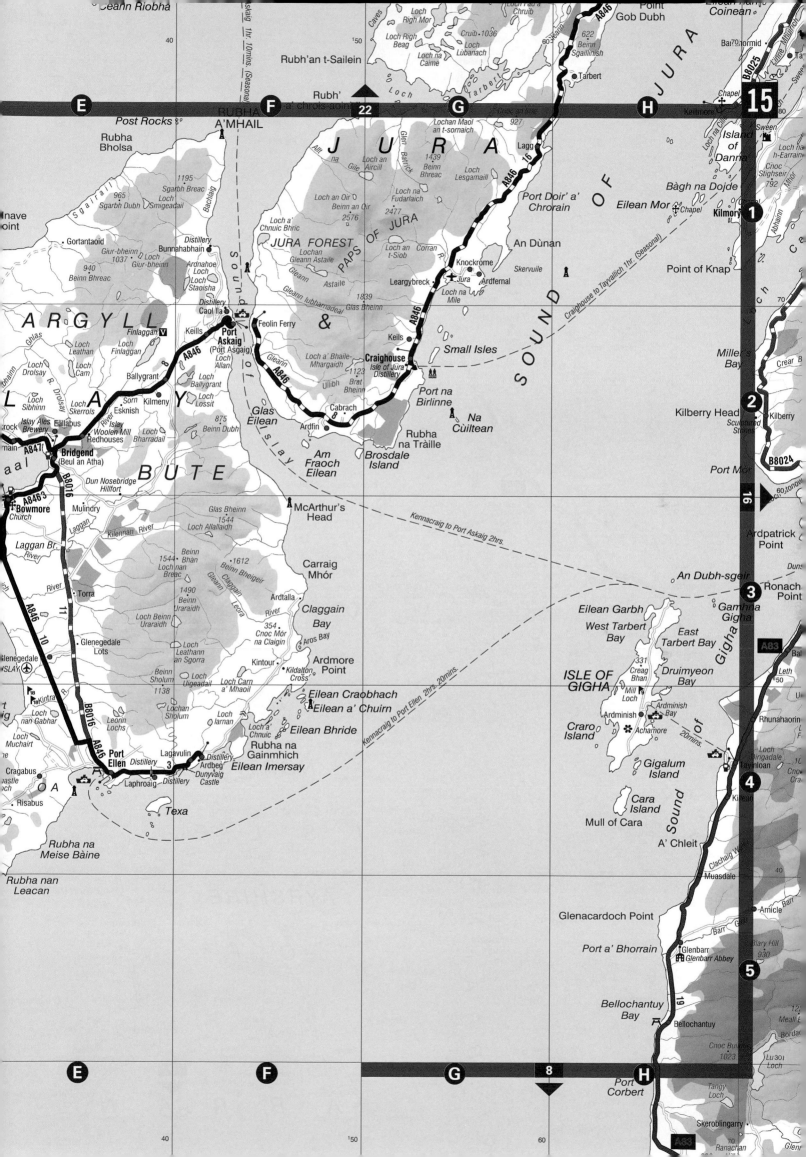

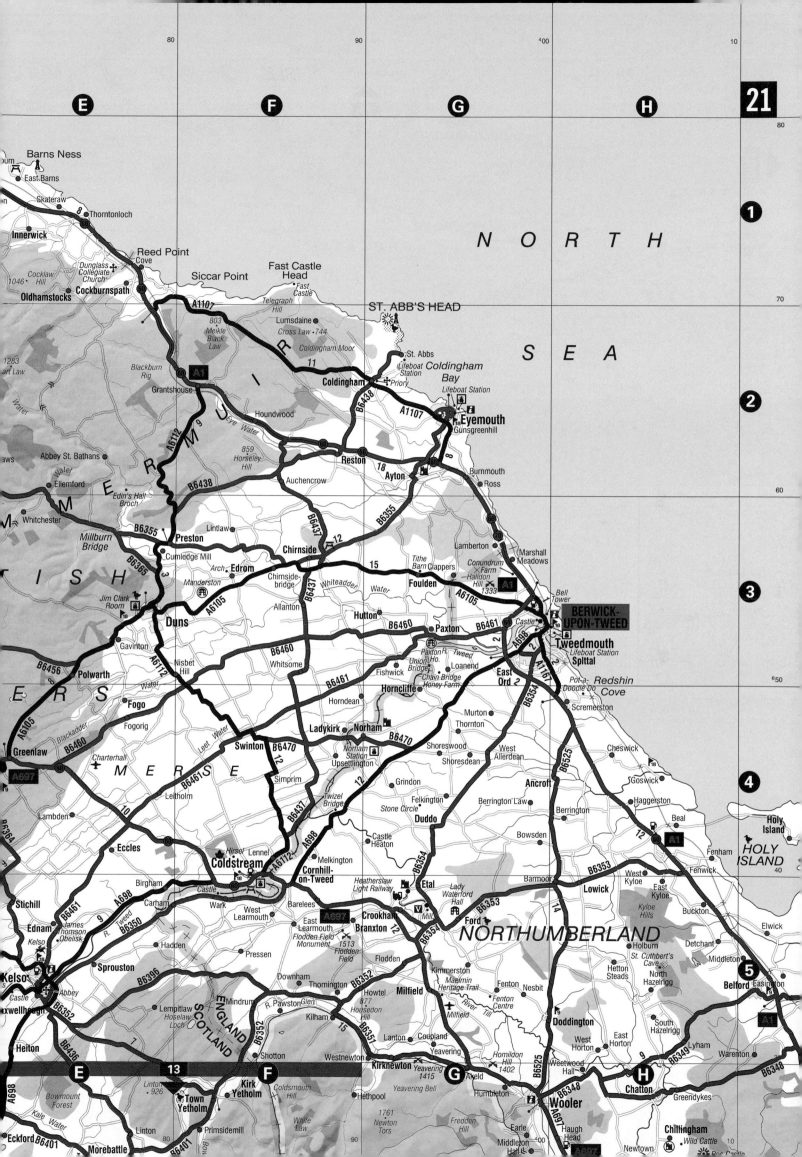

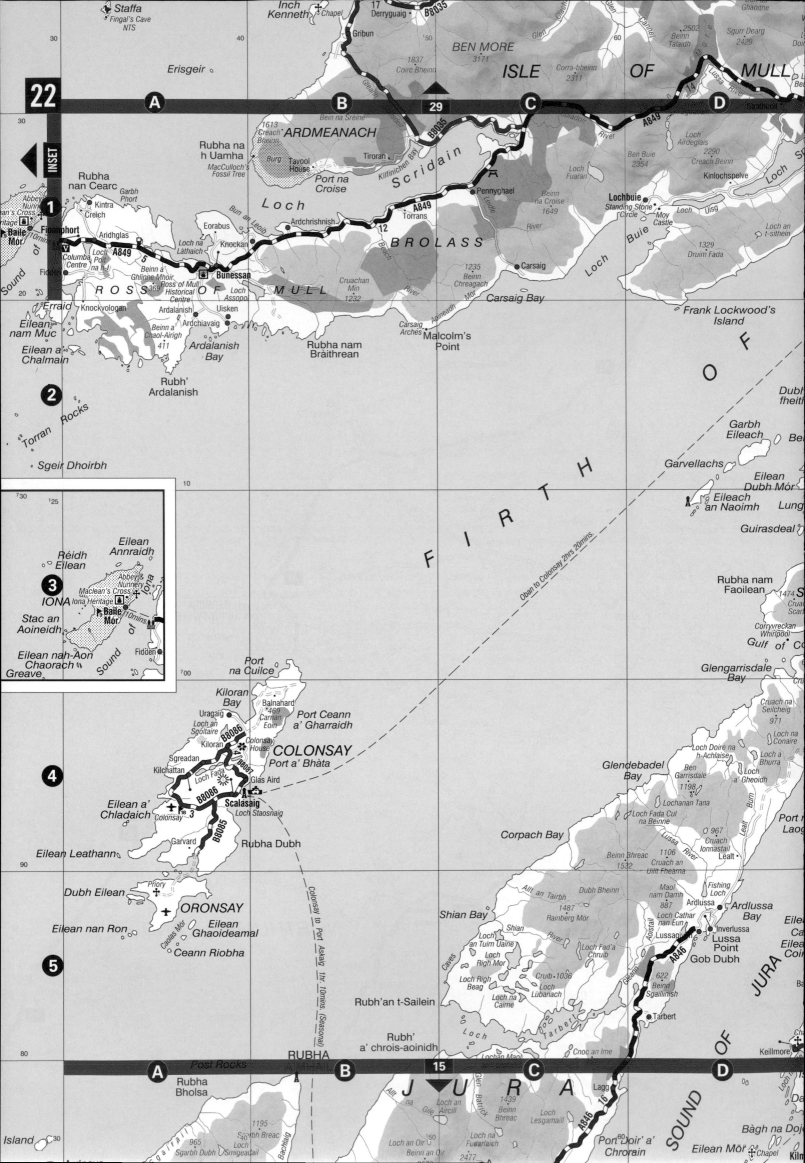

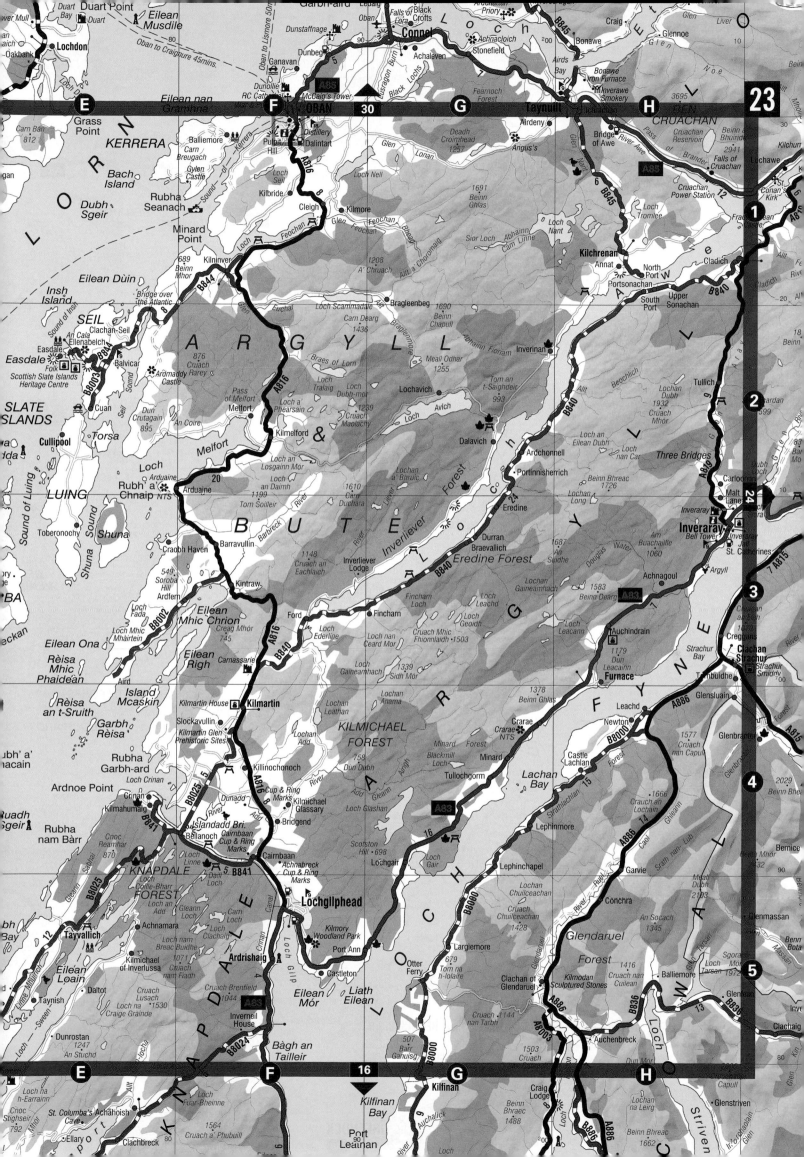

Oban to
Lochboisdale 5hrs. 20mins.
(Seasonal)

Oban to
Castlebay 5hrs.

1

2

Ca

Eag na
Maoile
Eile

Rubha Mór
Bousd
Cornaigmore
Sorisdale

Rubh'a' Bhinnein
B8072
Loch
Fada

COLL

Cliad Bay

Grishipoll
Rubha Hogh
B8071
Clabhach
Loch Cliad
Bagh Feisdlum

Hogh Bay
340
Ben
Nogh
B8071
Arinagour
Totronald V Stables
Loch nan
Cinneachan
Loch Fatharna

Tiree to
Barra 2hrs. 45mins.
(Seasonal)

3
Loch
Anlaimh
Acha
B8070
Eilean
Ornsay
Coll
Uig
5
Port na h-Eathar
Feall
Bay
Oban to Tiree 3hrs. 20mins. (Seasonal)

Calgary Point
Port na
h-Eathar
Gunna
Caolas Ban
Crossapol
Bay
Loch Breachacha
Friesland
Bay

Gunna
Port
a' Mhurain
Soa

Coll to Tiree 55mins.
Miodar
Carnan
Rubhà Dubh

H E B R

Hough
Skerries
Balephetrish
Bay
Vaul
Bay
Salum
Caolas
Cornaigmore
Balephetrish
Vaul
B8069
Ruaig
Sraid Ruadh
Loch
Riaghain
5
Kirkapol
Balevullin
Gott
Gott Bay
Hough
Kilmoluaig
Cornaigbeg
Kenovay
5
B8068
TIREE
(Port Adhair Thiriodh)

4
Kilkenneth
B8068
Loch an
Eilein
An Iodhlann
B8065
Scarinish
Baugh
Rubha Tràigh
an Duin
Sandaig
Moss
Heylipol
Crossapol
Heanish
Middleton
Barrapol
Island Life
B8065
2
Port Mor
Port
Bharrapool
Loch a'
Phuill
B8067
3
Hynish
Bay
TIREE
Balephuil
Balemartine
B8067
3
Mannal
Balephuil
Bay
West
Hynish
Hynish
Port Snoig
Skerryvore
Lighthouse

I N N E R

Treshnish Isle
Lun

Bac Mor or
Dutchman's Cap
Bac Beag

5

Eilea
Annrai
Réidh
Eilean
Abbey

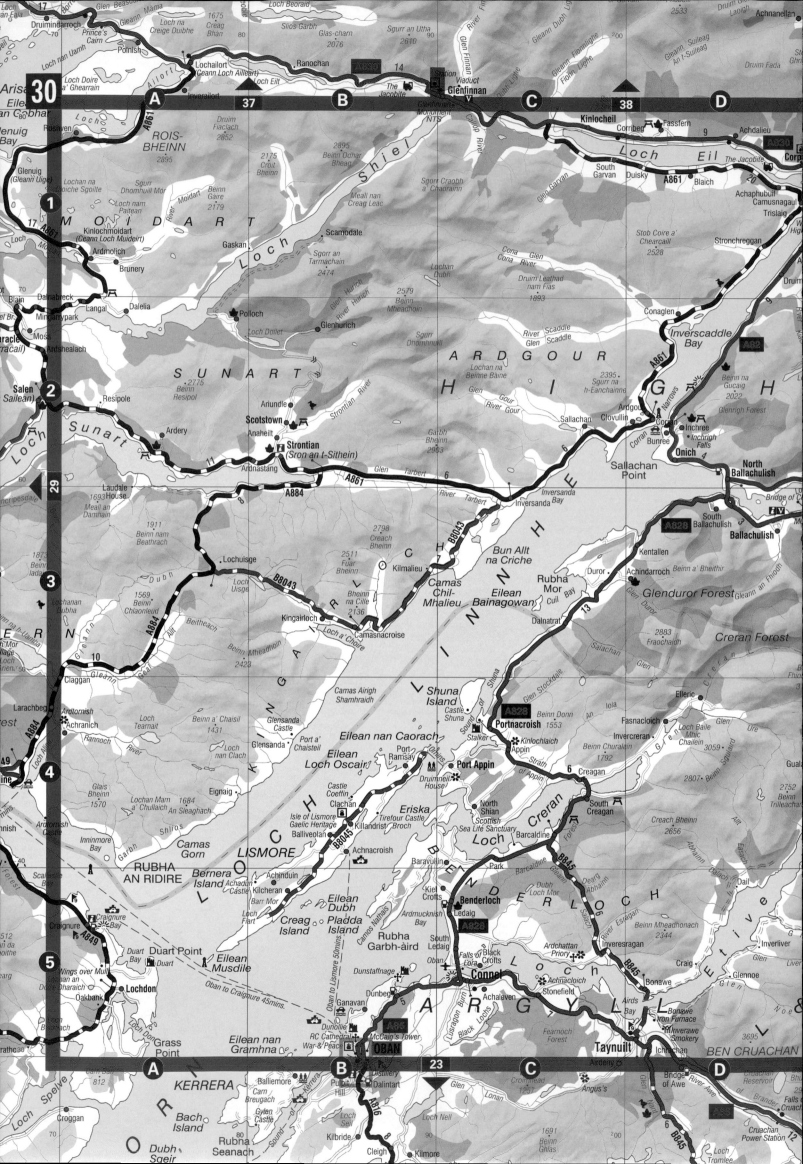

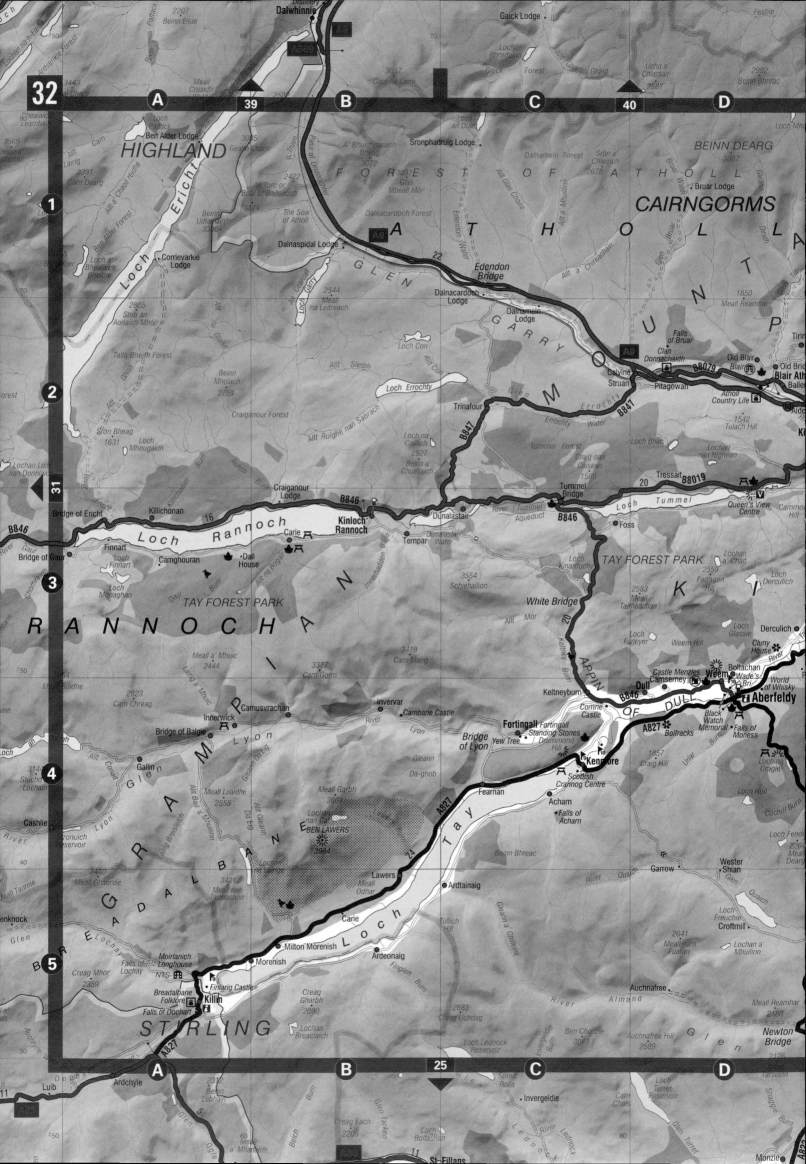

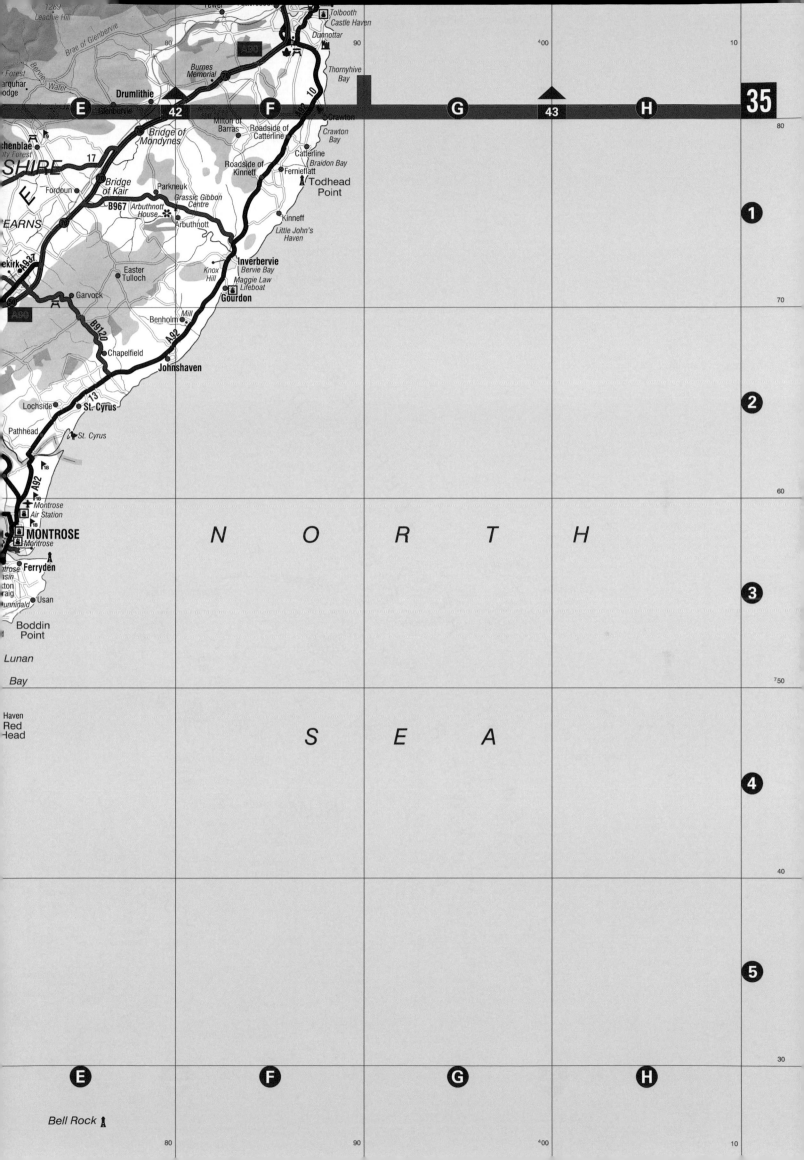

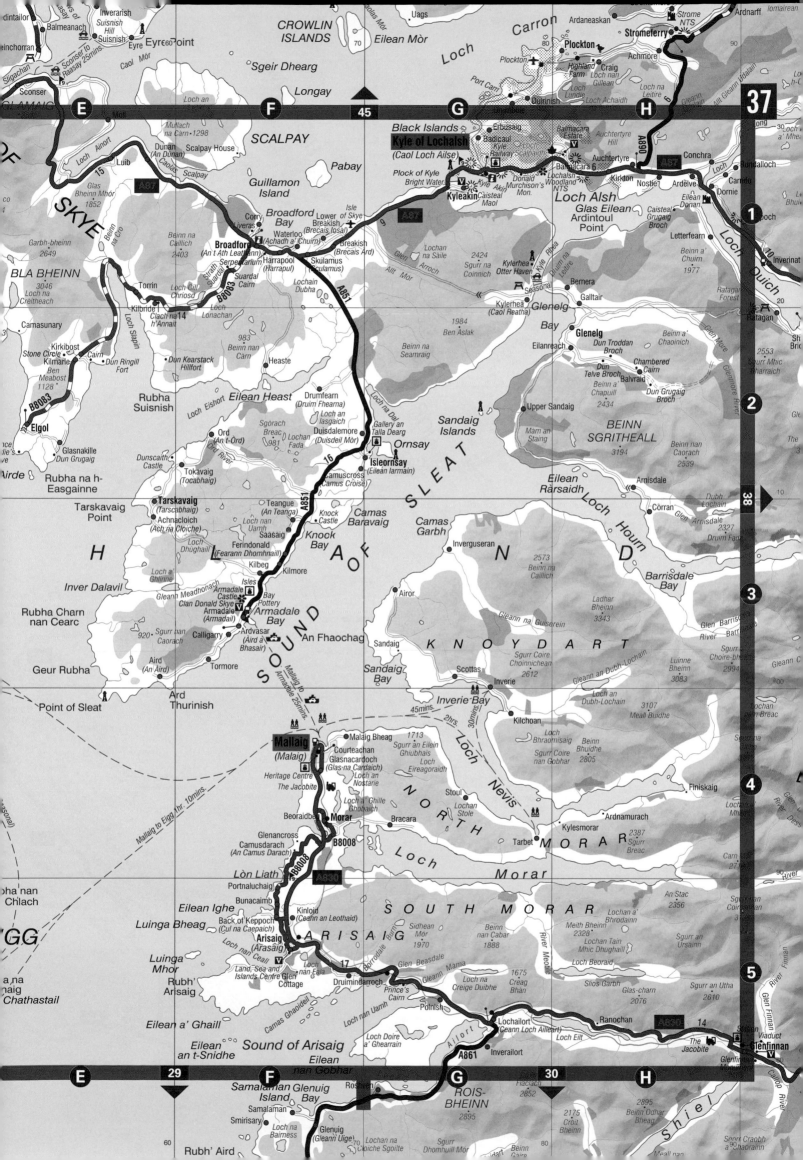

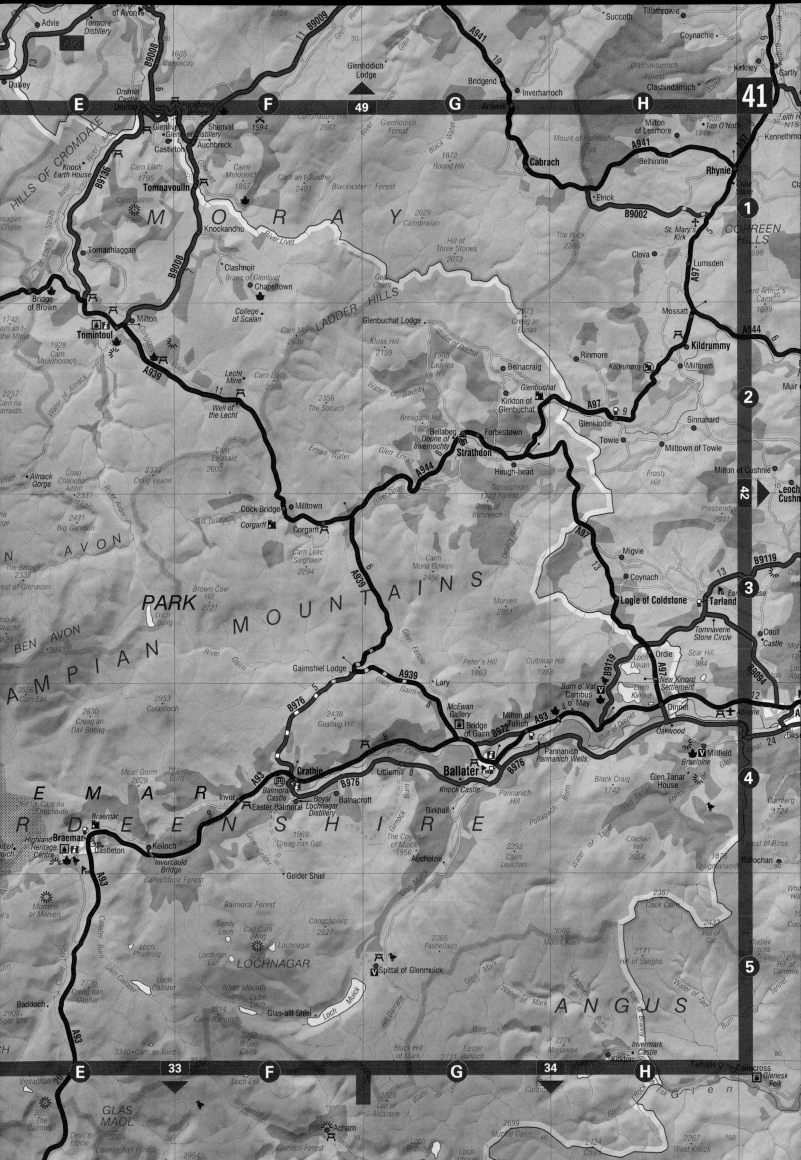

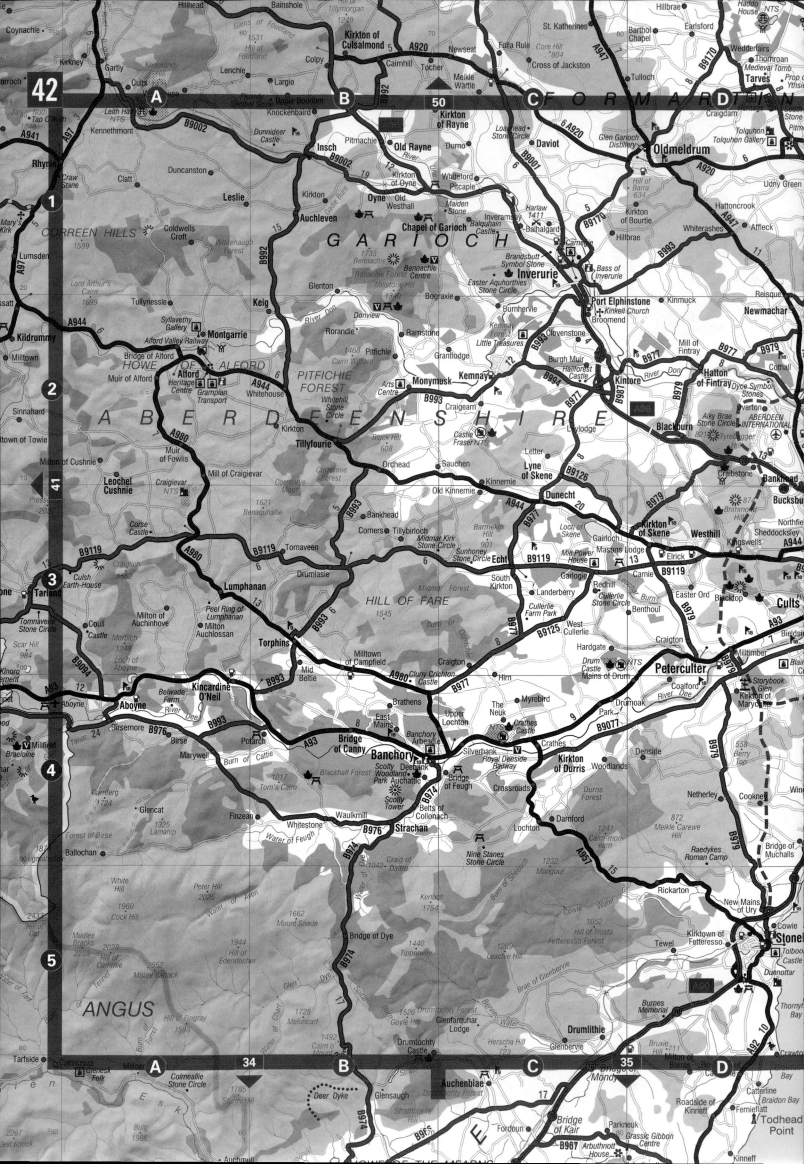

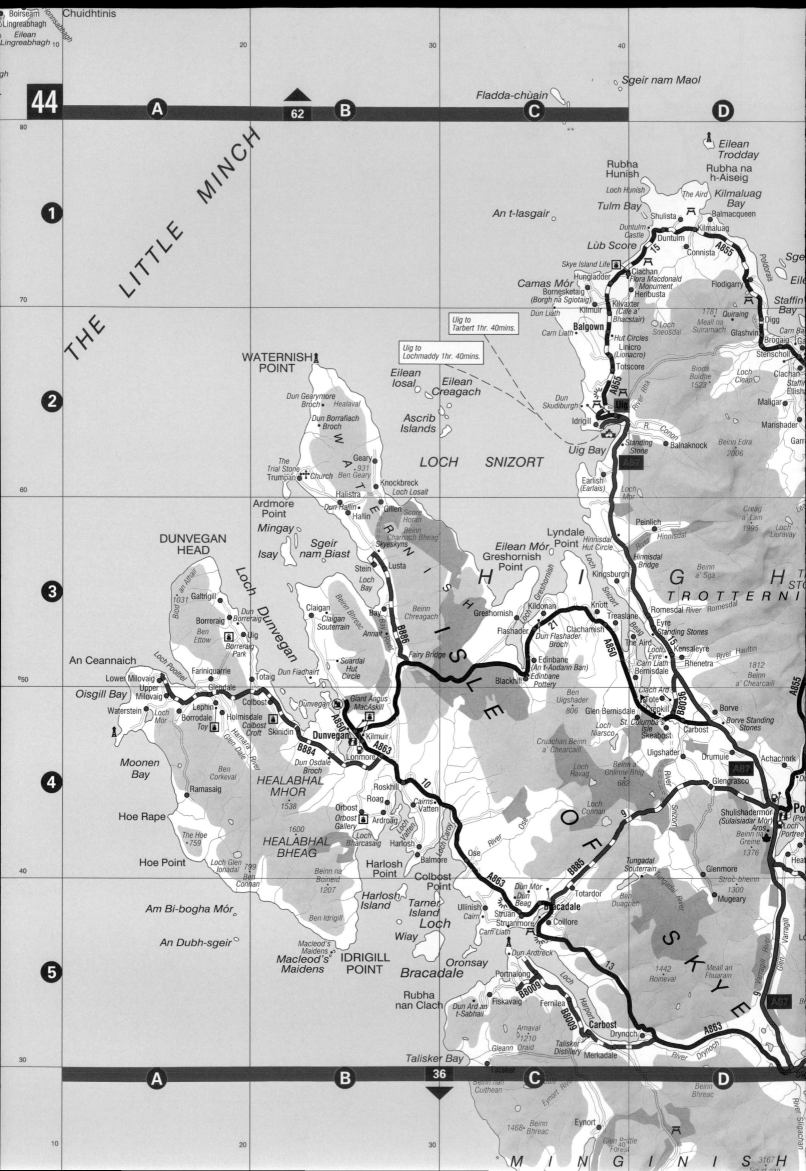

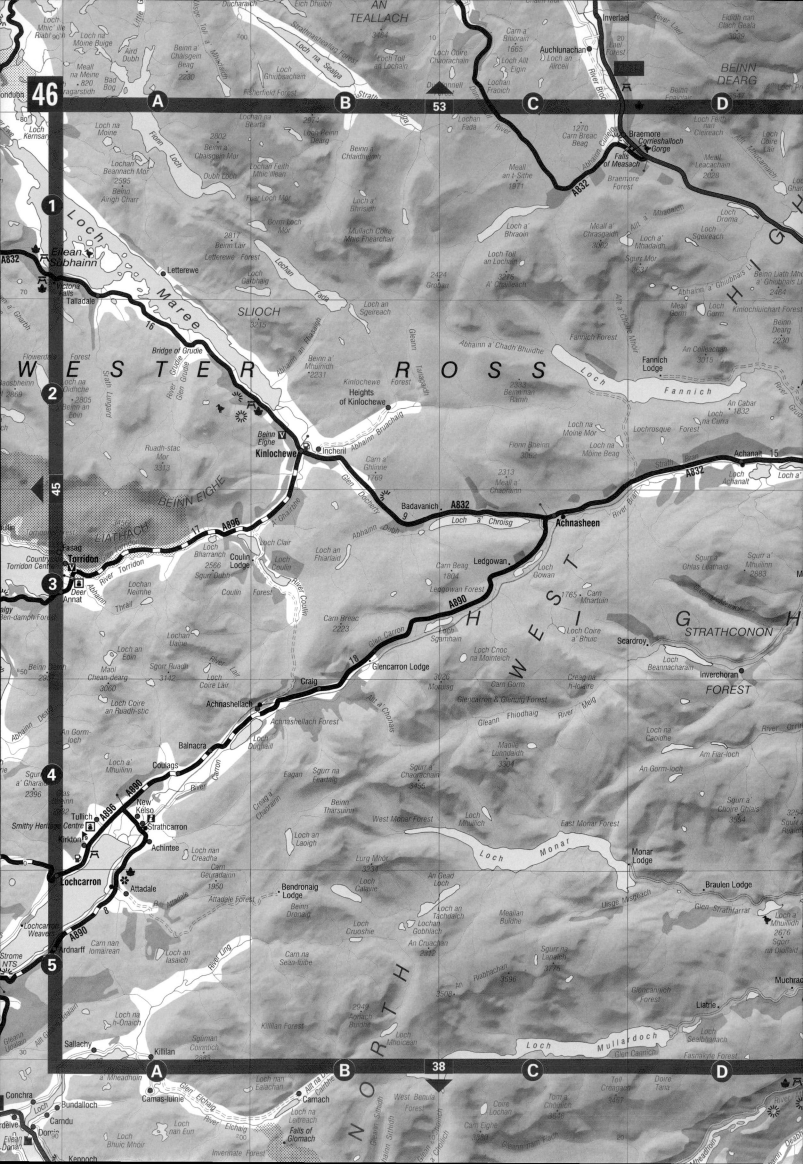

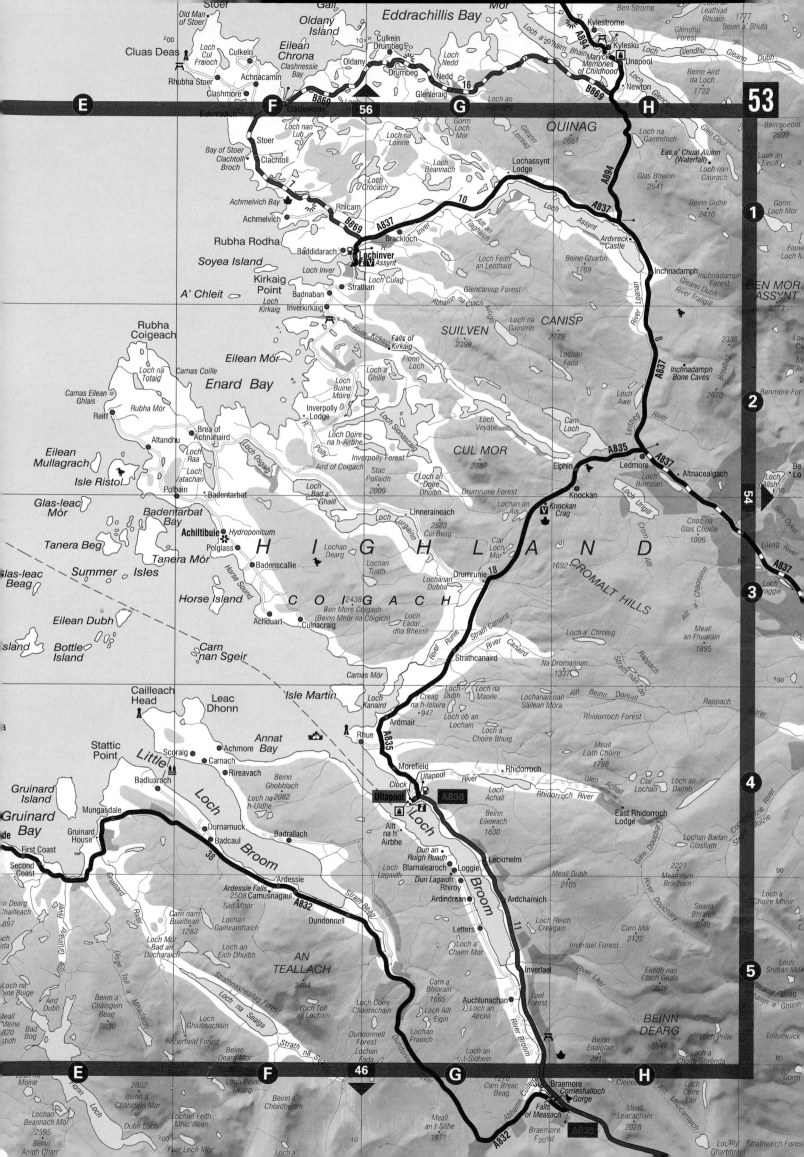

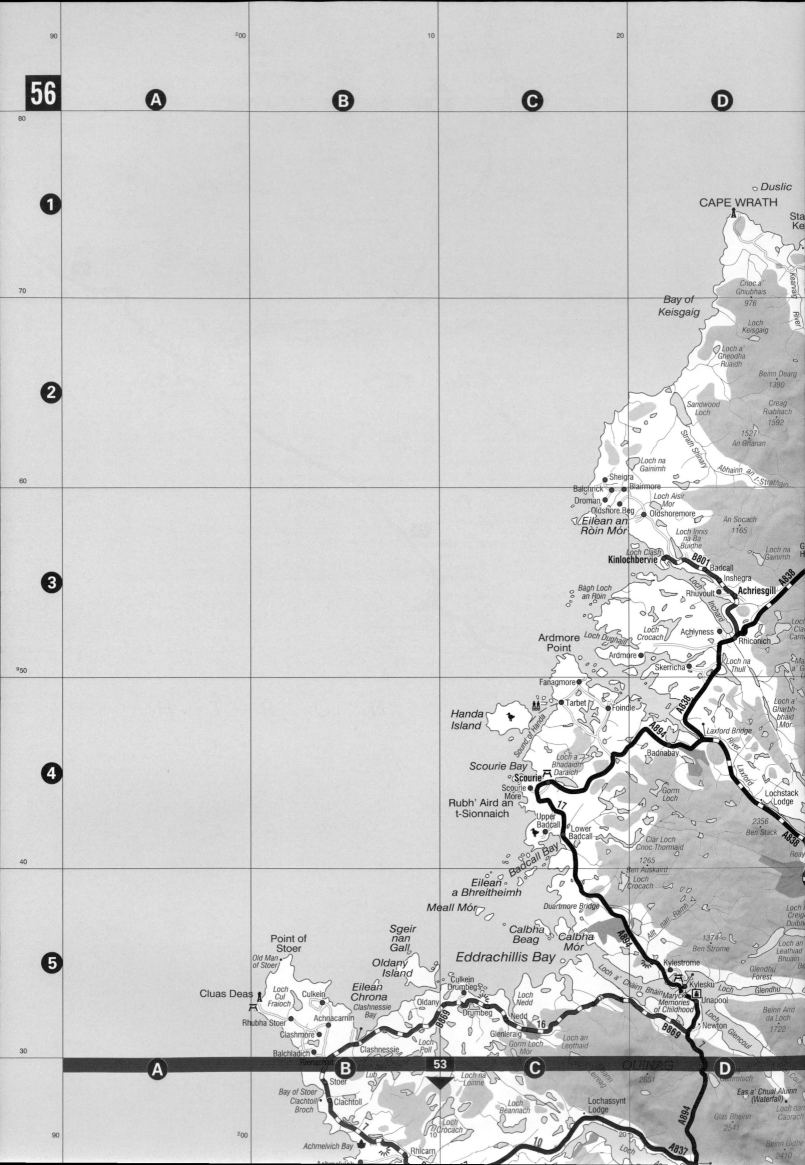

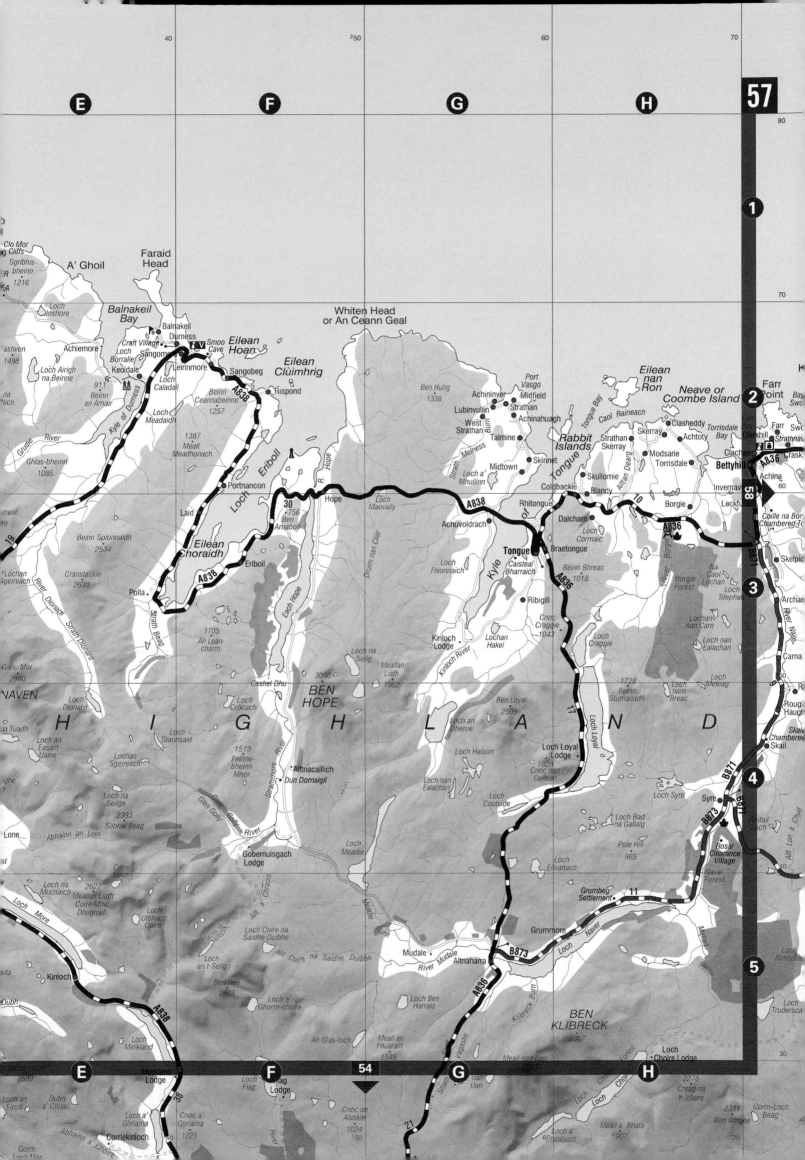

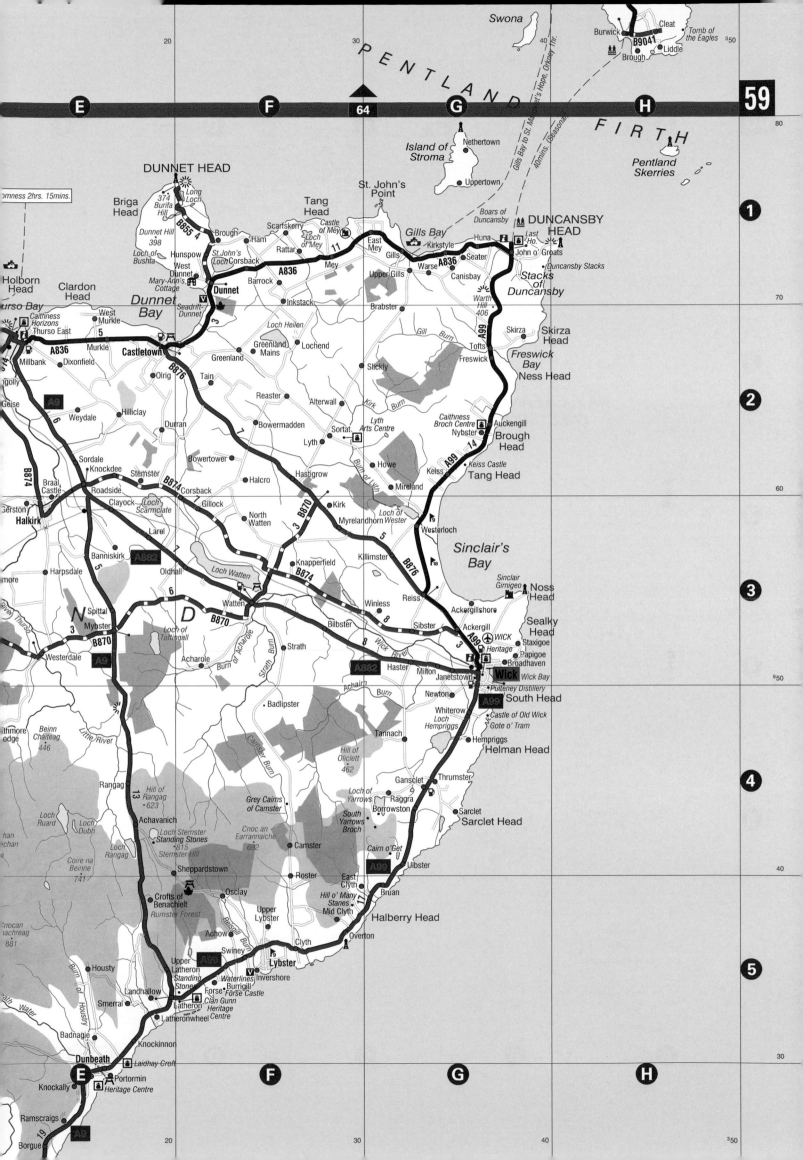

PENTLAND

FIRTH

Swona

Burwick
B904
Cleat
Tomb of the Eagles
³50
Liddle
Brough

E

F

64

G

H

80

Island of Stroma
Netherton
Uppertown

Gills Bay to St. Margaret's Hope, Orkney Thr.
40mins. (Seasonal)

Pentland Skerries

DUNNET HEAD

Briga Head

374 Burifa Hill
Long Loch

1

70

Dunnet Hill 398

B855 4

Brough

Scarfskerry

Castle of Mey

Tang Head

St. John's Point

Boars of Duncansby

Huna

DUNCANSBY HEAD

Holborn Head

Loch of Bushta

Hunspow

Ham

Rattar

Loch of Mey

East Mey

Gills Bay

Kirkstyle
John o' Groats

Last Ho.

Duncansby Stacks

Clardon Head

St. John's Loch

11

Mey

Gills

Warse

A836

Seater

Canisby

Stacks of Duncansby

urso Bay

West Dunnet

Corsback

A836

Upper Gills

Skirza

Skirza Head

Caithness Horizons

Mary-Ann's Cottage

Dunnet

Barrock

Brabster

Warth Hill 406

Tofts

Freswick

Freswick Bay

Ness Head

Thurso East

Dunnet Bay

Seadrift-Dunnet

West Murkle

Inkstack

A9

A836

Murkle

Castletown

Greenland

Loch Heilen

Lochend

Slickly

Gill Burn

2

60

Millbank

Dixonfield

B876

Olrig

Tain

Greenland Mains

Kirk Burn

Caithness Broch Centre

Auckengill
Nybster

Brough Head

Weydale

Hilliclay

Durran

Reaster

Bowermadden

Sortat

Lyth Arts Centre

Lyth

Howe

Kelss

A99

Keiss Castle

Tang Head

golly

Sordale

Knockdee

Bowertower

Halcro

Burn of Lyth

Mireland

14

Geise

B874

Stemster

B874

Corsback

Gillock

Kirk

Loch of Wester

Braal Castle

Roadside

Clayock

Loch Scarmclate

North Watten

Myrelandhorn

Wester

Westerloch

Gerston

Larel

B870

9

Sinclair's Bay

Halkirk

Banniskirk

A882

Oldhall

Loch Watten

B874

Knapperfield

Killimster

18

B876

Sinclair Girnigeo

Noss Head

3

50

Harpsdale

Loch of Toftingall

Watten

Winless

Reiss

Ackergillshore

Spittal

N

D

B870

Bilbster

Sibster

Ackergill

Sealky Head

Mybster

Acharole

Strath

8

Wick River

8

Haster

Milton

A99

WICK

Staxigoe

Papigoe

Broadhaven

3

Westerdale

B870

A9

Burn of Acharole

Strath Burn

Badlipster

Achairn Burn

Janetstown

Wick

Wick Bay

Pulteney Distillery

A882

thmore dge

Beinn Chaiteag 446

Little River

Acharn Burn

Newton

South Head

A99

Whiterow

Castle of Old Wick

4

40

han chan

Loch Ruard

Loch Dubh

Rangag

Hill of Rangag 623

Camster Burn

Grey Cairns of Camster

Hill of Oliclett 462

Loch of Yarrows

Raggra

Borrowston

Loch Hemprigg

Gansclet

Thrumster

Gote o' Tram

Hempriggs

Helman Head

Achavanich

Loch Stemster Standing Stones

Cnoc an Earrannaiche 692

South Yarrows Broch

Tannach

Sarclet

Sarclet Head

Coire na Beinne 741

Stemster Hill 815

Camster

Cairn o'Get

A99

Sheppardstown

Roster

Ulbster

5

30

Crofts of Benachielt

Rumster Forest

Osclay

East Clyth

Bruan

Achow

Upper Lybster

Hill o' Many Stanes

Mid Clyth

Halberry Head

cnocan nachreag 881

Housty

Upper Latheron Standing Stones

Boscall Burn

Swiney

Lybster

Clyth

Overton

Landhallow

Smerral

Waterlines

Forse

In, Invershore

Forse Castle

Burrigill

Clan Gunn Heritage Centre

A99

Badnagie

Latheron

Latheronwheel

Knockinnon

ath ter

Burn of Housdy

Dunbeath

Laidhay Croft

Knockally

Portormin

Heritage Centre

Ramscraigs

A9

19

Borgue

E

F

G

H

20

30

40

³50

³50

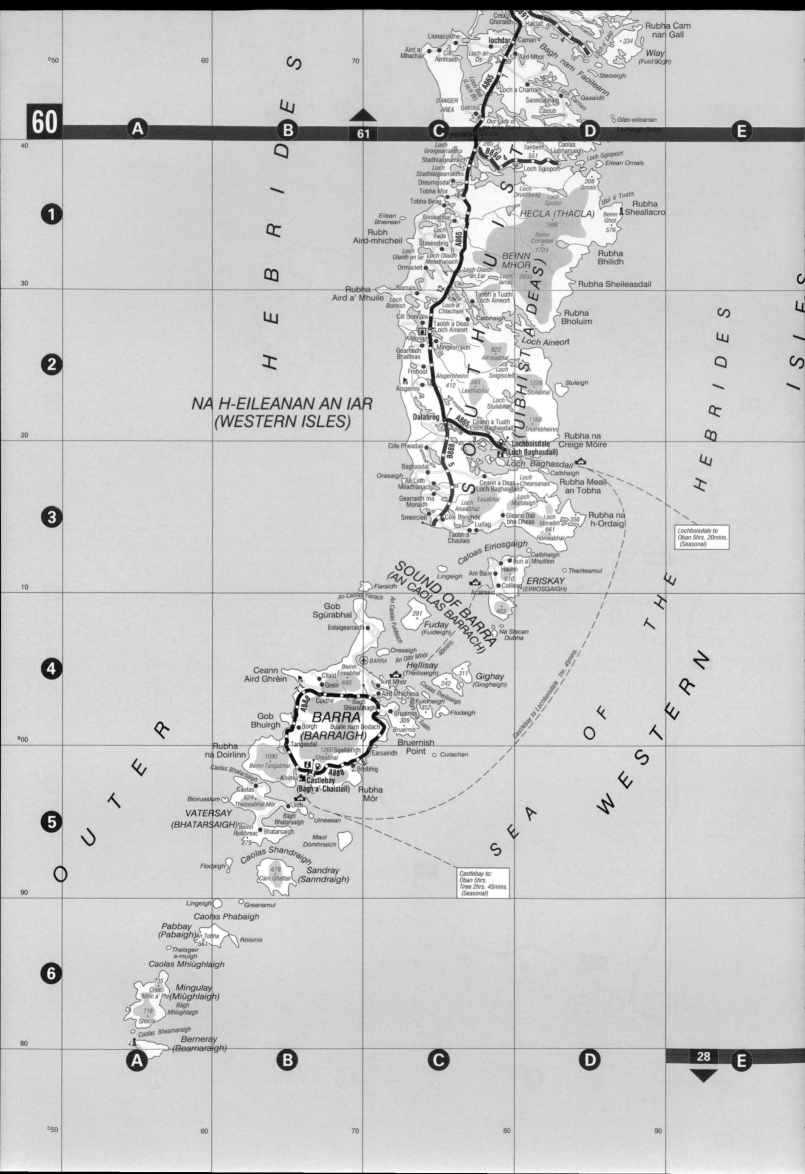

°50   60   70

1

HEBRIDES

2

NA H-EILEANAN AN IAR
(WESTERN ISLES)

3

OUTER

4

5

6

°50   60   70   80   90

Creag
Ghoraidh   Haclait   Rubha Cam
nan Gall
Lionacuidhe   Iochdar   Wiay
(Fuid 90gh)
Aird a'   Cill   Carnan   Aird-Mhor
Mhachair   Amhlaidh   Loch an   Bagh nam Faoileann
Os   Steiseigh
Loch Beag   A865   Loch a Chamain
(Loch Bì)   Sanndabhaig   Gasaidh
DANGER   Loch Carnan
AREA   Geirinis   Caslub
Our Lady of
the Isles Chalice   Glas-eileanan
Loch   A865   B890   Liunagan Dolan
Groigearraidh   Tairbeirt   Caolas   Eilean Ornais
Stadhlaigearraidh   551   Liubharsaigh
Loch   Loch Sgioport   Loch Sgioport
Stadhlaigearraidh   Eilean Ornais
Dreumasdal   208   Ornais
Tobha Mor   Loch   Mol a' Tuath
Tobha Beag   Loch   Beinn   Rubha
Druidibeag   Ghot   Sheallacro
Eilean   Sniseabhal   HECLA (THACLA)   576
Bheirean   1988
Rubh   Loch   Beinn   Rubha
Aird-mhicheil   Fada   Corradail   Bhilidh
Staoinebrig   1723
Loch   Loch Olaidh   BEINN   Rubha Sheileasdail
Olaidh an Iar   Meadhanach   MHOR
Ormacleit   Loch Olaidh   2033
an Ear   Loch
Bornais   Iarras   Rubha
Rubha   Taobh a Tuath   Bholuim
Aird a' Mhuile   Loch Aineort
Loch   A865   Calbhaigh
Bornish   Loch a   Rubha
Cill Donnain   Chlachain   Loch Aineort   Creige Mòire
Taobh a Deas
Kildonan   Loch Aineort
Gearraidh   Mingearraidh   822
Bhailteas   Airneabhal
Loch   Stulaigh
Frobost   Aisgerbheinn   Snigiscleit   1228
412   593   Stulabhal
Aisgernis   Leathabhal   1168
Loch   Truirebheinn
Dalabrog   Stulabhal   Rubha na
Ceann a Tuath   1168   Creige Mòire
A865   Loch Baghasdail
Cille Pheadair   Lochboisdale
(Loch Baghasdail)   Calbhaigh
Baghasdal   Ceann a Deas   Rubha Meall
Loch Chearsanais   an Tobha
Orasaigh   An Leth   Loch   Calbhaigh
Meadhanach   Baghasdail   Loch
Gearraidh na   Easabhal   Marulaigh   Rubha na
Monadh   Loch   h-Ordaig
Smeircleit   Aiseabhal   Loch
Cille Bhrighde   Moraibh   356
Ludag   Gleann Dail   661
Taobh a   bho Dheas   Roineabhal
Chaolais   Caolas Eiriosgaigh
Calbhaigh
Lingeigh   Bun a' Mhuillinn
Fiaraidh   Am Baile   Thairteamul
An Caolas Fiarach   610   ERISKAY
Gob   Haunn   (EIRIOSGAIGH)
Sgùrabhal   291   Acairseid   Coilleag
Eolaigearraidh   An Caolas Fuideach   403
Fuday   Na Stacan
(Fuideigh)   Dubha
40mins
Orasaigh   40mins
Ceann   An Oitir Mhòr
Aird Ghrèin   Beinn   BARRA   Hellisay   311   Gighay
Eireabhal   (Thèilisèigh)   (Gioghaigh)
Cliaid   Aird Mhor   242
Grein   680   Aird Mhichinis   Caolas Thèilisèigh
Cuidhir   Bàgh   1352   Flodaigh
Gob   Shiarabhagh   Bruairnis
Bhuirgh   BARRA   Fuidheigh
Borgh   Buaile nam Bodach   309
Tangasdal   (BARRAIGH)   Bruairnis
Rubha   1260   Sgallairidh   Bruernish
na Doirlinn   1090   Sgallairidh   Earsairidh   Point
Beinn Tangabhal   Sheabhal   Curachan
Caolas Bhatarsaigh   Breibhig
Kisimul   A888   Rubha
Castlebay   Mór
Caolas   (Bàgh a' Chaisteil)
Bioruaslam   624   Uidh
Theiseabhal Mòr   Uineasan
VATERSAY   Bàgh
(BHATARSAIGH)   Beinn   Bhatarsaigh
Ruilibreac   Bhatarsaigh
279   Maol
Dòmhnaich
Caolas Shandraigh
Flodaigh   678   Sandray
Càrn Ghaltair   (Sanndraigh)
Lingeigh   Greanamul
Caolas Phabaigh
Pabbay   An Tobha
(Pabaigh)   Ròisinis
561
Theisgeir
a-muigh
Caolas Mhiùghlaigh
735   Mingulay
Choc   (Miùghlaigh)
Mhic a' Phi   Bàgh
718   Mhiùghlaigh
Shecla
Caolas Bheàrnaraigh
Berneray
(Bearnaraigh)

A   B   C   D   28   E

Lochboisdale to
Oban 5hrs. 20mins.
(Seasonal)

Castlebay to Lochboisdale 1hr. 45mins
Castlebay to:
Oban 5hrs.
Tiree 2hrs. 45mins.
(Seasonal)

SOUND OF BARRA
(AN CAOLAS BARRACH)

SEA   OF   THE   WESTERN

HEBRIDES   ISLES

HEBRIDES

TARANSAY
(TARASAY)

61

Rubha
Leacach

Gloraig
Tharansaigh

877
Ben Ra

Dobell

Sound
(Caolas

Aird
Mhanais

Horgab

TOE HEAD
(GOB AN TOBHA)

Copaigh

Rubha
Sgeirigin

Rubha Màs
a' Chnuic

Taigh
Bhuirgh

Na Bui

1

62

Ceapabhal
1199

Scarasta
Sgarasta Mhor

90

SOUTH
(CEANN A

Rubh' an
Teampaill

MacGillivray
Centre

An Taobh
Tuath

Seallam!

Kyles Lodge

Leverburg
(An t-Ob)

150

A859

Roineav

Siolaigh
Bheag

Siolaigh

Shiolaigh

Caolas

Rubha Bhreinis

PABBAY
(PABAIGH)

643
Beinn a'
Charnain

Ensay
(Easaigh)

161

Eilean
Che

minis

Srannda

Caolas Spuir

Caolas

Phabaigh

Killegray
(Ceileagraigh)

147

Borghasdal

RENNISH
(Ro IBHA

Boreray
(Boraraigh)

BERNERAY
(BEÀRNARAIGH)

Brusta

Ruisigearraidh

Baile

Borgh

Rhaiteam

Rubha
Bhoisnis

Gilsaigh

Lingeigh

Groonaidh

Lingeigh

Sgarabhaigh

Aird a'
Mhòrain

Caolas a' Mhòrain

Caolas

Bhearnaraigh

Sgeir a' Chàil

Seòlaid Mhic Neacail

Opasaigh

Haskeir Island
(Eilean Hasgeir)

Haskeir Eagach

Rubha
Ghriminis

Rubha
Bheilis

Rubha
Mhànais

Taigh a'
Ghearraidh

Hogha
Gearraidh

Vàllay
(Bhalaigh)

Grìminis

Scolpaig

Ceathramh
Meadhanach

Tràigh
Bhalaigh

Orasaigh

Grelnetobht

Solas

A865

Lingeigh

Port nan Long

Baile
MhicPhail

Clachan
Shannda

624

Beinn Mhòr

B893

Sursaigh

Taghaigh

Loch
Mhic Phail

Loch
Amhlasaraidh

Tobha Beag

Thermatraigh

Bàgh a'
Chàise

Gròdaigh

Baile
Mhartainn

Loch Hosta

Cleitreabhal
a Deas

435

Glen Uroila

A865

13

Malacleit

Loch nan
Geireann

588

Crògearraidh Mor

Sgeallrabhal

332

756
Maireabhal

NORTH   UIST
(UIBHIST A TUATH)

Blathaisbhal

Loch
Fada

Rubha an
Dùine

70

Causamul

Aird an
Rùnair

Balranald

Baile Raghaill

Loch
Eubhal

A865

Loch
Scadabhagh

A867

Loch
Sgealtair

Sruth Mor

Lochmaddy
(Loch nam Madadh)

Loch nam Madadh

Rubha an
Fhigheadair

Lochportain

Rubha nam
Plèac

Rubha Port
Scolpaig

Paiblesgearraidh

Paibeil

Baile Mor

Cladach a
Chaolais

Uineabhal

458

Loch
Huna

Barpa Langass
Chambered Cairn

Sornach Coir' Fhinn
Stone Circle

9

Loch
Scadabhagh

Taigh Chearsabhagh

824
Li a Tuath

Loch
Thundair

920

Li a Deas

Lochmaddy to
Uig 1hr. 40mins.

Rubh' Arnal

Kirkibost Island
(Eilean Chircebost)

Cladach
Chirceboist

Bhorogaigh

Hebridean Smokehouse

Clachan na
Luib

Cladach
Iolaraigh

A865

A867

Langass

A894

Loch
Langais

3

An t-Aigeach

4

Deasker

Huskeiran

Ceann
Iar

Siolaigh

Stòcaidh

Ceann
Ear

SOUND
OF
MONACH
(CAOLAS
MHONACH)

Teanna Mhachair

Samhla

Loch Euphort

Saighdinis

Druim
Saighdinis

Loch

Euphort

Loch
Carabhat

Loch
Obasaraigh

Eigneig Mhòr

Eigneig
Bheag

60

THE LITTLE MINCH

ISLES

Heisker or Monach
Islands
(Theisgeir no na
H-Eileanan Monach)

NA H-EILEANAN AN IAR
(WESTERN ISLES)

Baleshare
(Baile Sear)

Bail'
Uachdraich

Cairinis

Cladach
Chairinis

EAVAL (EABHAL)
1139

Liernis

Flodaigh Beag

Flodaigh Mòr

Bail'
Iochdrach

Beul an Toirm
BENBECULA
(Bheinn na Faoghla)

Oitir
Mhór

A865

Baile Glas

Grimsay
(Griomasaigh)

Bagh Mor

379

Ceallan

Eilean
Fhlodaigh

325

Beinn
Rodagrich

Ronay
(Ronaigh)

Ròisinis

5

Baile
Mhanaich

B892

Uachdar

Gramasdail

Scotbheinn

Màtagaidh Mòr

Baile 'nan
Cailleach

Aird

Loch
Eilean Iain

Loch
Fada

408

Loch na
Deighe
fo Dheas

Grìminis

Loch
Mòr

Torlum

BENBECULA
(BEINN NA FAOGHLA)

Loch Uisgebhagh

Màithidh Riabhach

50

Borgh

B892

Loch Heouravay

Loch
Olabhat

Loch
Langabhat

Nan Eilean

Lionacleit

Creag
Ghoraidh

B891

Haclait

Rubha Cam
nan Gall

Lionacuidhe

Iochdar

Carnan

Bagh a' Laib

334

Wiay
(Fuidhaigh)

6

Aird a'
Mhachair

Cill
Amhlaidh

Loch an
Os

Aird-Mhor

Loch a Charnain

Steiseigh

Loch Carnan

Sanndabhaig

Loch Carnan

Gasaidh

Caslub

Glas-eileanan

Liursaigh Dubh

DANGER
AREA

Geirinis

A865

7

Our Lady of
the Isles Statue

Groigearraidh

Ruabhal

60

Eilean Ornais

Loch
Stadhlaigearraidh

Loch Sgioport

WESTERN

Dreumasdal

Tobha Mor

Tobha Beag

Sniseabhal

Eilean
Bheirean

Loch
Druidibeag

HECLA (THACLA)
1988

208
Ornais

Mol a' Tuath

Rubha
Sheallacro

Loch
Spotail

Beinn
Ghot

576

40

Rubh
Aird-mhicheil

A865

Loch
Fada

Staoinebrig

Beinn
Corradail

1723

ISLES

OUTER

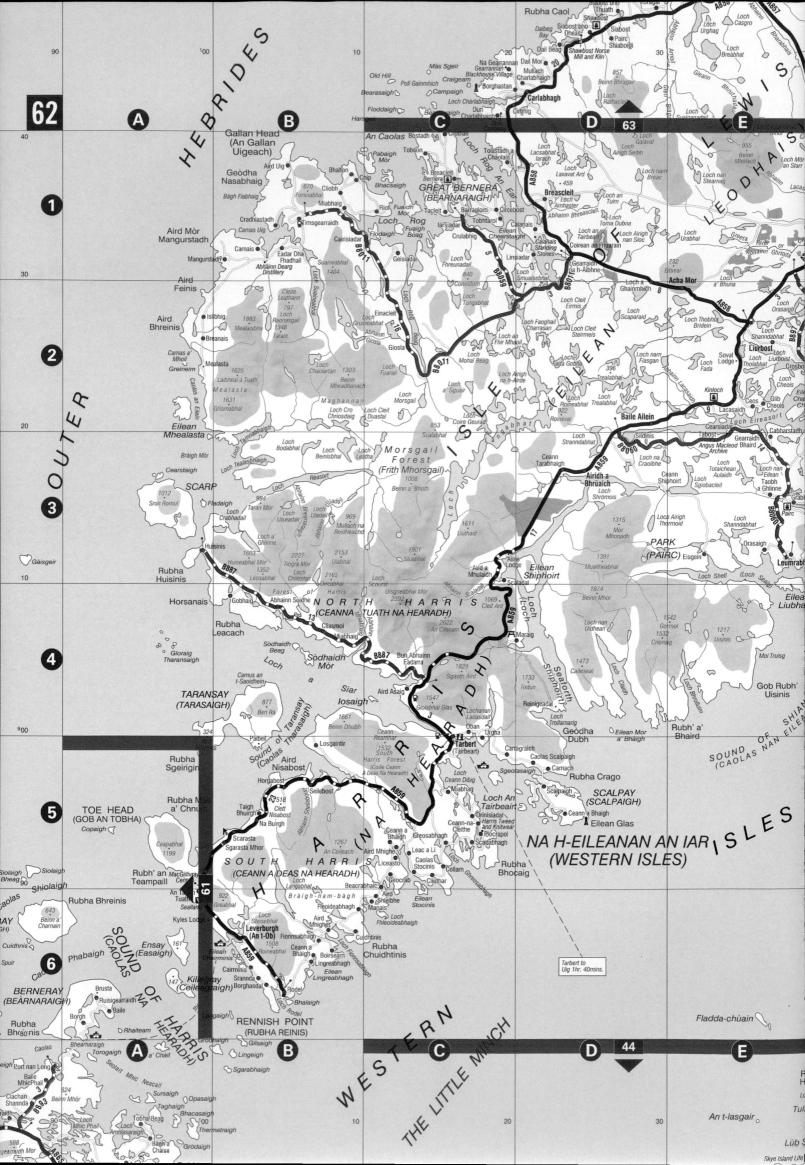

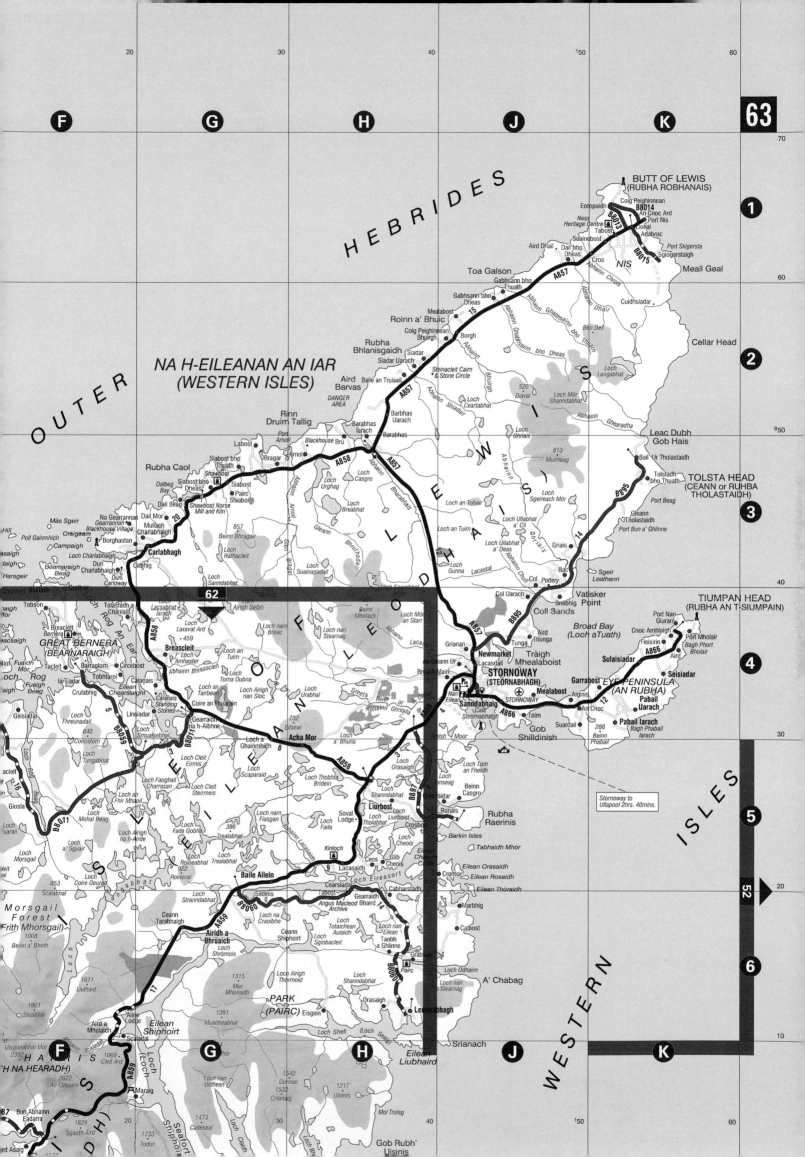

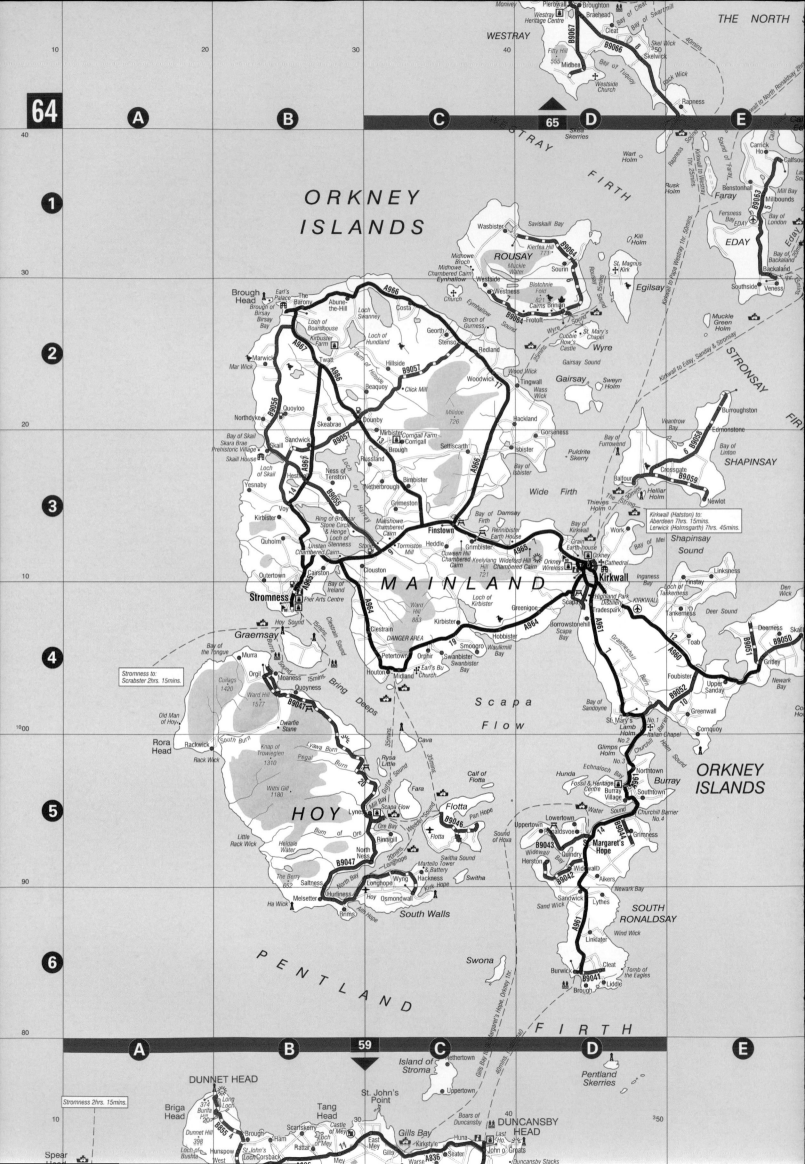

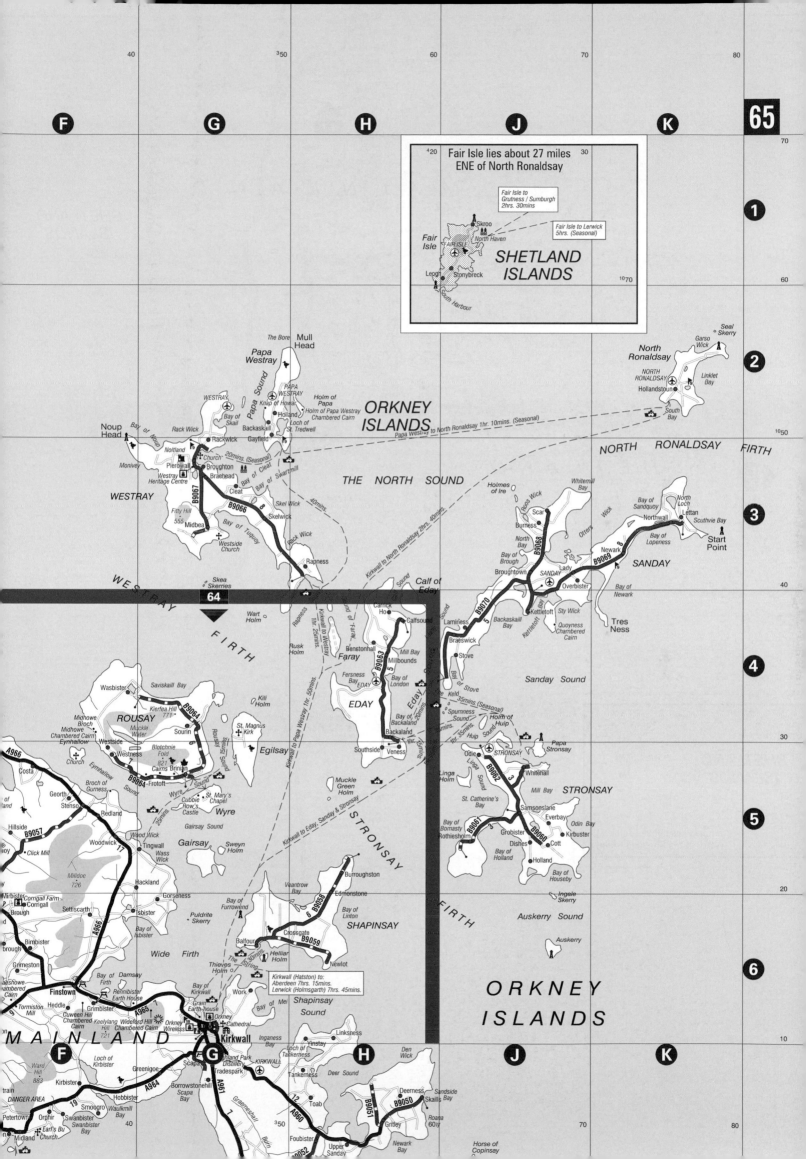

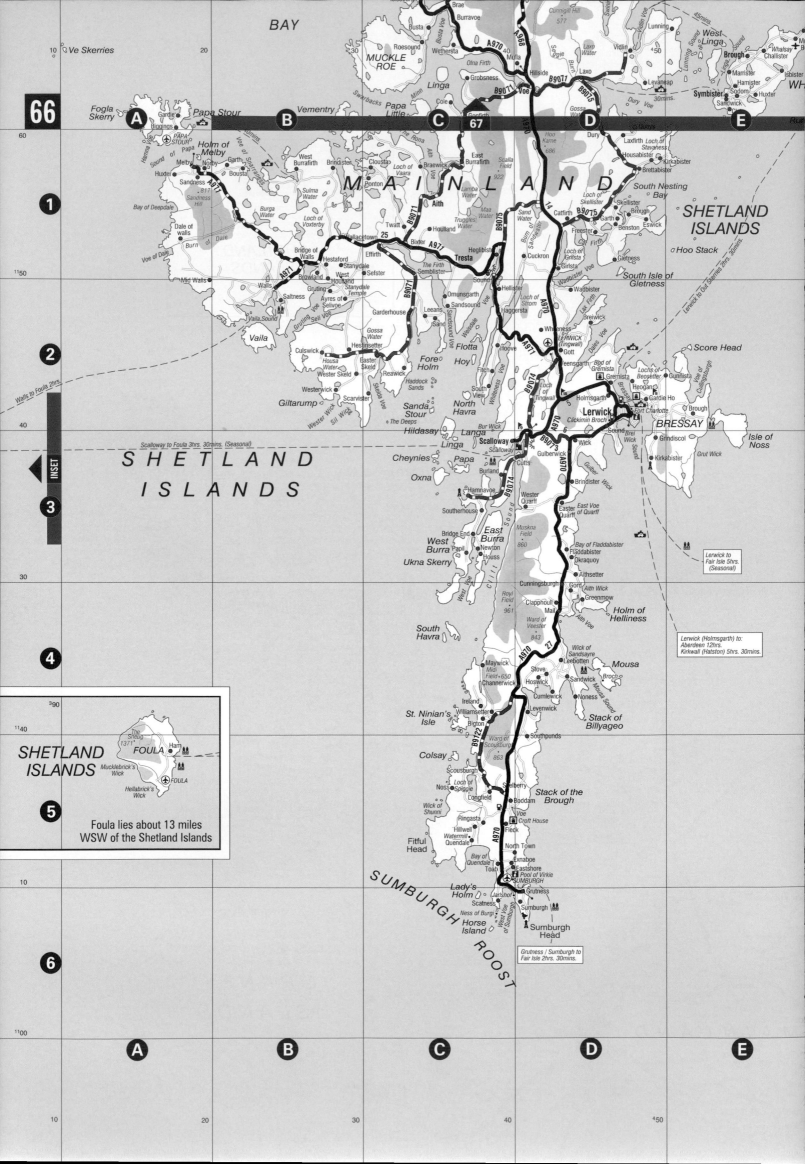

BAY

10 Ve Skerries 20

Fogla Skerry

A Papa Stour **B** Vementry **C** **67** **D** **E**

Gardie
Biggings
PAPA STOUR
Holm of Melby
Melby Norby Garth
Huxter Bousta
Sandness A971
Dale of walls
Burn of Dale
Mid Walls
Walls
Saltness

66

60

1150

40

30

INSET

SHETLAND
ISLANDS

Scalloway to Foula 3hrs. 30mins. (Seasonal)

1

2

3

4

Roesound
MUCKLE ROE
Wetherston
Linga
Grobsness
Swarbacks
Papa Little
Vementry
West Burrafirth
Brindister
Clousta
Loch of Vaara
Ponton
Aith
Twatt
Wallacetown 25
Bridge of Walls
Hestaford
Stanydale
Bixter A977
Browland
West Houland
Sefster
Stanydale Temple
Effirth
The Firth
Semblister
Gruting
Garderhouse
Leeans
Sandsound
Omunsgarth
Sand

Brae
Burravoe
Busta
Busta Voe
Muckle Voe
Olna Firth
Hillside
Voe

A970
A968
Cunnigill Hill
577
Lunning
West Linga
Vidlin Voe
45mins
Vidlin
Lunning Sound

Mulla
Laxo Water
Burn
Laxo
B9071
B9075
Gossa Water
Dury Voe
30mins
Brough
Challister
Marrister
Hamister
Huxter
Symbister
Sodom
Sandwick

East Burrafirth
Braewick
Scalla Field
922
Lamba Water
Maa Water
Truggles Water
Sand Water
Cuckron
14
Catfirth
B9075
Loch of Skellister
Skellister
Brough
Garth
Benston
Eswick
Freester
Girlsta
Loch of Grilsta
Gletness
Wadbister
Lax Firth

Loch of Strom
Hellister
Haggersta
Sound
Whiteness
Whiteness Voe
Hoove
Flotta
Hoy
Fitch
South Havra
North Havra
Bur Wick
Hildasay
Langa
Linga

M A I N L A N D

SHETLAND
ISLANDS

Hoo Stack

South Isle of Gletness

Lerwick to Out Skerries 2hrs. 30mins.

Breiwick
Wadbister Voe
A970
Dales Voe
LERWICK (Tingwall)
Gott
Veensgarth
Loch of Tingwall
Bod of Gremista
Gremista
Holmsgarth
5
Lerwick
Clickimin Broch
Fort Charlotte
Clickimin Broch
Score Head
Lochs of Beosetter
Heogan
Gardie Ho
Gunnista
Voe of Cullingsburgh
BRESSAY
Brough
Grindiscol
Brei Wick Sound
Kirkabister
Grut Wick
Isle of Noss

Scalloway
Cutts
Gulberwick
Wick
Gulber Wick
B9073
A970
6
Burland
Papa
Cheynies
Oxna
Hamnavoe
Southerhouse
West Burra
Bridge End
Papil
East Burra
Newton
Houss
Ukna Skerry

Wester Quarff
Easter Quarff
East Voe of Quarff

SHETLAND
ISLANDS

FOULA
The Sneug
1371
Ham
FOULA
Mucklebrick's Wick
Hellabrick's Wick

5

Foula lies about 13 miles
WSW of the Shetland Islands

390
1140

B9122
South Havra

Muskna Field
860
Royl Field
961
Ward of Veester
843
Cunningsburgh
Gord
Aith Wick
Clapphoull
Mail
Aith Voe
Greenmow
Holm of Helliness

Lerwick to
Fair Isle 5hrs.
(Seasonal)

Lerwick (Holmsgarth) to:
Aberdeen 12hrs.
Kirkwall (Hatston) 5hrs. 30mins.

Wick of Sandsayre
Leebotten
Stove
Sandwick
Hoswick
Cumlewick
Noness
Levenwick
Maywick
Midi Field 650
Channerwick
Ireland
Williamsetter
Bigton
St. Ninian's Isle
Ward of Scousburgh
863
Colsay
Scousburgh
Noss
Loch of Spiggie
Longfield
Wick of Shunni
Ringasta
Hillwell
Watermill
Quendale
Fitful Head
Bay of Quendale
Toab
Lady's Holm
Scatness
Ness of Burgi
Horse Island
West Voe of Sumburgh
Sumburgh Head

Mousa
Broch
Stack of Billyageo
Mousa Sound

27
A970
Southpunds
Spelberry
Boddam
Voe
Croft House
Fleck
North Town
Exnaboe
Eastshore
Pool of Virkie
SUMBURGH
Grutness
Jarlshof
Sumburgh

Stack of the Brough

Grutness / Sumburgh to
Fair Isle 2hrs. 30mins.

30

1100

10

A **B** **C** **D** **E**

10 20 30 40 450

S U M B U R G H   R O O S T

TOWN PLAN PAGES

REFERENCE

MOTORWAY	M8	AIRPORT	✈
MOTORWAY UNDER CONSTRUCTION		BUS STATION	➤
MOTORWAY PROPOSED		CAR PARK (Selection of)	P
MOTORWAY JUNCTIONS WITH NUMBERS	4 5	CHURCH	†
Unlimited Interchange **4**		CITY WALL	⏛
Limited Interchange **5**		FERRY (Vehicular)	⛴
PRIMARY ROUTE	A92	(Foot only)	👥
DUAL CARRIAGEWAYS		GOLF COURSE	⛳9 ⛳18
CLASS A ROAD	A804	HELIPORT	🚁
CLASS B ROAD	B700	HOSPITAL	H
MAJOR ROADS UNDER CONSTRUCTION		LIGHTHOUSE	🗼
MAJOR ROADS PROPOSED		MARKET	⚒
MINOR ROAD		NATIONAL TRUST FOR SCOTLAND PROPERTY	
SAFETY CAMERA (with Speed Limits)	30	(Open)	NTS
FUEL STATION	⛽	(Restricted Opening)	NTS
RESTRICTED ACCESS		PARK & RIDE	P+🚌
PEDESTRIANIZED ROAD & MAIN FOOTWAY		PLACE OF INTEREST	■
ONE-WAY STREET	→ →	POLICE STATION	▲
TOLL	TOLL	POST OFFICE	★
RAILWAY AND STATION	🚉	SHOPPING PRECINCT	▬
LEVEL CROSSING AND TUNNEL	╫ ---	SHOPMOBILITY	🦽
BUILT-UP AREA		TOILET	▽
ABBEY, CATHEDRAL, PRIORY ETC.	†	VISIT SCOTLAND INFORMATION CENTRE	i
		VIEWPOINT	※

ABERDEEN

Built almost entirely from granite, Aberdeen is the third largest city in Scotland. However, it is not only famed for its splendid granite architecture, Aberdeen has been a Royal Burgh since the 12th century, it is home to one of the oldest universities in Britain and it has an important maritime history and even today remains one of Britain's busiest harbours. To the north of the city is Old Aberdeen and though it has been incorporated with the main part of the city since 1891, it maintains its own ambience. Old Aberdeen is primarily associated with the university and the distinctive crown spire of Kings College, founded in 1495 by Bishop Elphinstone during the reign of King James IV. Later in 1860 King's college would combine with Marischal College in the main part of the city (see below) to form the University of Aberdeen. Today, most visitor attractions centre on the main part of the city along Union Street and its environs. From here it is a short walk to the harbour that has played a significant role in shaping Aberdeen's prosperity since the 12th century when shipping tithes were first introduced. Ferries to Orkney and the Shetlands leave from the quay and the fish market can be visited Monday to Friday. The Aberdeen International Youth Festival takes place each year usually at the beginning of August and attracts many young performers from around the world who descend on the city for ten days to showcase their talents. Aberdeen is a diverse city with a wide spectrum of attractions that make it an attractive tourist destination throughout the year.

PLACES OF INTEREST

Visit Scotland Information Centre (All Year) - 23 Union Street. AB11 5BP. Tel: (01224) 288828

◆ ABERDEEN ART GALLERY - This popular attraction houses an important fine art collection with paintings, sculptures and graphics from the 15th to 21st century, a rich and diverse applied art collection, an exciting programme of special exhibitions. Gallery shop and café. Schoolhill. ◆ ABERDEEN ARTS CENTRE - Small gallery exhibiting contemporary arts and crafts. 33 King Street. ◆ ABERDEEN CATHEDRAL - Perpendicular Gothic style episcopal church dating from 1817 and subsequently gaining Cathedral status in 1914. Within the cathedral is an exhibition that reflects the history of Christianity in the north east of Scotland. King Street. ◆ ABERDEEN MARITIME MUSEUM - The museum highlights the history of the North Sea using models, paintings and computer interactives. The offshore oil industry is brought to life using the world's largest oil platform model. This attraction includes one of Aberdeen's oldest buildings, Provost Ross's House, built in 1593. Shop. Shiprow. ◆ ABERDEEN MERCAT CROSS - Dating from 1686, Aberdeen's mercat cross is regarded as the finest example in Scotland. It depicts a unicorn mounted on a hexagonal base on which are panels with medallion heads of the ten Stuart monarchs together with heraldic coats-of-arms. Justice Street. ◆ ABERDEEN RC CATHEDRAL - Gothic revival Victorian cathedral dating from 1860-80. 20 Huntly Street. ◆ ABERDEEN TOLBOOTH MUSEUM - One of the city's oldest buildings, the Tolbooth was once a gaol. As a museum it describes the history of crime and punishment in Aberdeen. Visit the 17th & 18th Century cells with their original doors and barred windows. Interactive displays and exhibitions. Castle Street. ◆ KIRK OF ST NICHOLAS - Dating from the 12th century, this is the original parish church of Aberdeen. Only the transepts remain of the original structure and modifications have continued into the 20th century with the addition of Scottish stained glass. Back Wynd. ◆ MARISCHAL COLLEGE - Famed as the world's second largest granite structure. The present buildings date predominantly from the 19th century and the neo-Gothic west front is regarded as one of the world's finest architectural achievements in granite. Broad Street. (Currently occupied by Aberdeen City Council). ◆ MARISCHAL MUSEUM - Housed in the impressive Marischal College, the diverse collection of exhibits have been gathered by generations of university graduates from around the world. The displays illustrate the arts and customs of different cultures from ancient to modern times and include fine examples of Egyptian and Classical antiquities. Broad Street. (Closed for refurbishment). ◆ PEACOCK VISUAL ARTS - Contemporary art exhibitions and events. Digital, photography and printmaking workshops. 21 Castle Street. ◆ PROVOST SKENE'S HOUSE - This 16th century house captures the grandeur of earlier times with a stunning series of period room settings and Painted Gallery. Changing displays highlight local history and the Costume Gallery features fashions. Broad Street.

ENTERTAINMENT

◆ Casinos - G Casino, Exchanger Row. Gala Casino, Summer Street. Soul Casino, Union Street. ◆ Cinemas - 10 Ship Row. 49 Belmont Street. Union Square, Guild Street. Queen's Link Leisure Park (E of Aberdeen). ◆ Concerts - Aberdeen Exhibition and Conference Centre, Bridge of Don (N of Aberdeen). Aberdeen Music Hall, Union Street. Lemon Tree, 5 West North Street.
◆ Theatres - Aberdeen Arts Centre, King Street. His Majesty's Theatre, Rosemount Viaduct. Lemon Tree (as above).

SPORT & LEISURE

◆ Bowls - Bon Accord Indoor Bowling Centre (Within the Bon Accord Centre), George Street. ◆ Ice Rink - Linx Ice Arena, Beach Promenade (E of Aberdeen). ◆ Parks & Gardens - Union Terrace Gardens, Union Terrace. ◆ Sports Centres - Beach Leisure Centre, Beach Promenade (E of Aberdeen). Chris Anderson Stadium, Linksfield Road. Torry Youth & Sports Centre, Oscar Road (S of Aberdeen). ◆ Swimming Pools - Beach Leisure Centre (as above). ◆ Tennis Centre - Westburn Tennis Centre, Westburn Park, Westburn Road (W of Aberdeen). ◆ Ten-Pin Bowling - Cosmic Bowling, Codonas Amusement Park, Beach Boulevard (E of Aberdeen).

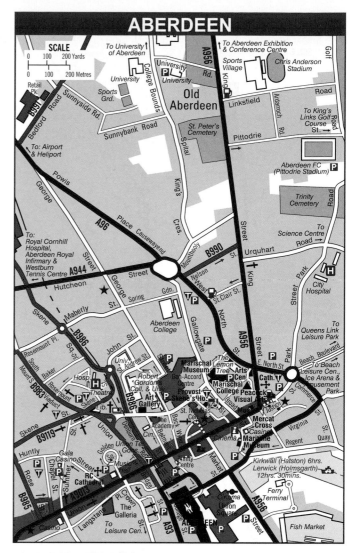

Aberdeen

Crathes Castle

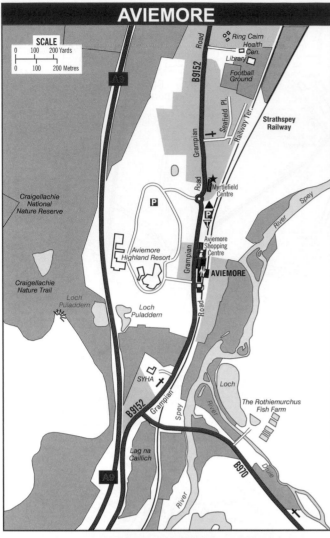

AVIEMORE

32 miles South of Inverness on the A9 lies the Highland resort of Aviemore, a picturesque village renowned for its spectacular mountain scenery. In close proximity to Britain's premier ski area, the Cairngorm Mountains, Aviemore is an ideal base from which to tour the Highlands offering the tourist a diverse range of quality accommodation along with leisure facilities and visitor attractions. To maintain its continued popularity as a UK holiday destination, Aviemore has embarked upon an ambitious programme of regeneration in order to reaffirm its status as a world class centre for tourism throughout the year.

PLACES OF INTEREST

Visit Scotland Information Centre (All year) - 7 The Parade, Grampian Road. PH22 1RH. Tel: (01479) 810930 ◆ CRAIGELLACHIE NATIONAL NATURE RESERVE & NATURE TRAIL - (Scottish National Heritage) 260 hectare National Nature Reserve containing a mixture of birchwood and moorland. ◆ STRATHSPEY RAILWAY - 9.5 mile standard gauge railway running between Aviemore, Boat of Garten and Broomhill passing within sight of some of the highest and most spectacular mountains in Scotland. Aviemore Station.

SPORT & LEISURE

◆ Skiing Facilities - The Ski & Snowboard School, Cairngorm Mountain, 9 miles SE of Aviemore.

AYR

Ayr is a busy shopping centre and commercial seaport. With its long stretches of sandy beach, backed by pleasant lawns behind the esplanade, it is also one of Scotland's premier coastal resorts. The town is centred around Alloway Street and High Street. Famous for its associations with Burns (born in Alloway immediately to the south and who described Ayr as the town of 'honest men and bonnie lasses'), the Tam O'Shanter Inn on the High Street & 'Twa Brigs' (Auld Brig, described below, and New Bridge built in 1788, rebuilt in 1877-9) feature in his works. Burns statue is near the railway station in Burns Statue Square. Of architectural interest are the restored 16th century Loudoun Hall on Boat Vennel off New Bridge Street, the oldest building in the town, and the Town Buildings surmounted by a slender spire built in the early 1820s, off the same road. Ayr Racecourse (in the east of the town) is Scotland's top horse racing centre.

PLACES OF INTEREST

Visit Scotland Information Centre (All year) - 22 Sandgate. KA7 1BW. Tel: (01292) 290300
◆ AULD BRIG - Bridge over River Ayr dating from c1470, subject of Burns' 'Twa Brigs'. For 300 years Ayr's only bridge, now pedestrianized. High Street / River Street.
◆ AULD KIRK - Fine church, also known as the New Church of St John, built in 1655 with money given by Cromwell to replace the 'Old Church' (see below) incorporated in his fort. Kirk Port, High Street.
◆ JOHN MCADAM MONUMENT - Monument to John McAdam, the road builder, born in Ayr in 1756, who gave his name to the word 'tarmacadam'. Wellington Square.
◆ NEWTON STEEPLE - Georgian (rare in this district) steeple of 1795, formerly at entrance to parish church. King Street.
◆ ST JOHN'S TOWER - Restored tower of Old Church of St John where the Scottish Parliament met after Bannockburn in 1315 to confirm the future of the Scottish Crown. Later absorbed into a large Cromwellian fort built in 1652. Views to island of Arran from top. By appointment. Bruce Crescent.
◆ WALLACE TOWER - Early 19th century neo-gothic tower, with statue of William Wallace in niche, built on site where Wallace, the Scottish patriot, is reputed to have been imprisoned in the early 1300s. High Street.

ENTERTAINMENT

◆ Cinemas - Burns Statue Square.
◆ Concerts - Town Hall, New Bridge Street. Gaiety Theatre, Carrick Street. Citadel Leisure Centre, South Harbour Street.
◆ Theatres - Gaiety Theatre (as above).

SPORT & LEISURE

◆ Parks & Gardens - Belleisle Park, Belleisle (S of Ayr). Craigie Park, Craigie Road. Low Green, Wellington Square. Rozelle Park, Monument Road (S of Ayr).
◆ Sports Centres - Citadel Leisure Centre, South Harbour Street.
◆ Swimming Pools - Citadel Leisure Centre (as above).
◆ Ten-Pin-Bowling - LA Bowl, Miller Road.

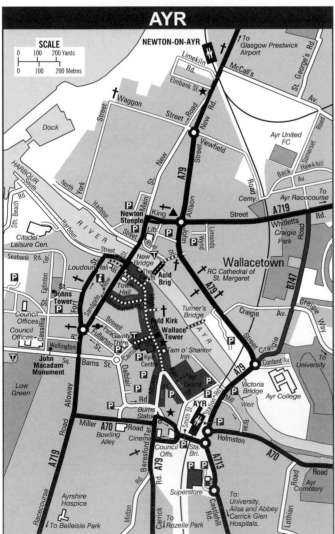

DUMFRIES

Dumfries is an attractive border town situated on the picturesque River Nith that divides it from Maxwelltown, with which it was amalgamated in 1929. With many of the houses painted in pastel colours or built of Lochar Briggs red sandstone and a modern shopping centre, it is the main centre for the region being given the status of a royal burgh as early as the 12th century. The town was the scene of the murder of 'the Red' Comyn by Robert Bruce in 1306 (marked by a plaque on a building in Castle Street), an event that started a change in the course of Scottish history that culminated with the defeat of the English at the battle of Bannockburn in 1314. Dumfries has been sacked many times, notably by the retreating Bonnie Prince Charlie in 1745 after his march on England, and consequently there is little from the medieval period to see, however a walk along the High Street and the waterfront at Whitesands is recommended. The Academy on Academy Street educated the playwright and novelist James Matthew Barrie, author of 'Peter Pan' whilst Robert Burns, Scotland's national poet lived here between 1791 and his death in 1796 during which time he wrote many of his poems and songs. The town contains many Burns sites of interest including (in addition to those listed below) a plaque marking his first home in Bank Street (then called Wee Vennel or 'Stinking Vennel' by Burns because of an open sewer which ran down the street to the river), a marble statue in front of Greyfriars church, Castle Street (built in 1867) and his family pew in St Michael's church, St Michael Street. Burns' favourite walk (now called 'Burns' Walk'), is on the east bank of the river off Nunholm Road in the north of the town.

PLACES OF INTEREST

Visit Scotland Information Centre (All year) - 64 Whitesands. DG1 2RS. Tel: (01387) 253862

◆ BURNS MAUSOLEUM - Built in 1815 in the style of a domed Grecian temple. Burns, his wife & several of his children are buried here. St Michael's Churchyard, St Michael Street.

◆ DEVORGILLA BRIDGE (OLD BRIDGE) - Six arched sandstone bridge of 1431, rebuilt in the 17th century after severe flood damage, now pedestrianized. Last in a succession of bridges here; the first wooden structure was built by Lady Devorgilla Balliol in the 13th century. Mill Road / Whitesands.

◆ DUMFRIES CAMERA OBSCURA - Astronomical instrument (one of only three in Scotland) installed in 1836 on the top floor of the old windmill tower at Dumfries Museum. Moving panoramic images are projected onto a table top screen allowing visitors to enjoy magnificent views of Dumfries & the surrounding countryside in a unique way. Dumfries Museum, The Observatory, Rotchell Road.

◆ DUMFRIES MUSEUM - History of South West Scotland. Exhibitions trace the history of the people of Solway, Dumfries & Galloway, early Christianity, prehistory, natural history & Victorian life. The Observatory, Rotchell Road.

◆ GLOBE INN - 17th century working inn; Burns' favourite tavern. Rooms are unchanged since the 1790s including the poet's chair & other memorabilia. 56 High Street.

◆ GRACEFIELD ARTS CENTRE - Large collection of Scottish paintings. Monthly exhibitions of contemporary art & craft. 28 Edinburgh Road.

◆ MID STEEPLE - Old Town Hall (or tolbooth) built between 1707 & 1708 marking the town centre. A table shows distances to important Scottish towns & to Huntingdon in England. High Street.

◆ OLD BRIDGE HOUSE MUSEUM - Museum of local life in sandstone building built in 1660 (the oldest house in Dumfries) adjoining Devorgilla Bridge. Period rooms include a Victorian nursery, kitchens from the mid 19th century & dentist's surgery. Devorgilla Bridge, Mill Road.

◆ ROBERT BURNS CENTRE - Set in an 18th century watermill, audio-visual presentations, exhibitions, original manuscripts & relics recount Burns' last years in Dumfries. The centre also includes a model of Dumfries in Burns' time, museum trails, activities for children, plus an award-winning café-restaurant. In the evenings the centre is home to the regional film theatre for Dumfries & Galloway. Mill Road.

◆ ROBERT BURNS HOUSE - Refurbished 18th century sandstone house, Burns' second home which he moved to in 1793 (& where he died in 1796 at the age of thirty-seven), containing his writing desk & chair, manuscripts & relics connected with the poet. Burns Street.

ENTERTAINMENT

◆ Cinemas - Shakespeare Street. Robert Burns Film Theatre, Robert Burns Centre (as above).
◆ Concerts - Easterbrook Hall, The Crichton Site, Bankend Road (SE of Dumfries).
◆ Theatres - Easterbrook Hall (as above). Theatre Royal, Shakespeare Street.

SPORT & LEISURE

◆ Parks & Gardens -Castledykes Park, Glencaple Road (S of Dumfries). Deer Park, Mill Road. Dock Park, St Michael's Bridge Road. Goldie Park, Glasgow Street. Greensands, Park Lane. Hamilton Stark Park, Moat Road (S of Dumfries). King George V Park, Glasgow Street. Mill Green, Mill Road. Noblehill Park, Annan Road (E of Dumfries).
◆ Sports Centres - David Keswick Athletic Centre, Marchmount (NE of Dumfries). DG One Leisure Complex, Hoods Loaning, Dumfries Ice Bowl, King Street. King George V Astro Arena, King George V Park, Glasgow Street.

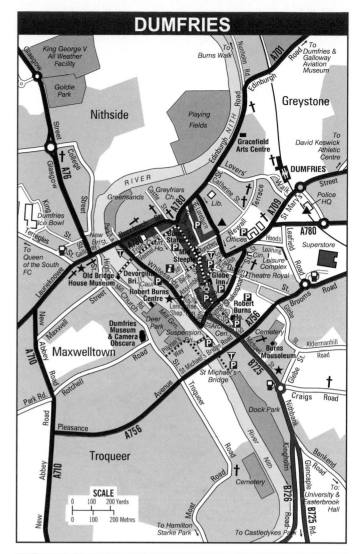

Devorgilla Bridge

Loch Ken

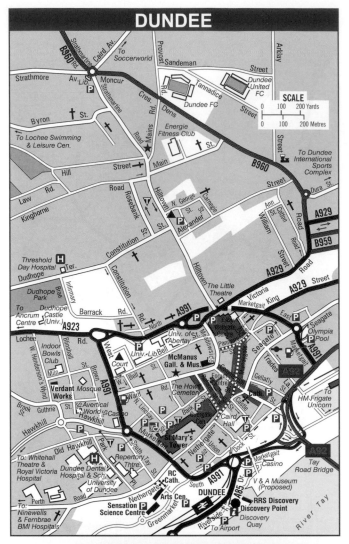

DUNDEE

With its picturesque setting on the River Tay, Dundee is the fourth largest city in Scotland. The history and fortunes of Dundee are inextricably linked to its maritime heritage. Dundee was once the United Kingdom's leading whaling port and maritime trading meant that goods from around the world were available. The emphasis on sea trading meant that ship construction was an important industry and today great vessels such as the RRS Discovery and HM Unicorn Frigate survive to reflect a vital part of Dundee's heritage. By the early 19th century the textile industry was thriving and Dundee became renowned as the jute capital of the world. Of historical interest Dundee has much to offer, The Howff, which was for three centuries until 1857 the city's primary burial ground, was given to the town in 1564 by Mary Queen of Scots. However, originally it was an adjoining orchard to a Franciscan monastery founded in 1270 by Devorguilla Balliol and destroyed in 1548.

Wishart Arch located on Cowgate is thought to date from 1548 and is the only surviving city gate. It is named in memory of George Wishart, a reformer who was burnt at St Andrews in 1546. During 1544, when Dundee was stricken by plague, Wishart preached from this gate in two directions; to those affected who were excluded from the town and those within whom remained unaffected. 1878 saw the construction of the Tay Rail Bridge, which at two miles long was the longest bridge in the world. However, it was not to be long before disaster struck and on the evening of December 28th the following year during a severe storm, the centrepiece of the bridge collapsed while a train was crossing it which resulted in the death of the 75 passengers on board. Engineering faults and poor construction were blamed for the disaster but this did not deter from reconstructing it, a project that commenced three years after the tragedy.

Today Dundee is a lively city to explore where industrial heritage has laid the foundations for an exciting range of modern tourist attractions. It is a popular University City, with a large student community it offers a vibrant nightlife. An exciting waterfront regeneration programme is currently under way including housing, hotels, leisure and retail facilities. The skyline will include a new Victoria & Albert Museum, a landmark stone building on the bank of the River Tay. Once completed the museum will showcase Scottish design talent and provide a venue for major international touring exhibits.

PLACES OF INTEREST

Visit Scotland Information Centre (All Year) - Discovery Point, Riverside Drive. DD1 4XA Tel: (01382) 527527

◆ DISCOVERY POINT & RRS DISCOVERY - Attraction centres around Captain Scott's famous Antarctic exploration ship, which was built in Dundee in 1901. Dramatic visual presentations recreate the events in the Discovery story and other exhibitions reveal what happened to the ship following the exploration. Discovery Quay.

◆ DUDHOPE CASTLE - Dating from the 13th century, the castle was once the hereditary home of the Constables of Dundee. Now owned by the Unviersity of Abertay who use it as offices and the Dundee Business School. (Exterior view only). Barrack Road.

◆ DUNDEE CATHEDRAL - Dating from 1853, this Scottish Episcopal Church was designed by Sir George Gilbert Scott. The Cathedral's 64 m (210 ft) high tower and spire is a renowned landmark. High Street.

◆ DUNDEE CONTEMPORARY ARTS - A hub for the contemporary art scene, the DCA houses five floors of galleries, cinemas, artists facilities, education resources, the University of Dundee visual research centre and the Café Bar. 152 Nethergate.

◆ DUNDEE ROMAN CATHOLIC CATHEDRAL - This Cathedral church dedicated to St Andrew was designed in the Gothic style and dates from 1836. Nethergate.

◆ DUNDEE ST MARY'S TOWER - The 15th century tower known also as the "Old Steeple" is the only surviving part of the pre-Reformation Church of St Mary. Nethergate.

◆ MCMANUS GALLERIES & MUSEUM - Housed in a Victorian Gothic building dating from 1867 is Tayside's main regional museum and art gallery. It houses a fine array of exhibits including collections of silver, glass and furniture. There are displays on local history and a fine art collection which includes the work of Scottish artists from the 19th and 20th centuries. Albert Square.

◆ SENSATION SCIENCE CENTRE - This innovative science centre offers an insight into the perception of the senses using state of the art displays and interactive exhibits. Gift shop and coffee shop. Greenmarket.

◆ VERDANT WORKS - This restored 19th century jute mill is one of a few surviving examples of the industry. Exhibitions reveal how Dundee became the jute capital of the world and the effect that the industry had in shaping the town's history. West Henderson's Wynd.

ENTERTAINMENT

◆ Casinos - G Casino, West Marketgait. Gala Casino, Discovery Point, Riverside Drive ◆ Cinemas - Kingsway West (NW of Dundee). Dundee Contemporary Arts, Nethergate. ◆ Concerts - Caird Hall, City Square. ◆ Theatres - Dundee Repertory Theatre, Tay Square. The Little Theatre, Victoria Road. Whitehall Theatre, Bellfield Street (W of Dundee).

SPORT & LEISURE

◆ Climbing Walls - Avertical World, Blinshall Street. ◆ Parks & Gardens - Dudhope Park, Dudhope Terrace. ◆ Ski Slope - Ancrum Outdoor Centre, Ancrum Road (NW of Dundee). ◆ Sports Centres -Dundee International Sports Complex, Mains Loan (NE of Dundee). Lochee Swim Centre, Lochee (W of Dundee). ◆ Swimming Pools - Lochee Swim Centre (as above). ◆ Ten-Pin Bowling - Dundee Megabowl, Harefield Road (NW of Dundee).

Dundee Museum

Arbroath Cliffs

Forth Bridge

Loch Lomond

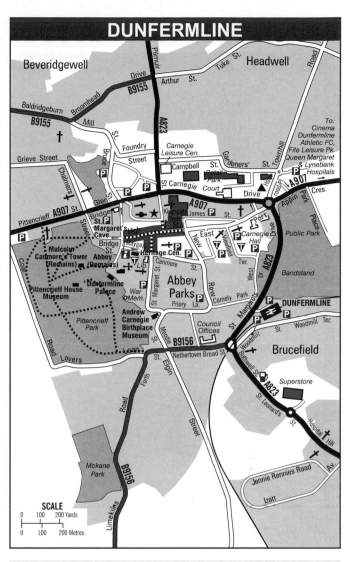

DUNFERMLINE

Scotland's ancient capital for over 500 years, Dunfermline was one of the early settlements of the Celtic Church and a favoured stronghold of the warrior King Malcolm Canmore. In 1070 King Malcolm married the saintly Saxon princess, Margaret whom while fleeing from the Normans was shipwrecked in the Forth and taken to Dunfermline. Together they founded their palace and later built a priory. In 1270 following her death, Margaret was proclaimed a saint and Dunfermline became one of the great centres of pilgrimage in Europe. The town is associated with the birth of numerous kings and queens and is the final resting place of Robert the Bruce. Aside from royalty, Dunfermline has benefited significantly from the generosity of Andrew Carnegie, the great philanthropist who did much to improve facilities available to the people of his native town. Today Dunfermline is a bustling town with a wealth of history to be discovered and a diverse range of visitor attractions.

PLACES OF INTEREST

Visit Scotland Information Centre (All Year) - 1 High Street. KY12 7DL.
Tel: (01383) 720999

◆ ABBOT HOUSE HERITAGE CENTRE - Located in the historic Maygate, the award-winning Abbot House takes the visitor through 1000 years of history from the Picts to the present day. Café, gift shop and garden. Maygate.

◆ ANDREW CARNEGIE BIRTHPLACE MUSEUM - Located in the house where Carnegie was born in 1835, the museum tells the extraordinary story of his rise from poverty to prominence when he emigrated to the United States and created the country's largest steel works. On the first Friday of every month visitors are able to enjoy demonstrations of a working Jacquard handloom reminiscent of the one used by Carnegie's father. The Memorial Hall, endowed by Mrs Louise Carnegie, adjoins the birthplace cottage and charts her husband's astounding business career from bobbin boy to the world's richest steel magnate. Touch-screen displays. Shop & café. Moodie Street.

◆ DUNFERMLINE ABBEY - (Historic Scotland) Remains of a Benedictine abbey founded by Margaret I in the 11th century. The foundations remain under the present Romanesque style nave built during the 12th century. A brass in the choir marks the grave of King Robert the Bruce. Pittencrieff Park.

◆ DUNFERMLINE PALACE - (Historic Scotland) Royal Palace developed out of the original abbey guest house. The palace was destroyed by fire in 1304 but was rebuilt by James IV in 1500. It was the birthplace of Charles I, the last monarch born in scotland in 1600. Pittencrieff Park.

◆ MALCOLM CANMORE'S TOWER - Ruin of a fortified tower alongside the burn where King Malcolm Canmore held court after the death of Macbeth. Pittencrieff Park.

◆ PITTENCRIEFF HOUSE MUSEUM - 17th century mansion house situated in Pittencrieff park was given to the town by Andrew Carnegie. Exhibits in the house include a collection of 19th & 20th Century clothing and displays of materials from the fife area. "Magic of the Glen" exhibition telling the story with photographs of how the park evolved. Pittencrief Park.

◆ ST MARGARET'S CAVE - 84 steps below the Glen Bridge Car Park is the cave where Margaret, an 11th century queen and saint sought refuge for prayer and meditation. Glen Bridge Car Park.

ENTERTAINMENT

◆ Cinemas - Fife Leisure Park (NE of Dunfermline).
◆ Concerts - Carnegie Hall, East Port.
◆ Theatres - Carnegie Hall (as above).

SPORT & LEISURE

◆ Parks & Gardens - Dunfermline Public Park, Appin Crescent. McKane Park, Limekilns Road. Pittencrieff Park, Pittencrieff Street.
◆ Sports Centres - Carnegie Leisure Centre, Pilmuir Street.
◆ Swimming Pools - Carnegie Leisure Centre (as above).

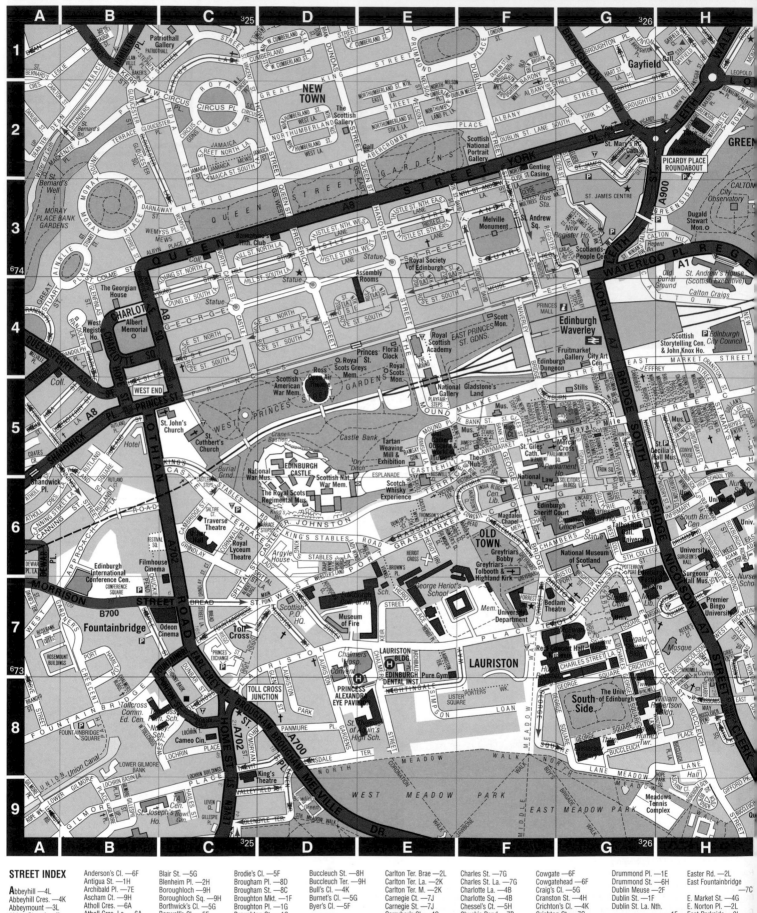

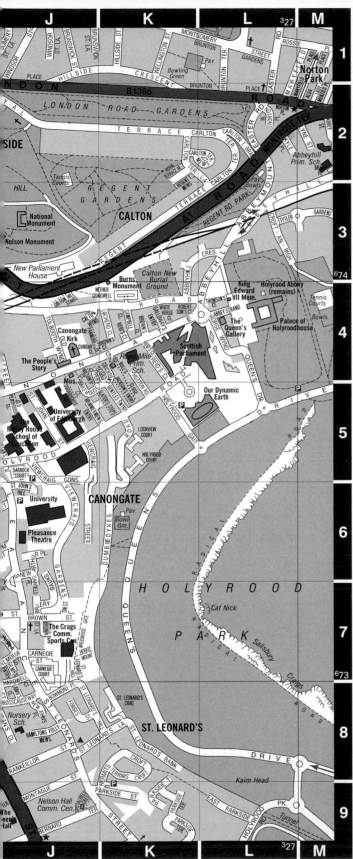

REFERENCE

One-way Street — Traffic flow on A Roads is also indicated by a heavy line on the driver's left.	⟶
Junction Name	WEST END
Restricted Access	
Pedestrianized Road	
Track & Footpath	
Residential Walkway	
Railway	Station ⊞ Tunnel
Edinburgh Trams	Stop
Built-up Area	ALBYN PL.
Car Park (selected)	P
Church or Chapel	†
Fire Station	■
Hospital	H
House Numbers (A & B Roads only)	

Visit Scotland Information Centre	i
National Grid Reference	325
Police Station	▲
Post Office	★
Toilet: without facilities for the Disabled	▽
with facilities for the Disabled	▽
Educational Establishment	■
Hospital or Healthcare Building	■
Industrial Building	■
Leisure or Recreational Facility	■
Place of Interest	■
Public Building	■
Shopping Centre or Market	■
Other Selected Buildings	■

SCALE : 1:9504 (6.66 inches to 1 mile)

0 — ¼ — ½ MILE
0 — 250 — 500 — 750 Metres

Hutton Rd. —4K
Hyndford's Cl. —5H

India Bldgs. —6F
India Pl. —2B
India St. —2C
Infirmary St. —6H
Inglis Ct. —6E

Jackson's Cl. —5G
Jackson's Entry —4K
Jamaica M. —2C
Jamaica St. —2C
  (not continuous)
Jamaica St. Nth. La.
  —2C
Jamaica St. Sth. La.
  —2C
James' Ct. —5F
James Craig Wlk. —3G
Jawbone Wlk. —9F
Jeffrey St. —4G
Johnston Ter. —6D

Keir St. —7E
Kerr St. —1B
Kincaid's Ct. —6G
King's Stables La. —6D
King's Stables Rd.
  —5C
Kyle Pl. —2L

Lady Lawson St. —6D
Lady Menzies Pl. —2M
Lady Stairs Cl. —5F
Lady Wynd —6D
Lamb's Cl. —8J
Lauriston Gdns. —7D
Lauriston Pk. —7D
Lauriston Pl. —7D
Lauriston St. —7D
Lauriston Ter. —7E
Lawnmarket —5F
Leamington Rd. —9A
Leith St. —3G
Leith Wlk. —2H
Leopold Pl. —1H
Leslie Pl. —1A
Leven Cl. —9C
Leven St. —9C
Leven Ter. —9C
Lister Sq. —8E
Lit. King St. —2H
Lochend Cl. —4K
Lochrin Basin La. —9B
Lochrin Bldgs. —8C
Lochrin Pl. —8C
Lochrin Ter. —8C
Lochview Ct. —5K
London Rd. —1H
Lonsdale Ter. —8D
Lothian Rd. —5B
Lothian St. —7H
Lwr. Gilmore Bank —8B
Lwr. Gilmore Pl. —9A
Lyne St. —2M
Lyon's Cl. —5G

Mackenzie Pl. —2A
Main Point —7D
Market St. —5F
Marshall's Ct. —2H
Marshall St. —7G
Maryfield —2L
Maryfield Pl. —2L

Meadow La. —8G
Melville Dr. —9D
Melville Pl. —4A
Melville St. —5A
Merchant St. —6F
Meuse La. —4F
Middle Mdw. Wlk. —9F
Milne's Ct. —5E
Montague St. —9J
Montgomery St. —1L
Montgomery St. La.
  —1H
Montrose Ter. —2L
Moray Pl. —3B
Morrison's Cl. —5H
Morrison St. —7A
Mound, The —4E
Mound Pl. —5E
Multrees Wlk. —3F

Nelson Pl. —2E
Nelson St. —2E
Nether Craigwell —4K
New Arthur Pl. —6J
New Broughton —1F
New John's Pl. —8J
New Skinner's Cl. —5H
New Steps, The —5F
New St. —4H
Nicolson Sq. —7H
Nicolson St. —6H
Niddry St. —5G
Niddry St. Sth. —6H
Nightingale Way —8E
Nth. Bank St. —5F
North Bri. —4G
North Bri. Arc. —5G
Nth. Castle St. —3C
Nth. Charlotte St. —4B
Nth. Clyde St. La. —2F
North E. Circus Pl.
  —2C
Nth. Gray's Cl. —5G
North Mdw. Wlk. —8D
Nth. Richmond St.
  —6H
Nth. St Andrew La.
  —3F
Nth. St Andrew St.
  —2F
Nth. St David St. —3F
Northumberland Pl.
  —2E
Northumberland Pl. La.
  —2E
Northumberland St.
  —2D
Northumberland St.
  Nth. East La. —2E
Northumberland St.
  Nth. West La. —2E
Northumberland St.
  Sth. East La. —2E
Northumberland St.
  Sth. West La. —2D
North West Circus Pl.
  —2B
North West
  Cumberland St. La.
  —1D

Oakfield Pl. —6J
Old Assembly Cl. —5K
Old Broughton —1F
Old Fishmarket Cl.
  —5G

Old Infirmary La. —6H
Old Playhouse Cl. —5J
Old Tolbooth Wynd
  —4J
Omni Cen. —2H

Paisley Cl. —5H
Panmure Cl. —4J
Panmure Pl. —8D
Parkside St. —9K
Parkside Ter. —9K
Parliament Sq. —5F
Patriothall —1B
Picardy Pl. —2G
Playfair Steps —5E
Pleasance —6J
Ponton St. —8C
Porters Wlk. —8F
Port Hamilton —7B
Portsburgh Sq. —6D
Potterrow —7J
Potterrow Port —6G
Princes Exchange —7C
Princes Mall —4F
Princes St. —5B

Quarry Cl. —8H
Queen's Dr. —4L
Queensferry St. —4A
Queensferry St. La.
  —5A
Queen St. —3C
Queen St. Gdns. East
  —2E
Queen St. Gdns. West
  —3D

Radical Rd. —6L
Ramsay Gdn. —5E
Ramsay La. —5E
Randolph Cres. —4B
Randolph La. —4B
Randolph Pl. —4B
Rankeillor St. —8J
Reekie's Ct. —7H
Regent Rd. —3H
Regent Ter. —3K
Regent Ter. M. —3K
Register Pl. —3F
Reid's Cl. —4K
Reid's Ct. —4K
Richmond La. —7H
Richmond Pl. —6H
Riddle's Ct. —5F
Riego St. —7C
Robertson's Cl. —6H
Robertson's Ct. —4K
Rope Wlk. —8H
Rosebank Cotts. —7A
Rosemount Bldgs.
  —7A
Rose St. —4C
Rose St. Nth. La. —4C
  (not continuous)
Rose St. Sth. La. —4C
  (not continuous)
Rossie Pl. —1L
Roxburgh Pl. —6H
Roxburgh's Cl. —5F
Roxburgh St. —6H
Royal Cir. —2C
Royal Ter. —2H
Royal Ter. M. —2K
Rutland Ct. —6B
Rutland Ct. La. —6B
Rutland Pl. —5B

Rutland Sq. —5B
Rutland St. —5B

St Andrew Sq. —3F
St Bernard's Cres.
  —1A
St Colme St. —4B
St David's Ter. —7A
St Giles St. —5F
St James Cen. —3G
St James Pl. —2G
St James Sq. —3G
St John's Hill —6J
St John St. —5J
St Leonard's Bank
  —8K
St Leonard's Crag
  —8K
St Leonard's Hill —7J
St Leonard's La. —8J
St Leonard's St. —8J
St Mary's St. —5H
St Ninian's Row —3G
St Patrick Sq. —8H
St Patrick St. —8H
St Stephen Pl. —1B
St Stephen St. —1B
St Vincent Pl. —1C
St Vincent St. —1C
Saltire Ct. —6C
Saunders St. —2B
Scotsman Bldgs. —5G
Semple St. —7B
Shandwick Pl. —5A
Simon St. —7H
Simpson Loan —8E
Slater's Steps —5K
Solicitors Bldgs. —6G
South Bri. —5H
Sth. Charlotte St. —4C
Sth. College St. —6G
South East Circus Pl.
  —2C
South East Cumberland
  St. La. —1D
Sth. Gayfield La. —1H
Sth. Gray's Cl. —5H
South Mdw. Wlk. —9D
South St Andrew St.
  —3F
South St David St.
  —3F
South West
  Cumberland St. La.
  —1D
Spittalfield Cres. —6H
Spittal St. —7C
Spittal St. La. —6D
Stafford St. —5A
Stevenlaw's Cl. —5G
Sugarhouse Cl. —5H
Surgeon's Hall —6H

Tarvit St. —8C
Terrars Cft. —8J
Teviot Pl. —7F
Thistle Ct. —3E
Thistle St. —3D
Thistle St. Nth.
  East La. —3E
Thistle St. Nth.
  West La. —3D
Thistle St. Sth.
  East La. —3E
Thistle St. Sth.
  West La. —3D

Thomson's Ct. EH1
  —6E
Thomson's Ct. EH8
  —4L
Thorny Bauk —7C
  (not continuous)
Tron Sq. —5G
Trunk's Cl. —5H
Tweeddale Ct. —5H
Tytler Gdns. —3L

Union Path —9A
Union Pl. —2H
Union St. —1G
Upper Bow —5F
Up. Dean Ter. —2A
Up. Gilmore Pl. —9B
Up. Greenside La. —2H

Valleyfield St. —9C
Vennel —6E
Victoria St. —6F
Victoria Ter. —6E
Viewcraig Gdns. —5J
Viewcraig St. —5J

Warden's Cl. —6F
Wardrop's Ct. —5F
Warriston's Cl. —5F
Waterloo Pl. —3G
Waverley Bri. —4F
Waverley Steps —4G
Webster's Land —6D
Wellington St. —1K
Wemyss Pl. —3C
Wemyss Pl. M. —3B
W. Adam St. —6H
West App. Rd. —7A
West Bow —6F
W. College St. —6G
West Crosscauseway
  —8H
West End —5B
W. Nicolson St. —7H
W. Norton Pl. —2L
W. Parliament Sq. —5F
West Port —7D
W. Register St. —3F
W. Register St. La.
  —3F
W. Richmond St. —7H
West Tollcross —8C
White Horse Cl. —4K
William St. —5A
Wilson's Ct. —4J
Windmill Cl. —8H
Windmill La. —8H
Windmill Pl. —8H
Windmill St. —8G
Windsor St. —1J
Windsor St. La. —1J
World's End Cl. —5H

York La. —2G
York Pl. —2F
Young St. —4C
Young St. Nth. La.
  —4C
Young St. Sth. La.
  —4C

Fountainbridge Sq.
  —8B
Fountain Cl. —5H
Frederick St. —3D

Gabriel's Rd. —3G
Galloway's Entry —4K
Gardner's Cres. —7B
Gayfield Cl. —1H
Gayfield Sq. —1H
Geddes Entry —5G
Gentle's Entry —4K
George IV Bri. —5F
George Sq. —8G
George Sq. La. —8F
George St. —4C
Gibbs Entry —7H
Gifford Pk. —9H
Gillespie Pl. —9C
Gillespie St. —9B

Gilmore Pk. —9A
Gilmore Pl. —9B
Gilmore Pl. La. —9B
Gilmour's Cl. —6E
Gilmour's Entry —7J
Gilmour St. —7J
Glanville Pl. —1B
Glenfinlas St. —4B
Glengyle Ter. —9C
Glen St. —8D
Gloucester La. —2B
Gloucester Pl. —2B
Gloucester Sq. —2B
Gloucester St. —2B
Grassmarket —6E
  (not continuous)
Gray's Ct. —7H
Gt. King St. —2D
Gt. Stuart St. —4A
Greenside End —2H
Greenside La. —2H
Greenside Pl. —2H
Greenside Row —3H
Greyfriars —6F
Greyfriars Pl. —6F
Grindlay St. —6D
Grindlay St. Ct. —7C
Grove St. —8A
Gullan's Cl. —5H

Haddon's Ct. —7H
Hailes St. —9C
Hamilton Folly M.
  —8J
Hamilton Pl. —1B
Hammermen's Entry
  —6H

Hanover St. —3E
Hardwell Cl. —7J
Hart St. —1G
Hart St. La. —1G
Hastie's Cl. —6G
Haugh St. —1B
Heriot Bri. —6F
Heriot Cross —6E
Heriot Mt. —7J
Heriot Pl. —7E
Heriot Row —3C
Hermits Cft. —8K
High Riggs —8C
High School Wynd
  —6H
High School Yards
  —6H
High St. —5F
Hill Pl. —7H
Hill St. —3C
Hillside Cres. —1J

Hillside St. —1K
Hill Sq. —6H
Hill St. —3C
Hill St. North La. —3C
Hill St. South La.
  —4C
Holyrood Cl. —5K
Holyrood Gait —5K
Holyrood Mt. —7J
Holyrood Pk. Rd.
  —9L
Holyrood Rd. —5J
Home St. —8C
Hope Pk. Sq. —8H
Hope St. —5B
Hope St. La. —5B
Horse Wynd —4L
Howden St. —7H
Howe St. —2D
Hunter's Cl. —6E
Hunter Sq. —5G

EDINBURGH

Referred to as the 'Athens of the North', Edinburgh is a flourishing city renowned for its history, style, diversity and prestigious annual festival, which is considered to be the most important and successful event of its kind in Britain. During the month of August, the city becomes a magnet for thousands of people from around the world intent on participating in the festival scene.

Edinburgh divides itself between the Old and New Town areas. The Old Town includes the ancient city centre, where the famous Royal Mile links the Castle and Holyrood, and the historical districts of Grassmarket and Greyfriars. The New Town, dating mainly from the 18th century extends north from Princes Street, Edinburgh's main shopping street, and comprises a continuous development of grand streets, squares, circuses and green spaces regarded as a masterpiece of urban architecture.

PLACES OF INTEREST

Visit Scotland Information Centre (All year), (4G 74) - 3 Princes Street. EH2 2QP. Tel: 0845 22 55 121. www.edinburgh.org

◆ **BRASS RUBBING CENTRE** (5H 74) - Housed in Trinity Apse, the only remaining part of the collegiate church founded in 1462. The centre holds a fine collection of replica brasses and Pictish stones from which rubbings can be made. Gift shop. off Chalmers Close. ◆ **BURNS MONUMENT** (4K 75) - A monument dedicated to Scotland's most beloved poet Robert Burns (1759-1796) built in 1830 by architect Thomas Hamilton. Regent Road. ◆ **CAMERA OBSCURA & WORLD OF ILLUSIONS** (5E 74) - This Victorian 'Eye in the Sky' has fascinated visitors for 150 years with its live moving panorama of the city. Enjoy access to free telescopes showing a spectacular 360° rooftop panorama and listen to your guide recount tales of Edinburgh's exciting past. In World of illusions you can immerse yourself in five floors of mind-boggling hands-on exhibits from shadow walls to bendy mirrors, seeing in 3D to shaking hands with your ghost. Gift shop. Castlehill. ◆ **CITY ART CENTRE** (4G 74) - A rich collection of fine art, almost entirely by Scottish artists, is housed within the six floors of the City Art Centre. The galleries display a wide range of media, including painting, drawing, print, sculpture, photography and installation art. Café and shop. 2 Market Street. ◆ **EDINBURGH CASTLE** (5D 74) - (Historic Scotland). The imposing fortress of Edinburgh Castle has dominated the cityscape since the Middle Ages, defiantly rooted to the ancient volcanic outcrop upon which it stands. Its strategic positioning and defensive structures have withstood countless sieges and provided successive Kings and Queens with refuge. The castle is home to the Scottish Crown Jewels, the Stone of Destiny and the famous 15th century siege gun Mons Meg. Of particular note is the remarkable St Margaret's Chapel, which has remained perfectly intact for 900 years, making it Edinburgh's oldest surviving building. Castlehill. ◆ **EDINBURGH DUNGEON, THE** (4F 74) - Experience 500 years of the capital's most blood-curdling history. Live actors, two hair-raising rides, shows and special effects transport visitors back to life in barbaric times. Market Street.

◆ **FLORAL CLOCK** (4E 74) - In 1903, John McHattie, the city's Park Superintendent, conceived the idea of the Floral Clock. The face and hands of the working clock are carpeted with thousands of small plants, all of which are replanted in Spring & Autumn. Princes Street. ◆ **FRUITMARKET GALLERY** (4G 74) - Exhibiting contemporary art of the highest quality, the gallery is committed to bringing the work of artists with both established and emerging international reputation to Scotland and presenting the work of Scottish artists. 45 Market Street. ◆ **GEORGIAN HOUSE** (4B 74) - (National Trust for Scotland) Situated on the north side of Charlotte Square, designed by Robert Adam in 1791, this house exemplifies the style of Edinburgh's New Town architecture. The rooms of No.7 (built in 1796) are furnished in period style. There is a video presentation "Living in a Grand Design" that reflects life in the New Town. The "Below Stairs" life of servants is also illustrated. Charlotte Square. ◆ **GLADSTONE'S LAND** (5F 74) - (National Trust for Scotland) Once the home of a wealthy merchant, this six-storey tenement building along the Royal Mile has been authentically restored to illustrate how 17th century people lived and worked. Gift shop. 477B Lawnmarket. ◆ **GREYFRIARS BOBBY** (6F 74) - Statue in memory of Greyfriars Bobby, the skye terrier who watched over his master's grave for 14 years after his death from 1858-1872. Candlemaker Row.

◆ **HOLYROOD ABBEY** (4L 75) - (Historic Scotland) The ruined nave is all that remains of this Abbey church founded for Augustinian canons during the late 12th and early 13th centuries. Beneath the Abbey the Royal Vault was the final resting place for a number of Scottish Kings, including David II (son of Robert the Bruce), James II, James V and Lord Darnley, Mary Queen of Scot's second husband. Canongate. ◆ **MUSEUM OF CHILDHOOD** (5H 74) - This museum houses an extensive collection of childhood memorabilia including toys, games, books and dolls. For the adult visitor there are exhibitions relating to the history of child welfare including health, education and upbringing. Gift shop. 42 High Street. ◆ **MUSEUM OF EDINBURGH** (4J 75) - A series of 16th to 18th Century buildings arranged around a close, provide the setting for exhibitions devoted to the local history of Edinburgh. The diverse range of artefacts include pottery, silverware, street signs and treasures of national importance. Watch the city evolve at your feet in Foundation Edinburgh, the museum's latest blacked-out theatre attraction. Gift shop. 142 Canongate. ◆ **MUSEUM OF FIRE** (7D 74) - Relating the history of the oldest municipal fire brigade in the UK. Exhibits include manual horse drawn, steam & motorised pumps dating from 1806 & fire engines dating from 1910. Lauriston Place. ◆ **MUSEUM ON THE MOUND** (5F 74) - Based in the headquarters of Scotland's oldest bank, this museum takes a fresh look at money; see a million pounds, crack a safe, or build the bank! Displays illustrate the story of banks, building societies, life assurance and more. North Bank Street. ◆ **NATIONAL LIBRARY OF SCOTLAND** (6F 74) - The world's foremost centre for the study of Scotland and the Scots, the National Library of Scotland is a treasure trove of knowledge, history and culture with millions of books, manuscripts and maps. George IV Bridge.

View from Edinburgh Castle

◆ **NATIONAL MONUMENT** (3J 75) - Built in 1826 to honour the Scottish who perished in the Napoleonic wars, this monument was designed to emulate the Parthenon, (temple dedicated to Athena, the Greek goddess of war). Unfortunately, it was never completed due to a collapse in funding and remains today unfinished. Calton Hill. ◆ **NATIONAL MUSEUM OF SCOTLAND** (6G 74) - Extensively re-developed in 2011, to include 16 galleries with displays exploring Scottish history, the natural world, world cultures, science and technology and art and design. With a wealth of interesting objects from fossils to future technology, meteorites to deep sea creatures, canoes to musical instruments and bicycles to space age rockets. Chambers Street. ◆ **NATIONAL WAR MUSEUM OF SCOTLAND** (5D 74) - This absorbing museum detailing 400 years of Scottish military history, reflects the experience of war, sourced from personal diaries, photographs and official documents. Other exhibits include uniforms, insignia and equipment, medals, decorations, weapons, paintings, ceramics and silverware. Edinburgh Castle. ◆ **NELSON MONUMENT** (3J 75) - Built between 1807 and 1815, this was one of the first monuments to Admiral Nelson. The climb to the top is rewarded with splendid panoramic views across the city. Exhibition, telling the story of the monument's history & the Battle of Trafalgar. 32 Calton Hill. ◆ **OUR DYNAMIC EARTH** (5K 75) - Through technology including a 3D and 4D experience, discover our planet's past, present and future. Be shaken by volcanoes, fly over glaciers, feel the chill of polar ice, get caught in a tropical rainstorm and debate the planet's future. A new gallery is planned, in which an interactive exhibition commemorates the life of James Hutton known as "The father of geology". 107 Holyrood Road. ◆ **PALACE OF HOLYROODHOUSE & HOLYROOD PARK** (4L 75) - At the eastern end of Edinburgh's historic Royal Mile stands the Palace of Holyroodhouse, the Queen's official Scottish residence. Today, tourists can visit the Royal apartments, the Throne room, the Royal Dining Room and the Great Gallery to experience the grandeur of this Royal residence. Changing exhibitions throughout the year. Canongate, Royal Mile. ◆ **PEOPLE'S STORY, THE** (4J 75) - Housed in the 16th century Tolbooth, this museum reflects working class life in Edinburgh since the 18th century. Sounds, sights, smells and reconstructed rooms combine to evoke an atmosphere of a bygone era. Canongate Tolbooth. ◆ **REID CONCERT HALL MUSEUM OF INSTRUMENTS** (7G 74) - An outstanding and diverse collection of over 1000 musical instruments from around the world chronicling the art of instrument making over the past 400 years. Changing exhibitions throughout the year. Bristo Square. ◆ **ROYAL SCOTS REGIMENTAL MUSEUM, THE** (6D 74) - The visitor is taken back to the raising of the regiment in 1663 and with displays of maps, tableaux and dioramas the story of the regiment is told, right up to the present day. Castlehill. ◆ **ROYAL SCOTTISH ACADEMY** (4E 74) - Presenting the cream of Scottish contemporary art through an ongoing programme of exciting exhibitions including painting, sculpture, printmaking, installation, photography, architecture, new media, film and performance art. The Mound. ◆ **ST. CECILIA'S HALL MUSEUM OF INSTRUMENTS** (5H 74) - St. Cecilia's Hall was built in 1763 and is the oldest concert hall in Scotland. On display are 50 highly important and well -preserved early keyboard instruments. There is also a display of harps, lutes, citterns and guitars. Cowgate. ◆ **ST. GILES' CATHEDRAL** (5F 74) - Founded in 1120, the mother church of Presbyterianism, most of the remaining architecture dates from the 14th and 15th centuries including the famous crown spire that dominates the city skyline. Royal Mile. ◆ **ST. MARY'S RC CATHEDRAL** (2G 74) - This Cathedral church of St. Mary was designed by James Gillespie Graham and dates from 1814 and 1890. The St. Andrews Altar contains the National Shrine to Scotland's patron saint. Broughton Street. ◆ **SCOTCH WHISKY EXPERIENCE, THE** (6E 74) - Enjoy a ride through history in a whisky barrel to discover the traditions and origins of whisky production. Hear stories recounting the magical craft and let the experts advise you on the perfect dram for your palate. 345 Castlehill. ◆ **SCOTTISH NATIONAL GALLERY** (5E 74) - Located in the heart of the city, the gallery has been open to the public since 1859. The collection comprises a comprehensive catalogue of work from the Renaissance era to the Post Impressionist period. The Mound. ◆ **SCOTTISH NATIONAL PORTRAIT GALLERY** (2F 74) - Visual history of Scotland from the 16th century to the present day depicted through portraits of figures who shaped it: royalty, philosophers, poets and rebels are included. The gallery also houses the National Collection of Photography. 1 Queen Street. ◆ **SCOTTISH PARLIAMENT** (4K 75) - Standing boldly at the eastern end of the historic Royal Mile, the new building is open to visitors Monday to Saturday. Take a free guided tour and learn about the work, history and procedures of the Scottish Parliament, as well as the design and architecture of this striking building. Canongate. ◆ **SCOTTISH STORYTELLING CENTRE** (5H 74) - Programme of live performances, visual arts & workshops celebrating Scotland's storytelling heritage. Also included in this attraction is John Knox House, associated with dramatic events in Scotland's turbulent history. James Mosman, goldsmith to Mary Queen of Scots, once lived here. 43-45 High Street. ◆ **SCOTT MONUMENT** (4F 74) - One of Edinburgh's most famous landmarks, this monument to Sir Walter Scott is 200 ft high and dates from 1840. The 287 steps lead to stunning panoramic views over the city centre. East Princes Street Gardens. ◆ **STILLS GALLERY** (5G 74) - Scotland's premier photographic gallery exhibits a comprehensive collection of contemporary photography. 23 Cockburn Street.

Edinburgh Tattoo

◆ **SURGEONS' HALL MUSEUMS** (6H 74) - Originally developed as a teaching museum for students of medicine and first opened to the public in 1832, the building houses one of the largest and most historic collections of surgical pathology material in the United Kingdom. It can also lay claim to being Scotland's oldest museum. Permanent displays include the Pathology Museum, the History of Surgery and the Dental Museum. Nicolson Street. ◆ **TALBOT RICE GALLERY** (6G 74) - Based at the University of Edinburgh, the Talbot Rice Gallery is one of Scotland's leading public galleries of contemporary visual art. South Bridge. ◆ **TARTAN WEAVING MILL AND EXHIBITION** (5E 74) - Housed in the former Castlehill Reservoir Cistern, this working mill allows visitors to view the entire production process of tartan from sheep to kilt. 555 Castlehill. ◆ **WRITERS' MUSEUM** (5F 74) - Located in the historic Lady Stair's House dating from 1622, the museum houses an exhibition that revolves around Scotland's three great writers; Robert Burns, Sir Walter Scott and Robert Louis Stevenson. Lady Stair's Close.

The following attractions are located outside the city centre map
◆ Arthur's Seat (Holyrood Park) 1 ½ miles South East of city centre.
◆ Royal Botanic Garden (Inverleith Row) 1 mile North of city centre.
◆ Royal Yacht Britannia (Leith Docks) 2 ½ miles North of city centre.
◆ Scottish National Gallery of Modern Art (Belford Road) 2 miles West of city centre.

ENTERTAINMENT
◆ Cinemas - Greenside Place. Home Street. 2 Lothian Road.
◆ Concerts - Assembly Rooms, George Street. Edinburgh Festival Theatre, Nicholson Street. Edinburgh Playhouse, Greenside Place. Queens Hall, Clerk Street. Ross Open Air Theatre, Princes Street Gardens. Usher Hall, Lothian Road.
◆ Theatres - Edinburgh Festival Theatre (as above). Edinburgh Playhouse (as above). King's Theatre, Leven Street. Royal Lyceum Theatre, Grindlay Street. Traverse Theatre, Cambridge Street.

SPORT & LEISURE
◆ Parks & Gardens - Calton Hill, Regent Road. East Meadow Park, Meadow Lane. East and West Princes Street Gardens, Princes Street. Holyrood Park, Queen's Drive. London Road Gardens, London Road. Moray Place Bank Gardens, Moray Place. Queen Street Gardens, Queen Street. Regent Gardens, Regent Terrace. Regent Road Park, Abbeymount. West Meadow Park, Melville Drive.

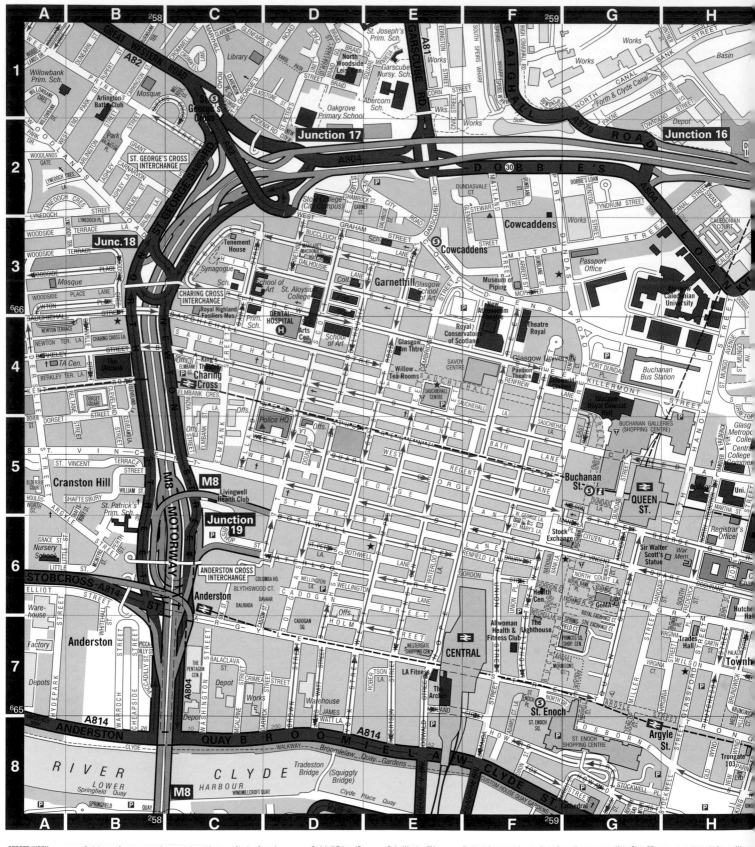

STREET INDEX

Adams Ct. La. —8F
Albion Ga. —7J
Albion St. —8J
 (not continuous)
Alexandra Pde.
 —4M
Allen Glen Pl. —5J
Anchor La. —6G
Anderston Quay —8B
Andrew Ure Hall —7K
Argyle St. —7C
Argyll Arc. —7F
Arlington Pl. —2B
Arlington St. —2B
Ashley La. —2B
Ashley St. —2B

Baird St. —3J
Balaclava St. —7C
Baliol La. —3B
Baliol St. —2B
Barrack St. —8M

Bath La. —4C
 (not continuous)
Bath St. —4C
Bell St. —7J
Beltane St. —4B
Berkeley St. —4A
Berkeley Ter. La. —4A
Birkbeck Ct. —5K
Bishop St. —6C
Blackfriars Rd. —7K
Blackfriars St. —7J
Black St. —3K
Blythswood Ct. —6C
Blythswood Sq. —5D
Blythswood St. —7D
Bothwell La. —6D
Bothwell St. —6D
Braid La. —1D
Braid St. —1D
Broomielaw —8D
Brown St. —7D
Brunswick La. —7H
Brunswick St. —7H
Buccleuch La. —3D

Buccleuch St. —3C
Buchanan Galleries
 (Shopping Cen.)
 —5G
Buchanan St. —7F
Burnbank Ter. —1B
Burrell's La. —6K

Cadogan La. —6D
Cadogan Sq. —7D
Cadzow St. —7C
Caledonian St. —3H
Calgary St. —3H
Cambridge St. —4E
Canal St. —2H
Candleriggs —8J
Carnarvon St. —2B
Carrick St. —8D
Carrington St. —1B
Castle St. —3M
Cathedral Sq. —6L
 (not continuous)
Cathedral St. —5G
Chancellors Hall —6K

Charing Cross La.
 —4B
Charles St. —2M
Cheapside St. —8B
Chisholm St. —8J
Citizen La. —6G
Civic St. —2E
Clarendon Pl. —1C
Clarendon St. —1C
Cleveland La. —4B
Cleveland St. —4B
Clyde Pl. —8D
Clyde St. —8F
Clyde Walkway —8B
Cochrane St. —6H
College La. —7K
College St. —7J
Collins St. —6L
Columba Ho. —6D
Corn St. —1E
Couper Pl. —3J
Couper St. —3J
Cowcaddens Rd.
 —3E

Craighall Rd. —1F
Crimea St. —7C
Cromwell La. —1C
Cromwell St. —1C
Custom Ho. Quay Gdns.
 —8F

Dalhousie La. —3D
Dalhousie St. —4D
Dalriada —6D
Davaar —6D
Dixon St. —8F
Dobbie's Loan —2F
 (not continuous)
Dobbie's Loan Pl.
 —4J
Dorset Sq. —4B
Dorset St. —5A
Douglas La. —5D
Douglas St. —7D
Dover St. —5A
Drury St. —6F
Duke St. —6K

Duke Wynd —7M
Dunblane St. —2F
 (not continuous)
Dundashill —1F
Dundas La. —5G
Dundas St. —5G
 (not continuous)
Dundasvale Ct. —2F
Dunearn St. —1B
Dunlop St. G1—8G
 (Howard St.)
Dunlop St. G4—8G
 (Osborne St.)

East Bath La. —5G
E. Campbell St.
 —8L
Edington St. —1E
Elderslie Ct. —5A
Elderslie St. —4A
Elliot St. —6A
Elmbank Cres. —4C
Elmbank Gdns —4C
Elmbank St. —5C

Elmbank St. La. —5C
Exchange Pl. —6G

Forbes Hall —6K
Fountainwell Rd. —1K
Fox St. —8F

Gallowgate —8J
Garnet Ct. —2D
Garnethill St. —3D
Garnet St. —4C
Garnett Hall —5K
Garscube Rd. —1E
Garth St. —7H
George V Bri. —8E
George Sq. —6G
Gibson Hgts. —6L
Gladstone St. —1C
Glasgow Bri. —8F
Glassford St. —7H
Glebe Ct. —4L
Glebe St. —3K
 (Black St.)

Glebe St. —4L
 (McAslin St.),
 not continuous)
Glenfarg St. —1C
Glenmavis St. —2F
Gordon La. —6F
Gordon St. —6F
Grace St. —6A
Grafton Pl. —4H
Grant St. —2B
Granville St. —4B
Great Dovehill —8K
Gt. Western Rd. —1B

Hanover Ct. —5H
Hanover St. —6G
Havannah St. —1L
Headline Building, The
 —6J
High Craighall Rd. —1F
High St. —8J
Hill St. —3C
Holland St. —5D
Holm St. —7D

Hope St. —7E
Houldsworth St. —5A
Howard St. —8F
Hunter St. —8L
Hutcheson St. —7H
Hydepark St. —7A

India St. —4C
Ingram St. —6G
Inner City Trad. Est.
 —3J

Jamaica St. —8F
James Blyth Ct. —6K
James Goold Hall
 —6K
James Watt La. —7D
James Watt St. —8D
James Young Hall —6L
John Knox St. —6M
John St. —6H

Karol Path —1D
Kennedy Path —4J

Kennedy St. —4H
Kent Rd. —4A
Killermont St. —4G
Kings Ct. —8H
King St. —8H
Kyle St. —3H

Ladywell Bus. Cen.
Ladywell Est. —6K
Lancefield Quay
 —8A
Larbert St. —3F
Lister Hgts. —6L
Lister St. —3K
Little Dovehill —8K
Little St. —6A
London Rd. —8J
London St. —8J
Lynedoch Cres.

Lynedoch Cres. La.

Lynedoch Pl. —1B

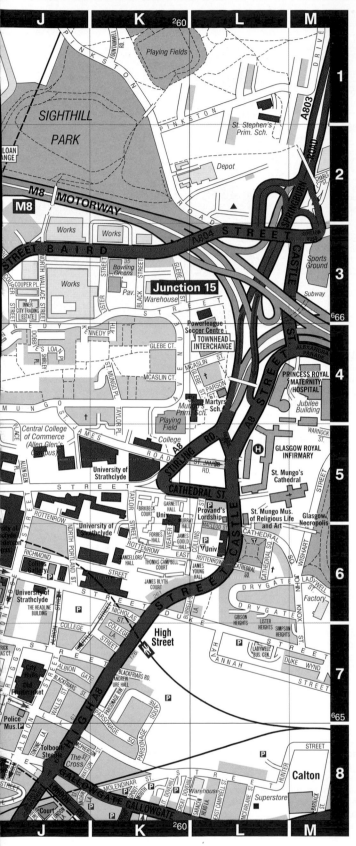

REFERENCE

One-way Street Traffic flow on A Roads is also indicated by a heavy line on the driver's left.	
Junction Name	DOBBIE'S LOAN INTERCHANGE
Restricted Access	
Pedestrianized Road	
Track & Footpath	
Residential Walkway	
Railway	Station ≡ Tunnel
Subway Station	Ⓢ
Built-up Area	CLYDE PL.
Car Park (selected)	P
Church or Chapel	†
Fire Station	■
Hospital	Ⓗ
House Numbers (A & B Roads only)	

Visit Scotland Information Centre	i
National Grid Reference	325
Police Station	▲
Post Office	★
Safety Camera with Speed Limit Fixed cameras and long term road works cameras Symbols do not indicate camera direction	30
Toilet:	
without facilities for the Disabled	▽
with facilities for the Disabled	▽
Educational Establishment	
Hospital or Healthcare Building	
Industrial Building	
Leisure or Recreational Facility	
Place of Interest	
Public Building	
Shopping Centre or Market	
Other Selected Buildings	

SCALE : 1:9504 (6.66 inches to 1 mile)

0 ¼ ½ MILE

0 250 500 750 Metres

George Square

GLASGOW

The history of Glasgow can be dated from the 6th century when a settlement developed around the church built by St Mungo on the banks of the Molendinar burn. His popularity earned him the name 'dear one' and to this day is the patron saint of the city. These first inhabitants named their settlement 'Glas Ghu' (dear green place) and with the city and its environs boasting no less than 70 parks and green spaces it certainly lives up to its name. In the period between the death of St Mungo and the granting of a charter in 1175 by William the Lion, little is known of the city's history, but from this date the city became a prosperous centre. In 1451 the university was founded which after St Andrew's is Scotland's oldest University and the 4th oldest in the UK and in 1611 Glasgow became a Royal Burgh. The city prospered through its ability to trade in tabacco, sugar and cotton with the American colonies but when the American Revolution affected this in 1775 the city turned to industry. With the advent of Industrialisation in the 19th century, Glasgow concentrated upon ship building and soon established a reputation for quality throughout the world that earned the city its reputation as 'Second City of the British Empire.' However, the onset of economic depression in post war England would contribute to the decline of industrial prestige. Depression of the industry was slowed down by the need for naval re-armament in the 1930s but by the 1950s demand was dwindling and combined with cheap foreign competition, Glasgow could no longer compete in the industrial arena.

With a rich heritage of cultural splendour, Glasgow realised that this was the key to renewed prosperity. Splendid Victorian architecture lay beneath the grime of an industrial age and once restored would revive the city as a cultural centre. Many of the city's buildings reflect the style of the talented Glasgow born architect, Charles Rennie Mackintosh (1868-1928) whose influential style contributed significantly to shaping the distinctive forms of Art Nouveau throughout Europe. Architecture became a focus for his artistic expression and in the city there is an abundance of public buildings, private buildings and tea rooms that display the familiar Mackintosh style. The Willow Tea Rooms on Sauchiehall Street, designed for Kate Cranston in 1903 have been restored to reflect Mackintosh's original design and the School of Art on Renfrew Street, architecturally one of Mackintosh's greatest achievements is still in use as an art school. In 1990 Glasgow was awarded the prestigious title of Cultural Capital of Europe and in 1999 was designated UK City of Architecture and design. Today, Glasgow is one of the UK's most visited cities offering visitors a wealth of cultural heritage and visitor attractions.

PLACES OF INTEREST
Visit Scotland Information Centre (All Year), (5G 78) - 172 Buchannan Street. G2 2LW Tel: (0141) 204 4400

◆ **CENTRE FOR CONTEMPORARY ARTS** (4D 78) - Inspiring and cutting edge centre for visual and performance art, film, music, and the spoken word. Housing six major Scottish and international exhibitions over a year. 350 Sauchiehall Street. ◆ **COLLINS GALLERY** (6J 79) - Affiliated to the University, the gallery mounts various exhibitions including contemporary, fine and applied art and photography. 22 Richmond Street. ◆ **GALLERY OF MODERN ART** (6G 78) - Elegant, neo-classical building situated in the heart of the city, the gallery offers a range of contemporary exhibitions and activities, displaying work by Scottish and International artists as well as addressing contemporary social issues. Café. Royal Exchange Square. ◆ **GLASGOW CITY CHAMBERS** (6H 78) - Built in 1883-88 by William Young, the imposing City Chambers is a magnificent example of 19th century architecture that occupies the east side of George Square. Today, it they are occupied by Glasgow City Council. George Square. ◆ **GLASGOW NECROPOLIS** (5M 79) - Adjacent to the Cathedral, this cemetery dating from 1883 is modelled on the famous Pere la Chaise in Paris and is renowned for its elaborate tombs. (Pre-booked tours - visit www.glasgownecropolis.org). Castle Street. ◆ **GLASGOW POLICE MUSEUM, THE** (7J 79) - Through the use of text boards and artefacts, the founding and history of the Glasgow Police is presented, along with a section on Police forces from around the world which includes insignia, headgear and uniforms. Bell Street. ◆ **GLASGOW ST ANDREW'S RC CATHEDRAL** (8G 78) - Built 1814-1817 to meet the needs of the growing Catholic population in Glasgow, the Cathedral was later considered "one of the finest ecclesiastical edifices in the city" and is one of the earliest examples of Gothic Revival architecture in the city. It is home to the Archibishop of Glasgow, the most important Roman Catholic figure in Scotland. Dunlop Street. ◆ **GLASGOW ST MUNGOS CATHEDRAL** (5L 79) - (Historic Scotland) Dating predominantly from the 15th century, the cathedral is regarded as one of Glasgow's most important buildings both architecturally and historically. (Guided tours). Castle Street.

◆ **LIGHTHOUSE, THE - SCOTLAND'S CENTRE FOR ARCHITECTURE, DESIGN & THE CITY** (7F 78) - Seeking to promote the disciplines of architecture and design throughout Scotland and abroad, the centre has attracted national and international recognition for its exhibition programmes. Also within the complex is the Mackintosh Interpretation Centre, which provides an insight into the work of the great Scottish artist. Café. 11 Mitchell Lane. ◆ **MITCHELL LIBRARY, THE** (4B 78) - Founded in 1874, this is one of the largest public reference libraries in Europe. Contained within its volumes can be found a wide range of literature relating to the culture and history of Glasgow and Scotland. North Street.

Glasgow University

◆ **MUSEUM AT THE NATIONAL PIPING CENTRE** (3F 78) - Museum houses an outstanding collection of bagpipes and exhibitions that trace the origins and history of piping through innovative displays. (Pre-booked tours - Tel: 0141 353 0220 or visit www.thebagpipeshop.co.uk). 30-34 McPhater Street. ◆ **PROVAND'S LORDSHIP** (5L 79) - Dating from 1471, this is the oldest house in Glasgow which was originally built as a manse to the adjacent St Nicholas Hospital. 3 Castle Street. ◆ **ROYAL HIGHLAND FUSILIERS REGIMENTAL MUSEUM** (3C 78) - Extensively refurbished in 2013 there are displays of medals, uniforms and records relating to the history of The Royal Scots Fusiliers, The Highland Light Infantry and the Royal Highland Fusiliers. 518 Sauchiehall Street. ◆ **ST MUNGO MUSEUM OF RELIGIOUS LIFE & ART** (5L 79) - Innovative museum offering an insight into religious faiths throughout the world through various art forms which aspire to promote understanding and respect between people of different faiths and of none. After exploring the world's major religions visitors can relax in contemplation in the peaceful Zen garden, the first of its kind in Britain. Changing exhibitions. Café. 2 Castle Street. ◆ **SCOTT'S STATUE** (6H 78) - The first monument erected to the great writer Sir Walter Scott (1771-1832). The stone carving dates from 1837. George Square. ◆ **TENEMENT HOUSE** (3C 78) - (National Trust for Scotland) Dating from the late 19th century, this is a typical example of a Victorian tenement flat. Many of the original furnishings remain to create a fascinating insight of life in the early part of the 20th century. 145 Buccleuch Street. ◆ **TOLBOOTH STEEPLE** (8J 79) - Dating from 1626, this seven storey tower with its distinctive crown at the summit of the 34 m (113 ft) high steeple marked the centre of Glasgow until Victorian times. Glasgow Cross. ◆ **TRADES HALL** (7H 78) - One of the most historic buildings in the city. Explore the Grand Hall and discover how the trade houses shaped the Glasgow of today. (Guided tours on Tuesdays). 85 Glassford Street. ◆ **TRONGATE 103** (8H 78) - A resource for the city, housed in an Edwardian warehouse. The centre spans six floors with a print studio, photoworks and two floors of galleries. Café Trongate.

The following attractions are located outside the city centre map
◆ Burrell Collection (Pollok Country Park) 3 miles SW of city centre.
◆ Glasgow Science Centre (Pacific Quay) 2 miles SW of city centre.
◆ Hunterian Museum (University of Glasgow) 2 miles NW of city centre.
◆ Kelvingrove Art Gallery & Museum (Argyle St.) 2 miles W of city centre.
◆ People's Palace (Glasgow Green) 1 mile SE of city centre.
◆ Riverside Museum (Pointhouse Place) 2 1/2 miles W of city centre.
◆ Scottish Exhibition & Conference Centre (SECC) (Exhibition Way) 1 1/2 miles W of city centre.
◆ The Tall Ship at Riverside (River Clyde) 2 1/2 miles W of city centre.

ENTERTAINMENT
◆ Cinemas - Glasgow Film Theatre, Rose Street. Renfrew Street.
◆ Concerts - Arches, The, Argyle Street. Glasgow Royal Concert Hall, Sauchiehall Street. The Mitchell, Granville Street. Old Fruitmarket, Candleriggs. ◆ Theatres - Arches, The (as above). King's Theatre, Bath Street. The Mitchell (as above). New Athenaeum Theatre (within Academy of Music & Drama), Renfrew Street. Pavilion Theatre, Renfield Street. Theatre Royal, Hope Street. Tron Theatre, Trongate.
SPORT & LEISURE
◆ Parks & Gardens - Sighthill Park, Pinkston Road. ◆ Swimming Pools - North Woodside Leisure Centre, Braid Square. (closed for refurbishment).

FALKIRK

The history of Falkirk begins with the arrival of the Romans in the first century AD. The area was once of strategic importance and this is illustrated by the construction of the Antonine Wall, the route of which (albeit predominantly obliterated) ran through the centre of Falkirk. Built in 140AD and named after the Roman Emperor of the time, Antonius Pius, who ordered its construction as a defence against the Northern tribes, the Antonine Wall (announced a UNESCO World Heritage Site in 2008) stretched for 36 miles from Old Kirkpartrick on the Clyde to Carriden on the Firth with forts interposed every 2 miles. The wall itself was a turf rampart on a stone base with a ditch to the north and a military road running parallel along the south side. The most significant remains around Falkirk can be viewed in Callendar Park (see below) and to the west of the town on Anson Avenue a short section of embankment can be viewed. Falkirks newest addition is the Falkirk Wheel. The Wheel is a boat lift which links the Forth and Clyde Canal at the point of which it lays 35 m (115 ft) below the level of the Union Canal.

PLACES OF INTEREST

Visit Scotland Information Centre (All year) - The Falkirk Wheel, Lime Road. FK1 4RS. Tel: (01324) 620244
◆ ANTONINE WALL - A section of ditch 40 ft wide, 10 ft deep and half a mile in length runs through Callendar Park and is easily visible. Callendar Road. ◆ CALLENDAR HOUSE & PARK - The 170 acres park has a beautiful bloom of spring daffodils and has the Park Gallery in the grounds. Callendar House displays 600 years of Scottish history through interactive displays and an authentic georgian working kitchen which is the centre of the experience. Callendar Road.◆ FALKIRK STEEPLE - The third incarnation of this Falkirk landmark was built in 1814. A part of the 140 ft high structure used to be the town's lockup. High Street.

ENTERTAINMENT

◆ Cinemas - Central Retail Park, Grahams Road. ◆ Concerts - Town Hall, West Bridge Street. ◆ Theatres - Town Hall (as above).
SPORT & LEISURE
◆ Parks & Gardens - Bellsmeadow Park, Bellsmeadow Road. Blinkbonny Park, Gartcows Road. Callendar Park, Callendar Road. Dollar Park, Camelon Road. Victoria Park, Thornhill Road. ◆ Sports Centres - Mariner Leisure Centre, Glasgow Road (W of Falkirk). Woodlands Games Hall, Cochrane Av. ◆ Swimming Pools - Mariner Leisure Centre (as above).

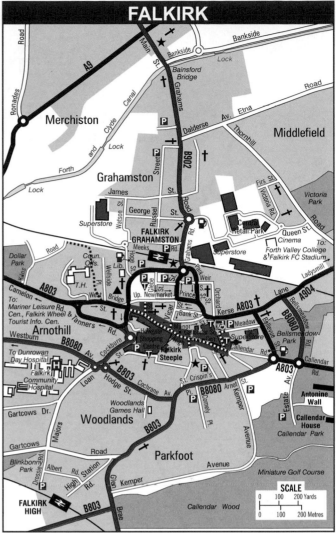

FORT WILLIAM

The history of Fort William can be dated from 1655 when General Monck built an earthwork fort here, the purpose of which to quote Johnson was to keep "savage clans and roving barbarians" at bay. This was later rebuilt under William III and, for a short time the town was renamed Maryburgh in honour of his queen. In both 1715 and 1745, the Jacobites failed to capture the fort and it was eventually pulled down during the late 19th century. For today's visitor, Fort William is synonymous with Ben Nevis and the town has become a popular holiday resort and base for the many people who wish to climb Britain's highest mountain.

PLACES OF INTEREST

Visit Scotland Information Centre (All Year) - 15 High Street. PH33 6DH Tel: (01397) 701801.
◆ JACOBITE, THE (FORT WILLIAM TO MALLAIG STEAM SERVICE) - Considered to be one of the 'greatest railway journeys of the world' the train travels the 84 miles round trip from Fort William to the West Coast fishing port of Mallaig and back. Steeped in history, the route encompasses breathtaking scenery with views of Ben Nevis, Britain's most westerly mainland railway station Ari Saig, Neptune's Staircase and the magnificent 21 arch Glenfinnan Viaduct. Fort William Station.
◆ LIME TREE GALLERY - A privately funded gallery showing both national art collections (this has included Goya) and local contemporary artists. Achintore Road.
◆ WEST HIGHLAND MUSEUM - Founded in 1922, exhibitions illustrate the history of traditional Highland life. The museum also houses a world famous Jacobite collection. Cameron Square.
◆ WEST HIGHLAND WAY - Long distance footpath covering 95 miles between Glasgow and Fort William.

ENTERTAINMENT

◆ Concerts - The Nevis Centre, An Aird.
◆ Theatres - The Nevis Centre (as above).

SPORT & LEISURE

◆ Sports Centres - Lochaber Leisure Centre, Belford Road. The Nevis Centre, An Aird.
◆ Swimming Pools - Lochaber Leisure Centre (as above).
◆ Ten Pin Bowling - The Nevis Centre (as above).

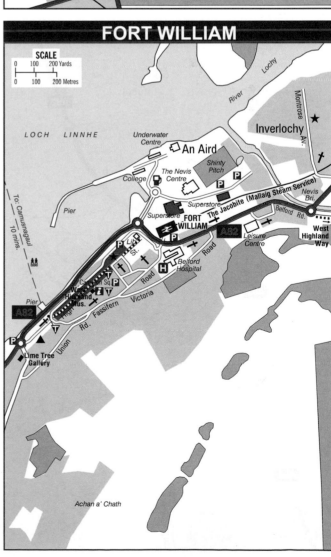

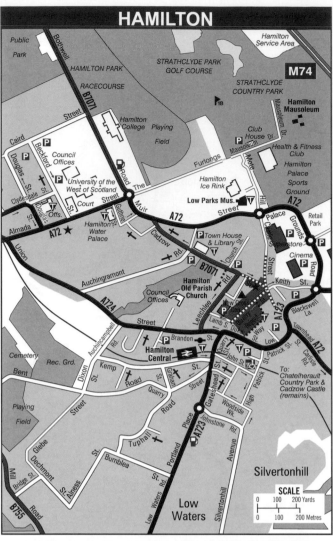

HAMILTON

There has been a settlement at Hamilton since prehistoric times, which was known as Cadzow, a name derived from the Celtic "Cadihou" meaning "beautiful castle." It was in 1445, that a charter granted by James II to the first Lord Hamilton gave permission for the official name of the town to be changed to that of his family. The town was once one of the main stopping places for the stagecoach that ran between England and Scotland and the town's museum (see below) is housed in a former coaching inn. With the rise of industrialisation, the town became the centre of a mining district, but closure of the pits forced diversification and today Hamilton is a thriving town that offers a wide range of visitor attractions and leisure facilities.

PLACES OF INTEREST
◆ HAMILTON MAUSOLEUM - Built in 1850 for the 10th Duke of Hamilton as a family chapel and crypt at an estimated cost of £150,000 the mausoleum is a spectacular structure designed by David Bryce. Tours booked with Low Parks Museum (see below). Strathclyde Country Park.
◆ HAMILTON OLD PARISH CHURCH - Dating from 1732-34, this church was designed by William Adam. Strathmore Road.
◆ HAMILTON PARK RACECOURSE - Considered to be one of the most picturesque racecourses in Britain, it once formed part of the Royal forest of Cadzow. The inaugural race meeting at Hamilton was held in August 1782 and today the racecourse offers a varied fixture list throughout the season that includes some evening meetings during the summer months. Bothwell Road.
◆ LOW PARKS MUSEUM - Museum was created through the amalgamation of the former District Museum with the Cameronians Regimental Museum and is housed in one of the town's oldest buildings, once a coaching inn which dates from 1696. Exhibitions include displays on the Clyde Valley and Hamilton Estate. 129 Muir Street.

ENTERTAINMENT
◆ Cinemas - Palace Grounds Road.
◆ Concerts - Town House, Cadzow Street.
◆ Theatres - Town House (as above).

SPORT & LEISURE
◆ Ice Rink - Hamilton Ice Rink, Muir Street.
◆ Parks & Gardens - Chatelherault Country Park (SE of Hamilton). Public Park, Bothwell Road. Strathclyde Country Park, The Furlongs.
◆ Sports Centres - Hamilton Palace Sports Ground, Mote Hill. Hamilton Water Palace, Almada Street.
◆ Swimming Pools - Hamilton Water Palace (as above).
◆ Ten-Pin Bowling - Cosmic Bowl, M & D's Theme Park (NE of Hamilton).

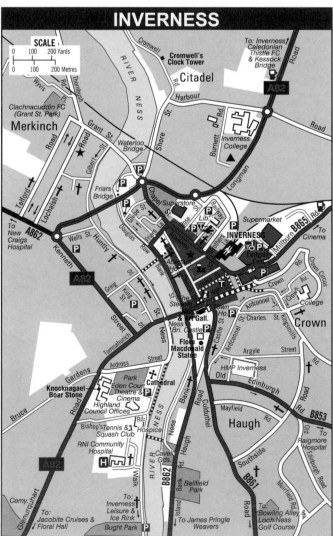

INVERNESS

For many years referred to as the 'Capital of the Highlands', Inverness became a city at the start of the new millennium and has therefore attained the status befitting its title. It is a bustling centre with a rich heritage and though the emphasis today lies with administration, commerce and industry, Inverness is still a worthy tourist destination. Lying on the shores of the Moray Firth and divided by the River Ness, the main part of the town occupies the right bank. Notable buildings include the magnificent castle, built in the 1830s which houses the Sheriff's Court, the Town House, a Victorian Gothic building dating from 1880, Abertarff House, built in 1592 which was restored by the National Trust for Scotland in 1963 and was until recently their highland office and Dunbar's Hospital, built in 1688 as an almshouse. Acting as a green oasis, the Ness Islands, linked by bridges, are a public park which also provide an alternative method of crossing the river where lies the Caledonian Canal, which runs from Fort William to Inverness and dates from 1822.

PLACES OF INTEREST
Visit Scotland Information Centre (All Year) - Castle Wynd. IV2 3BJ. Tel: (01463) 252401
◆ CROMWELL'S CLOCK TOWER - Site of Cromwell's Fort which was destroyed during the Restoration, the clock tower is all that remains. Cromwell Road.
◆ FLORA MACDONALD STATUE - This statue dedicated to the Jacobite heroine dominates the grounds of Inverness Castle. Inverness Castle. ◆ INVERNESS CASTLE - The current castle was built of red sandstone in 1836 by William Burn to replace the original which was destroyed by a fire in 1746. Overlooking the River Ness it is now the Sheriff's Court. Only the grounds are open to the public. Castle Street. ◆ INVERNESS CATHEDRAL - Built from red sandstone between 1866 & 1869, this gothic style cathedral was the first to be completed in Britain after the reformation. Lack of funding meant they were unable to add the planned 30 m spire. Ardross Street. ◆ INVERNESS MUSEUM & ART GALLERY - Displays of human and natural history are combined to reflect the history of Inverness and the Highlands. The collection also includes silver, weapons and period costume. Café. Castle Wynd. ◆ KNOCKNAGAEL BOAR STONE - Preserved within the Council Offices, the stone is inscribed with Pictish symbols which depict a mirror case and wild boar. Glenurquhart Road.

ENTERTAINMENT
◆ Cinemas - Eastfield Way (E of Inverness). Eden Court Theatre, Bishops Road.
◆ Concerts - Eden Court Theatre (as above). ◆ Theatres - Eden Court Theatre (as above).

SPORT & LEISURE
◆ Ice Rink - Inverness Ice Centre, Bught Park. ◆ Parks & Gardens - Bellfield Park, Island Bank Road. Bught Park (S of Inverness). Northern Meeting Park, Ardross St. Whin Park (S of Inverness). ◆ Sports Centres - Inverness Leisure, Bught Park. ◆ Swimming Pools - Inverness Leisure (as above). ◆ Ten-Pin Bowling - Rollerbowl, Culduthel Road (S of Inverness).

KILMARNOCK

Kilmarnock, a commercial town noted for its pedestrian friendly town centre, is reputed to have derived its name from the early Christian missionary St Marnock but the town only started to grow after receiving a Royal Charter in 1592. It was here that John Wilson (buried in Old High Kirk churchyard) published the first edition of Burns' poems in 1786, the site of his printing shop being marked by a plaque in Burns Precinct off The Cross. Other associations include Laigh Kirk, the former tower remaining with the rebuilt nave of 1802, situated off Bank Street in the oldest surviving part of the town.

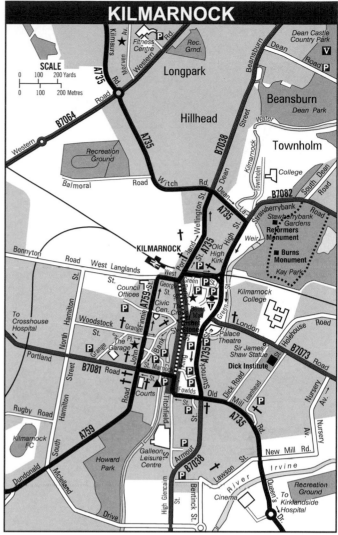

PLACES OF INTEREST

◆ BURNS MONUMENT - Monument to the poet with statue erected in 1879. Having been damaged by a fire in recent years, the monument has been redeveloped as the focal point of a new genealogy centre, the Burns Monument Centre. Kay Park, Strawberry Bank Road.
◆ DEAN CASTLE COUNTRY PARK - 200 acre park with visitor centre, walks, rivers, adventure playground and pets corner. Contains Dean Castle, built around a 14th century tower house, containing armour, tapestries, musical instruments and Burns manuscripts. Café. Dean Road.
◆ DICK INSTITUTE - Contains two art galleries and three museum galleries housing both temporary and permanent displays of natural sciences, industrial & local history and fine & contemporary art. Elmbank Avenue.
◆ NISBET STONE - Stone recalling the hanging here of John Nisbet in 1683 for supporting the Covenanters at the battle of Bothwell Bridge. The Cross.
◆ REFORMERS MONUMENT - Corinthian column erected in 1885 to commemorate Scottish pioneers of Parliamentary Reform. Kay Park, Strawberrybank Road.

ENTERTAINMENT

◆ Cinemas - Queen's Drive.
◆ Concerts - Palace Theatre, Green Street.
◆ Theatres - Palace Theatre (as above).

SPORT & LEISURE

◆ Ice Rink - Galleon Leisure Centre, Titchfield Street.
◆ Parks & Gardens - Dean Park, Dean Road. Dean Castle Country Park, Dean Road. Howard Park, Dundonald Road. Kay Park, Strawberrybank Road. Strawberry Gardens, Strawberrybank Road.
◆ Sports Centres - Galleon Leisure Centre (as above). Hunter Fitness Centre, Western Road.
◆ Swimming Pools - Galleon Leisure Centre (as above).
◆ Ten-Pin Bowling - The Garage, Grange Street.

KIRKCALDY

With a historical past dating back to the 11th century, Kirkcaldy has an important industrial heritage. During the 19th century, Kirkcaldy was the first town to use the power loom which would revolutionise the textile industry and it was world renowned for its manufacture of linoleum. Though little remains of this era there is still much to discover around the town. The main street that extends along the waterfront for over 4 miles gave rise to Kirkcaldy becoming known as the 'Lang toun of Fife' and even today it is still referred to as this. In the town centre the Town House dating from 1939-56 is topped by Kirkcaldy's patron, St Bryce. Near the harbour is Sailor's Walk, a row of 17th century houses restored by the National Trust for Scotland. The town has numerous famous associations; it was the birth place of the architect, Robert Adam in 1728 and Adam Smith was born here in 1723, returning later to write his influential work, 'Wealth of Nations'. Thomas Carlyle is also associated with the town for the period he spent teaching at the burgh school. In April Kirkcaldy hosts the famous Links Market along the Esplanade. Incorporating over a mile of fairground attractions and rides, the market dates from 1304 and is considered to be the longest street fair in Britain.

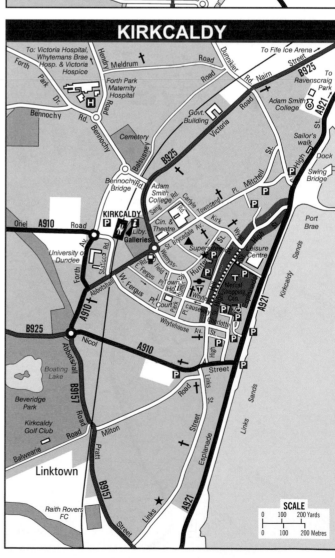

PLACES OF INTEREST

Visit Scotland Information Centre (All Year) - Kirkcaldy Galleries, Abbotshall Road. KY1 1YG. Tel: (01592) 267775
◆ KIRKCALDY GALLERIES - Exhibits a fine collection of 19th & 20th century Scottish paintings, including works by William McTaggart and the Colourist artist S J Peploe. The Glasgow Boys are also well represented. There are also fascinating displays of local and natural history, a changing programme of exhibitions, café and shop. War Memorial Gardens.

ENTERTAINMENT

◆ Cinemas - Adam Smith Theatre, St Brycedale Avenue.
◆ Concerts - Adam Smith Theatre (as above).
◆ Theatres - Adam Smith Theatre (as above).

SPORT & LEISURE

◆ Ice Rink - Fife Ice Arena, Rosslyn Street (NE of Kirkcaldy).
◆ Parks & Gardens - Beveridge Park, Abbotshall Road. Ravenscraig Park (NE of Kirkcaldy). War Memorial Gardens, Kirkcaldy Station.
◆ Sports Centres - Kirkcaldy Leisure Centre, Esplanade.
◆ Swimming Pools - Kirkcaldy Leisure Centre (as above).

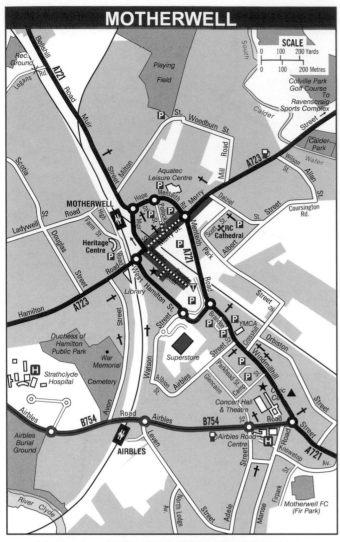

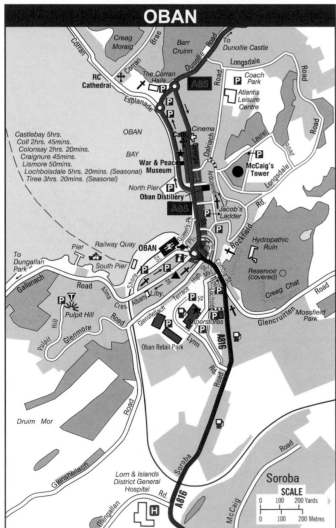

MOTHERWELL

Located at the head of the Clyde Valley, Motherwell is well situated to discover a remoter part of Scotland that is becoming increasingly popular as a tourist destination. The town was once famous for its iron, steel and engineering works and was home to the great Dalzell works, founded in 1871 by David Colville.

PLACES OF INTEREST
◆ MOTHERWELL HERITAGE CENTRE - Multi-media exhibition illustrates the history of Motherwell and the effects of industry on the area from the 19th century to the present day. There is also a fifth floor viewing tower with spectacular views up and down the Clyde Valley and on a clear day Ben Lomond can be seen. High Road.
◆ MOTHERWELL RC CATHEDRAL - Dates from the 1900's and became a cathedral in 1947. Coursington Road.

ENTERTAINMENT
◆ Concerts - Motherwell Concert Hall & Theatre, Windmillhill Street.
◆ Theatres - Motherwell Concert Hall & Theatre (as above).
SPORT & LEISURE
◆ Parks & Gardens - Calder Park, Merry Street. Duchess of Hamilton Public Park, Avon Road. ◆ Sports Centres - Aquatec Leisure Centre, Menteith Road. Ravenscraig Sports Complex (NE of Motherwell). ◆ Swimming Pools - Aquatec Leisure Centre (as above).

Oban Bay

OBAN

Well situated on the shore, flanked by the island of Kerrera which provides protection against Atlantic storms, Oban is regarded as the 'unofficial capital of the West Highlands' and 'The Gateway to the Isles'. The town revolves around its busy port with fishing craft and leisure boats filling the harbour with colour and activity. Since 2010 a bi-annual "Festival of the Sea" has been held in late May to celebrate the importance of the sea to the towns economy. Cruises are an important part of Oban's tourist industry and it is the main port for ferries bound for the Inner Hebrides with numerous other trips available to the islands of Coll, Tiree, Barra, South Uist, Colonsay and Islay. Obscured from view from the bay, the remains of Dunollie Castle to the north of Oban affords stunning views to the harbour by way of a short, but steep walk along a partially hidden path.

PLACES OF INTEREST
Visit Scotland Information Centre (All Year) - Argyll Square. PA34 4AN.
Tel: (01631) 563122
◆ MCCAIG'S TOWER - This folly dating from 1897 was commissioned by a local banker who aspired to alleviate unemployment whilst simultaneously perpetuating his own name. Though never completed, the tower stands as a monument to the McCaig family and the short walk up Jacobs Ladder to the viewing platform offers an excellent vantage point with outstanding views across the Bay to the Isle of Kerrera. Laurel Road. ◆ OBAN DISTILLERY - Built in 1793, the distillery combines guided tours which reveal the ancient craft of distilling with exhibitions and an audio-visual presentation reflecting the history of Oban. Stafford Street. ◆ OBAN EPISCOPAL CATHEDRAL - Consisting of the original church of 1864 with its partially-built 1910 replacement, the Cathedral has suffered from a lack of funds throughout its existence, yet retains a dignified presence. George St. ◆ OBAN ROMAN CATHOLIC CATHEDRAL - Modern granite building dating from 1932, built by Sir Giles Gilbert Scott. Corran Esplanade. ◆ WAR & PEACE MUSEUM - Collection of artefacts and memorabilia dating predominantly from the Second World War. Learn about the fishing and maritime industries, the railways and local sports such as Shinty. Old Oban Times Building. Corran Esplanade.

ENTERTAINMENT
◆ Cinemas - Highland Theatre, George Street. ◆ Concerts - The Corran Halls, Corran Esplanade. ◆ Theatres - The Corran Halls (as above).
SPORT & LEISURE
◆ Parks & Gardens - Dungallan Park, Gallanach Road. Mossfield Park, Glencruitten Road. ◆ Sports Centres - Atlantis Leisure, Dalriach Road.
◆ Swimming Pools - Atlantis Leisure (as above).

PAISLEY

With the White Cart Water flowing through the town centre, Paisley is a constantly developing town that is far more than a satellite of nearby Glasgow. Like so many other towns, Paisley flourished during the 19th century with the Industrial Revolution acting as a catalyst to providing prosperity for the town. British and French soldiers returning from India at the end of the 18th century brought with them fine Kashmir shawls which provided the inspiration for the development of a flourishing industry. The Kashmir designs were copied and Paisley soon became world renowned for its distinctively woven shawls.

PLACES OF INTEREST

Visit Scotland Information Centre (All Year) - 9A Gilmour Street. PA1 1DD. Tel: (0141) 887 1007

◆ COATS OBSERVATORY - Dating from 1883 the displays in the centre offer an insight into the history of astronomy, astronautics and meteorology. 49 Oakshaw Street West.

◆ PAISLEY ABBEY - A Cluniac Abbey Church originally founded in 1163, though destroyed by fire in 1307. The remaining structure dates mainly from the 15th century and within the church is displayed the Barochan Cross, a 10th century Celtic cross which is under the care of Historic Scotland. Abbey Close.

◆ PAISLEY MUSEUM & ART GALLERIES - The museum is home to the world's largest paisley shawl collection. Other exhibitions include displays on local industry and natural history. The Pillar Gallery re-opened in November 2012 following a complete refurbishment. Along with displays of work from Scottish artists and writers there are innovative computer displays and an interactive experience. High Street.

◆ PAISLEY RC CATHEDRAL - Built in 1932 in the neo-romanesque style and replacing the church of 1809, this cathedral church is dedicated to St Mirin, a 17th century Irish abbot who worked, died and was laid to rest here. Incle Street.

◆ PAISLEY THREAD MILL MUSEUM - Housed in part of the Mile End Mill, the collection includes artefacts and photographs of the mills from the 19th and 20th centuries. Seedhill Road.

◆ SMA' SHOT COTTAGES - Experience life in the 18th century in three weaver's cottages furnished in period style and containing the original looms. 11-17 George Place.

ENTERTAINMENT

◆ Cinemas - Phoenix Business Park (W of Paisley). ◆ Concerts - Town Hall, Abbey Close. ◆ Theatres - Paisley Arts Centre, New Street, Town Hall (as above).

SPORT & LEISURE

◆ Parks & Gardens - Barshaw Park, Glasgow Road (E of Paisley). Brodie Park, Braids Road (S of Paisley). East End Park, Seedhill Road. Fountain Gardens, Love Street. Saucelhill Park, Hunterhill Road.

◆ Sports Centres - Lagoon Leisure Centre, Mill Street. St Mirren Sport & Leisure Complex, Love Street (located under football stands). ◆ Swimming Pools - Lagoon Leisure Centre (as above).

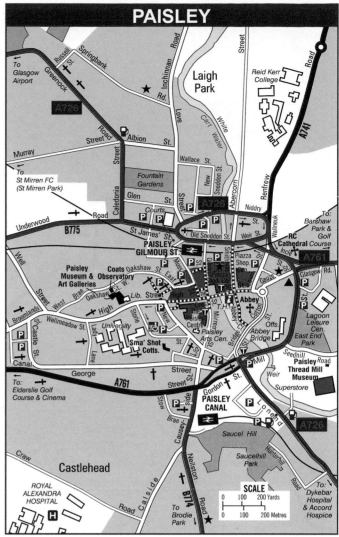

PERTH

Lying on the west bank of the River Tay, the Royal burgh of Perth is thought to have originated from a Roman camp and though there is dispute as to the validity of this, the rectangular street patterns seem to suggest that it may have been. Once the capital of Scotland, Perth was an important centre and coupled with its favourable location on the navigable River Tay, has maintained its pre-eminence as both a favourable tourist destination and busy harbour. There is a rich heritage to be discovered around the town with a diverse range of visitor and recreational attractions. The riverside North Inch Park is the notorious location of the 1396 'Battle of the Clans' when the Chattan and Kay clans fought each other to the death as a result of King Robert III unsuccessful attempt to curtail feuding between Highlanders. It was this battle that inspired Sir Walter Scott's novel, 'The Fair Maid of Perth.' The annual Perth Festival of the Arts held at the end of May encompasses the whole spectrum of performing arts and is considered to be one of the finest festivals of its kind in Scotland.

PLACES OF INTEREST

Visit Scotland Information Centre (All Year) - Lower City Mills. West Mill Street. PH1 5QR. Tel: (01738) 450600

◆ BLACK WATCH REGIMENTAL MUSEUM - Housed in Balhousie Castle, dating from 1860's as it stands, exhibitions illustrate the history of the 42nd / 73rd Highland regiment from 1740 to the present day. Displays include silver, colours, uniforms and medals. Hay Street.

◆ FERGUSSON GALLERY - Former waterworks converted into gallery, devoted to exhibiting the work of Scottish colourist painter, John Fergusson (1874-1961) who was an influential figure in the development of 20th century art in Scotland. Three galleries exhibit changing thematic displays of his work. Marshall Place.

◆ PERTH CATHEDRAL - Episcopal Cathedral founded in 1850 to serve the diocese of St Andrews, Dunkeld and Dunblane. North Methven Street.

◆ PERTH MUSEUM & ART GALLERY - Diverse range of displays covering fine and applied art, local and social history, natural history and archaeology. A changing programme of temporary exhibitions runs throughout the year. 78 George Street.

◆ ST JOHN'S KIRK - Founded in 1126 by David I and with much of the existing building dating from the 15th century, the kirk is the oldest standing building in Perth. John Knox preached here during the Reformation and in later years the kirk was divided into three separate churches, the reunification only occuring in 1923 in memory of the men of Perth who died in WW1. St. John Street.

ENTERTAINMENT

◆ Cinemas - Murray Street. ◆ Concerts - Perth Concert Hall, Mill Street. ◆ Theatres - Perth Theatre, High Street.

SPORT & LEISURE

◆ Ice Rink - Dewars Centre, Glover Street. ◆ Parks & Gardens - Bellwood Park, Dundee Road. North Inch Park, Hay Street. South Inch Park, King's Place. ◆ Sports Centres - Bells Sports Centre, Hay Street. ◆ Swimming Pools - Perth Leisure Pool, Glasgow Road.

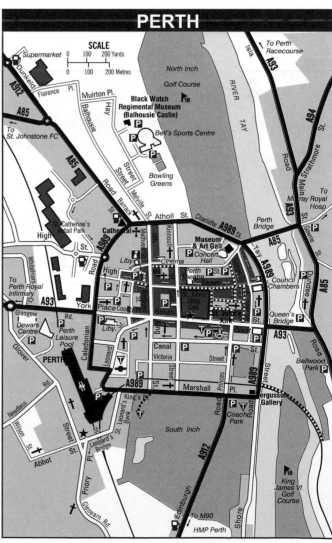

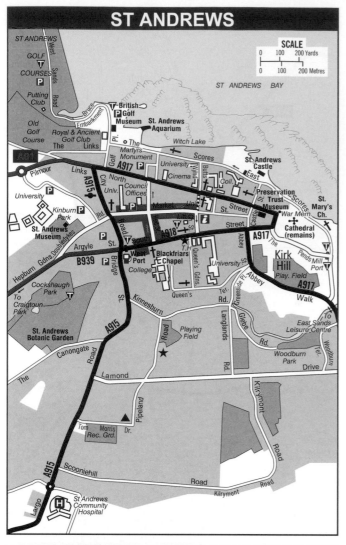

ST ANDREWS

St Andrews

St Andrews 18th Green

ST ANDREWS

According to legend, the town of St Andrews derives its name from the namesake saint whose remains were brought to this place by St Rule, a Greek monk. It was from here that a settlement developed with Celtic monks building St Mary's Church. The town became an important pilgrimage site with many people making the journey to visit the shrine of St Andrew, who became the patron saint of Scotland.

It is not only as a religious centre that St Andrews is worldly famous; it is heralded as the golfing capital of the world with numerous premier courses interspersed around the area. The game prospered in St Andrews and the Society of St Andrews Golfers was founded in 1754 to organise an annual competition, this later became known as the Royal and Ancient Golf club and today it is recognised as the governing body for the games rules in most countries. Twice annual golf events are held, which are organised by Links Golf St Andrews attracting golfers from around the world.

Originally a market town, St Andrews was appointed a Royal Burgh in 1620 and is home to the oldest University in Scotland, founded in 1412 by Bishop Henry Wardlaw. St Salvator's on North Street was founded in 1450 and St Leonards dates from 1512 with the two being merged in 1747. St Mary's College founded in 1537 is home to the theology faculty. West Sands, one of Scotland's best beaches and location for some of the scenes in the film Chariots of Fire is also popular with visitors.

PLACES OF INTEREST

Visit Scotland Information Centre (All Year) - 70 Market Street. KY16 9NU. Tel: (01334) 472021

◆ BLACKFRIARS CHAPEL - A vaulted side apse is all that remains of this 1525 chapel that was formerly part of a Dominican friary founded in 1274. South Street.

◆ BRITISH GOLF MUSEUM - The museum presents a chronological exploration of the development of golf spanning the last 500 years. An extensive collection of golfing memorabilia is combined with explanatory displays and innovative exhibitions covering all golfing aspects including tournaments, players and the evolution of golfing equipment. Bruce Embankment.

◆ ST ANDREWS AQUARIUM - The aquatic habitats of the world are explored here, from the crabs, starfish, sharks and octopus of our own seas, to the angelfish, clownfish and poisonous wolf fish from the tropics. Amazonian piranhas, poison dart frogs and hairy spiders are also present. Humbolt Penguins from the warm seas off South America. Seal enclosure pool and observation platform with seal feeding sessions twice a day. Land animals are also represented with a growing family of Meerkats. Gift shop and café. The Scores.

◆ ST ANDREWS BOTANIC GARDEN - Discover a hidden treasure of almost 8000 species of ferns, herbaceous plants, shrubs and trees laid out in different areas including the Water Garden, Rock Garden and Heath Garden. The Canongate.

◆ ST ANDREWS CASTLE - (Historic Scotland) Overlooking the sea are ruins of the 13th century stronghold, once belonging to the Archbishops of St Andrews. Today, notable features that remain include a 24 ft deep bottle dungeon hollowed out of solid rock from which death was allegedly the only escape and a mine and counter mine remaining from a siege in 1546. The visitor centre incorporates a fascinating multi-media exhibition that illustrates the history of the castle. The Scores.

◆ ST ANDREWS CATHEDRAL and ST RULE'S TOWER - (Historic Scotland) Founded in 1160 by Bishop Arnold, this was once the largest cathedral in Scotland and the centre of the medieval Scottish church. The Cathedral museum houses an important collection of Early Christian and medieval artefacts found on the site. The Pends.

◆ ST ANDREWS MUSEUM - Housed in Kinburn House, a Victorian mansion, the museum traces the history of the St Andrews area from the Bronze Age to the present. Doubledykes Road.

◆ ST ANDREWS PRESERVATION TRUST MUSEUM - Collection reflects the social history of the burgh and includes a 1950's reconstruction of a grocery shop with period furniture, photographs and paintings. 12 North Street.

◆ ST ANDREWS WEST PORT - Dating from 1589, with renovations in 1843, this is one of the few remaining city gates in Scotland. Exterior view only. South Street.

◆ ST MARY'S CHURCH - Perched on the cliff edge behind the cathedral, little remains of this cruciform church which was the earliest collegiate church in Scotland. East Scores.

ENTERTAINMENT

◆ Cinemas - New Picture House, North Street.
◆ Concerts - Town Hall, South Street. Younger Hall, Music Centre, University of St Andrews, North Street.

SPORT & LEISURE

◆ Parks & Gardens - Cockshaugh Park, Hepburn Gardens. Craigtoun Park (SW of St Andrews). Kinburn Park, Doubledykes Road. Woodburn Park, Glebe Road.
◆ Sports Centres - East Sands Leisure Centre, St Mary Street.
◆ Swimming Pool - East Sands Leisure Centre (as above).

STIRLING

Situated on the River Forth, Stirling 'The Gateway to the Highlands' has from Medieval times been strategically regarded as the most important place in Scotland. Through time, the centrality of its location ensured that whoever held Stirling controlled the nation and it is therefore inevitable that much of Scotland's history intrinsically revolves around the ancient capital. The 13th & 14th century Wars of Independence, Wallace's victory over the English at Stirling Bridge in 1297 when he outmaneuvered the English by taking advantage of the river as a natural defence to divide the English army and force their retreat and numerous other battles were fought in close proximity to the Burgh. It was the victory at Stirling Bridge that inspired the fight for autonomy from English domination and though Wallace was later defeated at Falkirk in 1298, betrayed and brutally executed in London, his determination to free Scotland would live on. It was in 1314 that the reward came when King Robert the Bruce led his nation to freedom at the Battle of Bannockburn. An uneasy peace was born out of the 1314 victory and slowly the castle made the transition from fortification to Royal residence. Today, much of Stirling's heritage is still visible, the old town centering around Broad Street and St John's Street retains its charm with cobbled streets and numerous historic buildings. The National Wallace Monument stands to the north east of Stirling, overlooking the site of the Battle of Stirling Bridge. The Back Walk offers a scenic route through the town to Gowan Hill and during the summer months open top heritage bus tours operate which provide a fascinating insight into this historic town.

PLACES OF INTEREST

Visit Scotland Information Centre (All Year) - 41 Dumbarton Road. FK8 2QQ. Tel: (01786) 475019

◆ ARGYLL & SUTHERLAND HIGHLANDERS REGIMENTAL MUSEUM - Reflects history of the Regiment from 1794 to the present day. Displays include uniforms, paintings, a collection of medals dating from Waterloo and a realistic model of a World War I trench. Stirling Castle.

◆ ARGYLL'S LODGING - (Historic Scotland) Built in 1630, this renaissance mansion is regarded as Scotland's most impressive surviving building of its period. Castle Wynd.

◆ BEHEADING STONE - This former execution site reflects a bygone era of gruesome capital punishment. Many important figures were slain at this site, amongst whom were Murdoch Stewart, regent of Scotland during the imprisonment of James I in England. Gowan Hill.

◆ COWANE'S HOSPITAL - Known also as Stirling Guildhall, the hospital was built between 1634 & 1649 by John Cowane to provide for the aged members of the Guild of Merchants. Outside is a statue of its founder. Coffe shop. St John Street.

◆ KING'S KNOT - (Historic Scotland) The remaining octagonal mound once formed part of a magnificant 17th century formal knot garden below the castle. King's Park.

◆ LADIES ROCK - Once a popular vantage point for the ladies of the court to watch the Royal Tournaments, the rock allows panoramic views across to the Trossachs and Ben Lomond. Valley Cemetery.

◆ MAR'S WARK - (Historic Scotland) Standing at the head of the town, this renaissance building was commisioned by the Earl of Mar in 1569 and would have been built using stone from the ruined Cambuskenneth Abbey. It was damaged by cannon fire during the 1740's and the shell is all that remains. Castle Wynd.

◆ STAR PYRAMID - Monument in memory of Martyrs seeking religious freedom. Castle Wynd.

◆ STIRLING CASTLE - (Historic Scotland) Perched 250ft on a volcanic outcrop commanding a dominant position over the burgh, Stirling Castle considered by many to be the grandest of all Scottish castles both in location and architecture. Favoured royal residence of the Stuart Monarchs, it stands as the focal point of Stirling's turbulent history. Upper Castle Hill.

◆ STIRLING CHURCH OF THE HOLY RUDE - Church where coronation of James VI was conducted in 1567. St John Street.

◆ STIRLING MERCAT CROSS - The Mercat Cross in Broad Street was once the focal point of the town's trading activity. The unicorn figure on top of the cross is known locally as 'the puggy'. Broad Street.

◆ STIRLING OLD BRIDGE - (Historic Scotland) Dating from 1400, this bridge was once of strategic importance as the most southerly crossing point across the River.

◆ STIRLING SMITH ART GALLERY & MUSEUM - Award winning museum & gallery presents a diverse exhibition programme along with a permanent collection of fine art. Visit 'The Stirling Story' a history of the city from its origins to the present day. Dumbarton Road.

ENTERTAINMENT

◆ Cinemas - Forthside Way.
◆ Concerts - Albert Halls, Dumbarton Road.
◆ Theatres - Tolbooth Theatre, Broad Street.

SPORT AND LEISURE

◆ Ice Rink - The Peak at Stirling Sports Village (E of Stirling).
◆ Parks & Gardens - Royal Gardens, Dumbarton Road. King's Park (Stirling Golf Club), Queens Road.
◆ Sports Centres - The Peak at Stirling Sports Village (as above).
◆ Swimming Pool - The Peak at Stirling Sports Village (as above).
◆ Ten Pin Bowling - AMF Bowling, Forth Street.

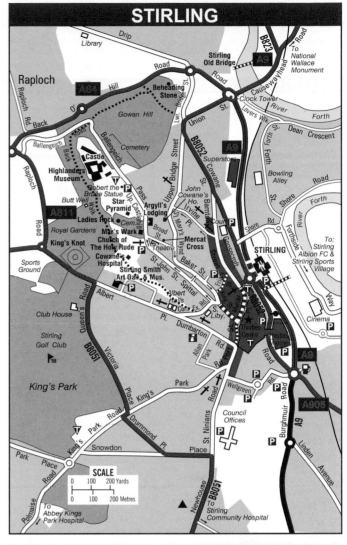

View from Stirling Castle

Stirling Castle

INDEX TO CITIES, TOWNS, VILLAGES, HAMLETS & LOCATIONS

(1) A strict alphabetical order is used e.g. Craig Lodge follows Craiglockhart but precedes Craigmalloch.

(2) The map reference given refers to the actual map square in which the town spot or built-up area is located and not to the place name.

(3) Where two or more places of the same name occur in the same County or Unitary Authority, the nearest large town is also given;
e.g. Achiemore. *High* . . . 2E **57** (nr. Durness) indicates that Achiemore is located in square 2E on page **57** and is situated near Durness in the Unitary Authority of Highland.

(4) Major towns are shown in bold, i.e. **Aberdeen**. *Aber* . . . . 3E **43** & **69**. Where they appear on a Town Plan a second page reference is given.

COUNTIES AND UNITARY AUTHORITIES with the abbreviations used in this index

Aberdeen : *Aber*
Aberdeenshire : *Abers*
Angus : *Ang*
Argyll & Bute : *Arg*
Clackmannanshire : *Clac*
Cumbria : *Cumb*
Dumfries & Galloway : *Dum*
Dundee : *D'dee*
East Ayrshire : *E Ayr*
East Dunbartonshire : *E Dun*
East Lothian : *E Lot*
East Renfrewshire : *E Ren*
Edinburgh : *Edin*
Falkirk : *Falk*
Fife : *Fife*
Glasgow : *Glas*
Highland : *High*
Inverclyde : *Inv*
Midlothian : *Midl*
Moray : *Mor*
North Ayrshire : *N Ayr*
North Lanarkshire : *N Lan*
Northumberland : *Nmbd*
Orkney : *Orkn*
Perth & Kinross : *Per*
Renfrewshire : *Ren*
Scottish Borders : *Bord*
Shetland : *Shet*
South Ayrshire : *S Ayr*
South Lanarkshire : *S Lan*
Stirling : *Stir*
West Dunbartonshire : *W Dun*
Western Isles : *W Isl*
West Lothian : *W Lot*

A

Abbey St Bathans. *Bord* . . . 2E **21**
Abbeytown. *Cumb* . . . 3E **7**
Aberarder. *High* . . . 1H **39**
Aberargie. *Per* . . . 2C **26**
Aberchalder. *High* . . . 3E **39**
Aberchirder. *Abers* . . . 3B **50**
Abercorn. *W Lot* . . . 1F **19**
Abercrombie. *Fife* . . . 3G **27**
Aberdalgie. *Per* . . . 1B **26**
Aberdeen. *Aber* . . . 3E **43** & **69**
Aberdeen International Airport. *Aber* . . . 2D **42**
Aberdour. *Fife* . . . 5C **26**
Aberfeldy. *Per* . . . 4D **32**
Aberfoyle. *Stir* . . . 3E **25**
Aberlady. *E Lot* . . . 1B **20**
Aberlemno. *Ang* . . . 3C **34**
Abernethy. *Per* . . . 2C **26**
Abernyte. *Per* . . . 5H **33**
Aberuthven. *Per* . . . 2A **26**
Abhainn Suidhe. *W Isl* . . . 4B **62**
Abington. *S Lan* . . . 1G **11**
Aboyne. *Abers* . . . 4A **42**
Abriachan. *High* . . . 5G **47**
Abronhill. *N Lan* . . . 1C **18**
Abune-the-Hill. *Orkn* . . . 2B **64**
Acairseid. *W Isl* . . . 4C **60**
Acha. *Arg* . . . 3C **28**
Achachork. *High* . . . 4D **44**
Achadh a' Chuirn. *High* . . . 1F **37**
Achahoish. *Arg* . . . 1A **16**
Achaleven. *Arg* . . . 5C **30**
Achallader. *Arg* . . . 4G **31**
Acha Mor. *W Isl* . . . 2E **62**
Achanalt. *High* . . . 2D **46**
Achandunie. *High* . . . 1H **47**
Ach'an Todhair. *High* . . . 1D **30**
Achany. *High* . . . 3C **54**
Achaphubuil. *High* . . . 1D **30**
Acharacle. *High* . . . 2H **29**
Acharn. *Ang* . . . 1H **33**
Acharn. *Per* . . . 4C **32**
Acharole. *High* . . . 3F **59**
Achateny. *High* . . . 2G **29**
Achavanich. *High* . . . 4E **59**
Achdalieu. *High* . . . 1D **30**
Achduart. *High* . . . 3F **53**
Achentoul. *High* . . . 5B **58**
Achfary. *High* . . . 5D **56**
Achfrish. *High* . . . 2C **54**
Achgarve. *High* . . . 4D **52**
Achiemore. *High* . . . 2E **57** (nr. Durness)
Achiemore. *High* . . . 3B **58** (nr. Thurso)
A'Chill. *High* . . . 3B **36**
Achiltibuie. *High* . . . 3F **53**
Achina. *High* . . . 2A **58**
Achinahuagh. *High* . . . 2G **57**
Achindarroch. *High* . . . 3D **30**
Achinduich. *High* . . . 3C **54**
Achinduin. *Arg* . . . 5B **30**
Achininver. *High* . . . 2G **57**
Achintee. *High* . . . 4A **46**
Achintraid. *High* . . . 5H **45**
Achleck. *Arg* . . . 4F **29**
Achlorachan. *High* . . . 3E **47**
Achluachrach. *High* . . . 5D **38**
Achlyness. *High* . . . 3D **56**
Achmelvich. *High* . . . 1F **53**
Achmony. *High* . . . 5G **47**
Achmore. *High* . . . 5H **45** (nr. Stromeferry)
Achmore. *High* . . . 4F **53** (nr. Ullapool)
Achnacarnin. *High* . . . 5B **56**
Achnacarry. *High* . . . 5C **38**
Achnaclerach. *High* . . . 2F **47**
Achnacloich. *High* . . . 3E **37**
Ach na Cloiche. *High* . . . 3E **37**
Achnaconeran. *High* . . . 2F **39**
Achnacroish. *Arg* . . . 4B **30**
Achnafalnich. *Arg* . . . 1B **24**
Achnagarron. *High* . . . 1H **47**
Achnaha. *High* . . . 2F **29**
Achnahanat. *High* . . . 4C **54**
Achnahannet. *High* . . . 1C **40**
Achnairn. *High* . . . 2C **54**
Achnamara. *Arg* . . . 5E **23**
Achnanellan. *High* . . . 5B **38**
Achnangoul. *Arg* . . . 3H **23**
Achnasheen. *High* . . . 3C **46**
Achnashellach. *High* . . . 4B **46**
Achosnich. *High* . . . 2F **29**
Achow. *High* . . . 5F **59**
Achranich. *High* . . . 4A **30**
Achreamie. *High* . . . 2D **58**
Achriabhach. *High* . . . 2E **31**
Achriesgill. *High* . . . 3D **56**
Achrimsdale. *High* . . . 3G **55**
Achscrabster. *High* . . . 2D **58**
Achtoty. *High* . . . 2H **57**
Achuvoldrach. *High* . . . 3G **57**
Achvaich. *High* . . . 4E **55**
Achvoan. *High* . . . 3E **55**
Ackergill. *High* . . . 3G **59**
Ackergillshore. *High* . . . 3G **59**
Adabroc. *W Isl* . . . 1K **63**
Addiewell. *W Lot* . . . 2E **19**
Addinston. *Bord* . . . 3C **20**
Advie. *High* . . . 5E **49**
Adziel. *Abers* . . . 3E **51**
Ae. *Dum* . . . 5G **11**
Affleck. *Abers* . . . 1D **42**
Affric Lodge. *High* . . . 1C **38**
Aglionby. *Cumb* . . . 3H **7**
Aiginis. *W Isl* . . . 4J **63**
Aikers. *Orkn* . . . 5D **64**
Aiketgate. *Cumb* . . . 4H **7**
Aikhead. *Cumb* . . . 4F **7**
Aikton. *Cumb* . . . 3F **7**
Aird. *Arg* . . . 3E **23**
Aird. *Dum* . . . 2B **4**
Aird. *High* . . . 1G **45** (nr. Port Henderson)
Aird. *High* . . . 3E **37** (nr. Tarskavaig)
Aird. *W Isl* . . . 5H **61** (on Benbecula)
Aird. *W Isl* . . . 4K **63** (on Isle of Lewis)
Àird a Bhasair. *High* . . . 3F **37**
Aird a Mhachair. *W Isl* . . . 6H **61**
Aird a Mhulaidh. *W Isl* . . . 3C **62**
Aird Asaig. *W Isl* . . . 4C **62**
Aird Dhail. *W Isl* . . . 1J **63**
Airdens. *High* . . . 4D **54**
Airdeny. *Arg* . . . 1G **23**
Aird Mhidhinis. *W Isl* . . . 4C **60**
Aird Mhighe. *W Isl* . . . 5C **62** (nr. Ceann a Bhaigh)
Aird Mhighe. *W Isl* . . . 6B **62** (nr. Fionnsabhagh)
Aird Mhor. *W Isl* . . . 4C **60** (on Barra)
Aird Mhor. *W Isl* . . . 6J **61** (on South Uist)
Airdrie. *N Lan* . . . 2C **18**
Aird Shleibhe. *W Isl* . . . 6C **62**
Aird, The. *High* . . . 3D **44**
Aird Thunga. *W Isl* . . . 4J **63**
Aird Uig. *W Isl* . . . 1B **62**
Airidh a Bhruaich. *W Isl* . . . 3D **62**
Airies. *Dum* . . . 2A **4**
Airntully. *Per* . . . 5F **33**
Airor. *High* . . . 3G **37**
Airth. *Falk* . . . 5A **26**
Aisgernis. *W Isl* . . . 2C **60**
Aith. *Shet* . . . 3K **67** (on Fetlar)
Aith. *Shet* . . . 1C **66** (on Mainland)
Aithsetter. *Shet* . . . 3D **66**
Akeld. *Nmbd* . . . 5G **21**
Alcaig. *High* . . . 3G **47**
Aldclune. *Per* . . . 2E **33**
Aldochlay. *Arg* . . . 4C **24**
Aldoth. *Cumb* . . . 4E **7**
Alexandria. *W Dun* . . . 5C **24**
Alford. *Abers* . . . 2A **42**
Aline Lodge. *W Isl* . . . 3C **62**
Alladale Lodge. *High* . . . 5B **54**
Allanbank. *N Lan* . . . 3D **18**
Allanton. *N Lan* . . . 3D **18**
Allanton. *Bord* . . . 3F **21**
Allerby. *Cumb* . . . 5D **6**
Alligin Shuas. *High* . . . 3H **45**
Alloa. *Clac* . . . 4H **25**
Allonby. *Cumb* . . . 4D **6**
Alloway. *S Ayr* . . . 2A **10**
Alltgobhlach. *N Ayr* . . . 4B **16**
Alltnacaillich. *High* . . . 4F **57**
Allt na h-Airbhe. *High* . . . 4G **53**
Alltour. *High* . . . 5D **38**
Alltsigh. *High* . . . 2F **39**
Almondbank. *Per* . . . 1B **26**
Alness. *High* . . . 2H **47**
Alnessferry. *High* . . . 2H **47**
Altandhu. *High* . . . 2E **53**
Altanduin. *High* . . . 1F **55**
Altass. *High* . . . 3B **54**
Alterwall. *High* . . . 2F **59**
Altgaltraig. *Arg* . . . 1D **16**
Altnabreac. *High* . . . 4D **58**
Altnacealgach. *High* . . . 2H **53**
Altnafeadh. *High* . . . 3F **31**
Altnaharra. *High* . . . 5G **57**
Altonhill. *E Ayr* . . . 5H **17**
Altrua. *High* . . . 4D **38**
Alva. *Clac* . . . 4H **25**
Alves. *Mor* . . . 2E **49**
Alvie. *High* . . . 3B **40**
Alwinton. *Nmbd* . . . 3H **13**
Alyth. *Per* . . . 4H **33**
Amatnatua. *High* . . . 4B **54**
Am Baile. *W Isl* . . . 3C **60**
Amisfield. *Dum* . . . 5H **11**
Amulree. *Per* . . . 5E **33**
Anaheilt. *High* . . . 2B **30**
An Àird. *High* . . . 3E **37**
An Camus Darach. *High* . . . 4F **37**
An Cnoc. *W Isl* . . . 4J **63**
An Cnoc Ard. *W Isl* . . . 1K **63**
An Coroghon. *High* . . . 3B **36**
Ancroft. *Nmbd* . . . 4H **21**
Ancrum. *Bord* . . . 1F **13**
An Dùnan. *High* . . . 1E **37**
Angerton. *Cumb* . . . 3F **7**
An Gleann Ur. *W Isl* . . . 4J **63**
Ankerville. *High* . . . 1B **48**
An Leth Meadhanach. *W Isl* . . . 3C **60**
Annan. *Dum* . . . 2F **7**
Annat. *Arg* . . . 1H **23**
Annat. *High* . . . 3H **45**
Annathill. *N Lan* . . . 1C **18**
Annbank. *S Ayr* . . . 1B **10**
An Sailean. *High* . . . 2H **29**
Anston. *S Lan* . . . 4F **19**
Anstruther Easter. *Fife* . . . 3G **27**
Anstruther Wester. *Fife* . . . 3G **27**
An Taobh Tuath. *W Isl* . . . 2K **61**
An t-Aodann Ban. *High* . . . 3C **44**
An t Ath Leathann. *High* . . . 1F **37**
An Teanga. *High* . . . 3F **37**
Anthorn. *Cumb* . . . 3E **7**
An t-Ob. *W Isl* . . . 6B **62**
An t-Òrd. *High* . . . 2F **37**
Anwoth. *Dum* . . . 3G **5**
Appin. *Arg* . . . 4C **30**
Applecross. *High* . . . 4G **45**
Applegarthtown. *Dum* . . . 5A **12**
Applethwaite. *Cumb* . . . 5F **7**
Appletreehall. *Bord* . . . 2E **13**
Arabella. *High* . . . 1B **48**
Arasaig. *High* . . . 5F **37**
Arbeadie. *Abers* . . . 4B **42**
Arbirlot. *Ang* . . . 4D **34**
Arbroath. *Ang* . . . 4D **34**
Arbuthnott. *Abers* . . . 1F **35**
Arcan. *High* . . . 3G **47**
Archargary. *High* . . . 3A **58**
Archiestown. *Mor* . . . 4F **49**
Ardachu. *High* . . . 3D **54**
Ardalanish. *Arg* . . . 2A **22**
Ardaneaskan. *High* . . . 5H **45**
Ardarroch. *High* . . . 5H **45**
Ardbeg. *Arg* . . . 5A **24** (nr. Dunoon)
Ardbeg. *Arg* . . . 4F **15** (on Islay)
Ardbeg. *Arg* . . . 2D **16** (on Isle of Bute)
Ardcharnich. *High* . . . 5G **53**
Ardchiavaig. *Arg* . . . 2A **22**
Ardchonnell. *Arg* . . . 2G **23**
Ardchrishnish. *Arg* . . . 1B **22**
Ardchronie. *High* . . . 5D **54**
Ardchullarie. *Stir* . . . 2E **25**
Ardchyle. *Stir* . . . 1E **25**
Ard-dhubh. *High* . . . 4G **45**
Ardechive. *High* . . . 4C **38**
Ardelve. *High* . . . 1H **37**
Arden. *Arg* . . . 5C **24**
Ardendrain. *High* . . . 5G **47**
Ardentinny. *Arg* . . . 5A **24**
Ardeonaig. *Stir* . . . 5B **32**
Ardersier. *High* . . . 3A **48**
Ardery. *High* . . . 2A **30**
Ardessie. *High* . . . 5F **53**
Ardfern. *Arg* . . . 3F **23**
Ardfernal. *Arg* . . . 1G **15**
Ardfin. *Arg* . . . 2F **15**
Ardgartan. *Arg* . . . 3B **24**
Ardgay. *High* . . . 4C **54**
Ardgour. *High* . . . 2D **30**
Ardheslaig. *High* . . . 3G **45**
Ardindrean. *High* . . . 5G **53**
Ardlamont House. *Arg* . . . 2C **16**
Ardler. *Per* . . . 4H **33**
Ardlui. *Arg* . . . 2C **24**
Ardlussa. *Arg* . . . 5D **22**
Ardmair. *High* . . . 4G **53**
Ardmay. *Arg* . . . 3B **24**
Ardminish. *Arg* . . . 4H **15**
Ardmolich. *High* . . . 1A **30**
Ardmore. *High* . . . 3D **56** (nr. Kinlochbervie)
Ardmore. *High* . . . 5E **55** (nr. Tain)
Ardnacross. *Arg* . . . 4G **29**
Ardnadam. *Arg* . . . 5A **24**
Ardnagrask. *High* . . . 4G **47**
Ardnamurach. *High* . . . 4H **37**
Ardnarff. *High* . . . 5H **45**
Ardnastang. *High* . . . 2B **30**
Ardoch. *Per* . . . 5F **33**
Ardochy House. *High* . . . 3D **38**
Ardpatrick. *Arg* . . . 2A **16**
Ardrishaig. *Arg* . . . 5F **23**
Ardroag. *High* . . . 4B **44**
Ardross. *High* . . . 1H **47**
Ardrossan. *N Ayr* . . . 4F **17**
Ardshealach. *High* . . . 2H **29**
Ardslignish. *High* . . . 2G **29**
Ardtalla. *Arg* . . . 3F **15**
Ardtalnaig. *Per* . . . 5C **32**
Ardtoe. *High* . . . 1H **29**
Arduaine. *Arg* . . . 2E **23**
Ardullie. *High* . . . 2G **47**
Ardvasar. *High* . . . 3F **37**
Ardvorlich. *Per* . . . 1F **25**
Ardwell. *Dum* . . . 4C **4**
Ardwell. *Mor* . . . 5G **49**
Arean. *High* . . . 1H **29**
Aridhglas. *Arg* . . . 1A **22**
Arinacrinachd. *High* . . . 3G **45**
Arinagour. *Arg* . . . 3D **28**
Arisaig. *High* . . . 5F **37**
Ariundle. *High* . . . 2B **30**
Arivegaig. *High* . . . 2H **29**
Armadail. *High* . . . 3F **37**
Armadale. *High* . . . 3F **37** (nr. Isleornsay)
Armadale. *High* . . . 2A **58** (nr. Strathy)
Armadale. *W Lot* . . . 2E **19**
Armathwaite. *Cumb* . . . 4H **7**
Arncroach. *Fife* . . . 3G **27**
Arnicle. *Arg* . . . 5A **16**
Arnisdale. *High* . . . 2H **37**
Arnish. *High* . . . 4E **45**
Arniston. *Midl* . . . 2A **20**
Arnol. *W Isl* . . . 3H **63**
Arnprior. *Stir* . . . 4F **25**
Aros Mains. *Arg* . . . 4G **29**
Arpafeelie. *High* . . . 3H **47**
Arrochar. *Arg* . . . 3B **24**
Arscaig. *High* . . . 2C **54**
Artafallie. *High* . . . 4H **47**
Arthrath. *Abers* . . . 5E **51**
Arthurstone. *Per* . . . 4H **33**
Ascog. *Arg* . . . 2E **17**
Ashfield. *Stir* . . . 3G **25**
Ashgill. *S Lan* . . . 4C **18**
Ashgrove. *Mor* . . . 2F **49**
Ashkirk. *Bord* . . . 1D **12**
Ashton. *Inv* . . . 1F **17**
Aspatria. *Cumb* . . . 4E **7**
Astle. *High* . . . 4E **55**
Athelstaneford. *E Lot* . . . 1C **20**
Ath-Tharracail. *High* . . . 2H **29**
Attadale. *High* . . . 5A **46**
Aucharnie. *Abers* . . . 4B **50**
Auchattie. *Abers* . . . 4B **42**
Auchavan. *Ang* . . . 2G **33**
Auchbreck. *Mor* . . . 1F **41**
Auchenback. *E Ren* . . . 3A **18**
Auchenblae. *Abers* . . . 1E **35**
Auchenbrack. *Dum* . . . 4E **11**
Auchenbreck. *Arg* . . . 5H **23**
Auchencairn. *Dum* . . . 3A **6** (nr. Dalbeattie)
Auchencairn. *Dum* . . . 5G **11** (nr. Dumfries)
Auchencarroch. *W Dun* . . . 5D **24**
Auchencrow. *Bord* . . . 2F **21**
Auchendennan. *W Dun* . . . 5C **24**
Auchendinny. *Midl* . . . 2H **19**
Auchengray. *S Lan* . . . 3E **19**
Auchenhalrig. *Mor* . . . 2G **49**
Auchenheath. *S Lan* . . . 4D **18**
Auchenlochan. *Arg* . . . 1C **16**
Auchenmade. *N Ayr* . . . 4G **17**
Auchenmalg. *Dum* . . . 3D **4**
Auchentiber. *N Ayr* . . . 4G **17**
Auchenvennel. *Arg* . . . 5B **24**
Auchindrain. *Arg* . . . 3H **23**
Auchininna. *Abers* . . . 4B **50**
Auchinleck. *Dum* . . . 1F **5**
Auchinleck. *E Ayr* . . . 1C **10**
Auchinloch. *N Lan* . . . 1B **18**
Auchinstarry. *N Lan* . . . 1C **18**
Auchleven. *Abers* . . . 1B **42**
Auchlochan. *S Lan* . . . 5D **18**
Auchlunachan. *High* . . . 5G **53**
Auchmillan. *E Ayr* . . . 1C **10**
Auchmithie. *Ang* . . . 4D **34**
Auchmuirbridge. *Per* . . . 3D **26**
Auchmull. *Ang* . . . 1C **34**
Auchnacree. *Ang* . . . 2B **34**
Auchnafree. *Per* . . . 5D **32**
Auchnagallin. *High* . . . 5D **48**
Auchnagatt. *Abers* . . . 4E **51**
Aucholzie. *Abers* . . . 4G **41**
Auchreddie. *Abers* . . . 4D **50**
Auchterarder. *Per* . . . 2A **26**
Auchteraw. *High* . . . 3E **39**
Auchterderran. *Fife* . . . 4D **26**
Auchterhouse. *Ang* . . . 5A **34**
Auchtermuchty. *Fife* . . . 2D **26**
Auchterneed. *High* . . . 3F **47**
Auchtertool. *Fife* . . . 4D **26**
Auchtertyre. *High* . . . 1H **37**
Auchtubh. *Stir* . . . 1E **25**
Auckengill. *High* . . . 2G **59**
Auds. *Abers* . . . 2B **50**
Aughertree. *Cumb* . . . 5F **7**
Auldearn. *High* . . . 3C **48**
Auldgirth. *Dum* . . . 5G **11**
Auldhouse. *S Lan* . . . 3B **18**
Ault a' chruinn. *High* . . . 1A **38**
Aultbea. *High* . . . 5D **52**
Aultdearg. *High* . . . 2C **46**
Aultgrishan. *High* . . . 5C **52**
Aultguish Inn. *High* . . . 1E **47**
Aultibea. *High* . . . 1H **55**
Aultiphurst. *High* . . . 2B **58**
Aultivullin. *High* . . . 2B **58**
Aultmore. *Mor* . . . 3H **49**
Aultnamain Inn. *High* . . . 5D **54**
Avielochan. *High* . . . 2C **40**
Aviemore. *High* . . . 2B **40** & **70**
Avoch. *High* . . . 3A **48**
Avonbridge. *Falk* . . . 1E **19**
Ayr. *S Ayr* . . . 1A **10** & **70**
Ayres of Selivoe. *Shet* . . . 2B **66**
Ayton. *Bord* . . . 2G **21**
Aywick. *Shet* . . . 4J **67**

B

Bac. *W Isl* . . . 3J **63**
Backaland. *Orkn* . . . 1E **64**
Backaskaill. *Orkn* . . . 2G **65**
Backfolds. *Abers* . . . 3F **51**
Backhill. *Abers* . . . 5C **50**
Backhill of Clackriach. *Abers* . . . 4E **51**
Backies. *High* . . . 3F **55**
Backmuir of New Gilston. *Fife* . . . 3F **27**
Back of Keppoch. *High* . . . 5F **37**
Badachonacher. *High* . . . 1H **47**
Badachro. *High* . . . 1G **45**
Badanloch Lodge. *High* . . . 5A **58**
Badavanich. *High* . . . 3C **46**
Badcall. *High* . . . 3D **56**
Badcaul. *High* . . . 4F **53**
Baddidarach. *High* . . . 1F **53**
Baddoch. *Abers* . . . 5E **41**
Badenscallie. *High* . . . 3F **53**
Badenscoth. *Abers* . . . 5C **50**
Badentarbat. *High* . . . 2F **53**
Badicaul. *High* . . . 1G **37**
Badlipster. *High* . . . 4F **59**
Badluarach. *High* . . . 4E **53**
Badnaban. *High* . . . 1F **53**
Badnabay. *High* . . . 4D **56**
Badnagie. *High* . . . 5E **59**
Badnellan. *High* . . . 3F **55**
Badninish. *High* . . . 4E **55**
Badrallach. *High* . . . 4F **53**
Bàgh a Chàise. *W Isl* . . . 3K **61**
Bàgh a' Chaisteil. *W Isl* . . . 5B **60**
Baghasdal. *W Isl* . . . 3C **60**
Bagh Mor. *W Isl* . . . 5J **61**
Bagh Shiarabhagh. *W Isl* . . . 4C **60**
Baile. *W Isl* . . . 2K **61**
Baile Ailein. *W Isl* . . . 2D **62**
Baile an Truiseil. *W Isl* . . . 2H **63**
Baile Boidheach. *Arg* . . . 1A **16**
Baile Glas. *W Isl* . . . 5J **61**
Bailemeonach. *Arg* . . . 4H **29**
Baile Mhanaich. *W Isl* . . . 5H **61**
Baile Mhartainn. *W Isl* . . . 3H **61**
Baile MhicPhail. *W Isl* . . . 3J **61**
Baile Mor. *Arg* . . . 3A **22**
Baile Mor. *W Isl* . . . 4H **61**
Baile nan Cailleach. *W Isl* . . . 5H **61**
Baile Raghaill. *W Isl* . . . 4H **61**
Baileyhead. *Cumb* . . . 5E **13**
Bailiesward. *Abers* . . . 5H **49**
Bail' Iochdrach. *W Isl* . . . 5J **61**
Baillieston. *Glas* . . . 2B **18**
Bail' Uachdraich. *W Isl* . . . 4J **61**
Bail Ur Tholastaidh. *W Isl* . . . 3K **63**
Bainsford. *Falk* . . . 5H **25**
Bainshole. *Abers* . . . 5B **50**
Baintown. *Fife* . . . 3E **27**
Balachuirn. *High* . . . 4E **45**
Balbeg. *High* . . . 5F **47** (nr. Cannich)
Balbeg. *High* . . . 1F **39** (nr. Loch Ness)
Balbeggie. *Per* . . . 1C **26**
Balblair. *High* . . . 4C **54** (nr. Bonar Bridge)
Balblair. *High* . . . 2A **48** (nr. Invergordon)
Balblair. *High* . . . 4G **47** (nr. Inverness)
Balcathie. *Ang* . . . 5D **34**
Balchladich. *High* . . . 5B **56**
Balchraggan. *High* . . . 4G **47**
Balchrick. *High* . . . 3C **56**
Balcurvie. *Fife* . . . 3E **27**
Baldinnie. *Fife* . . . 2F **27**
Baldwinholme. *Cumb* . . . 3G **7**
Balearn. *Abers* . . . 3F **51**
Balemartine. *Arg* . . . 4A **28**
Balephetrish. *Arg* . . . 4B **28**
Balephuil. *Arg* . . . 4A **28**
Balerno. *Edin* . . . 2G **19**
Balevullin. *Arg* . . . 4A **28**
Balfield. *Ang* . . . 2C **34**
Balfour. *Orkn* . . . 3D **64**
Balfron. *Stir* . . . 5E **25**
Balgaveny. *Abers* . . . 4B **50**
Balgonar. *Fife* . . . 4B **26**
Balgowan. *High* . . . 4H **39**
Balgown. *High* . . . 2C **44**
Balgrochan. *E Dun* . . . 1B **18**
Balgy. *High* . . . 3H **45**
Balhalgardy. *Abers* . . . 1C **42**
Baliasta. *Shet* . . . 2K **67**
Baligill. *High* . . . 2B **58**
Balintore. *Ang* . . . 3H **33**
Balintore. *High* . . . 1B **48**
Balintraid. *High* . . . 1H **47**
Balkeerie. *Ang* . . . 4A **34**
Balknakulish. *High* . . . 3D **30**
Ballachulish. *High* . . . 3D **30**
Ballantrae. *S Ayr* . . . 5F **9**
Ballater. *Abers* . . . 4G **41**
Ballencrieff. *E Lot* . . . 1B **20**
Ballencrieff Toll. *W Lot* . . . 1E **19**
Ballentoul. *Per* . . . 2D **32**
Balliemore. *Arg* . . . 5H **23** (nr. Dunoon)
Balliemore. *Arg* . . . 1F **23** (nr. Oban)
Ballieward. *High* . . . 5D **48**
Ballimore. *Stir* . . . 2E **25**
Ballingry. *Fife* . . . 4C **26**
Ballinluig. *Per* . . . 3E **33**
Ballintuim. *Per* . . . 3G **33**
Balliveolan. *Arg* . . . 4B **30**
Balloan. *High* . . . 3C **54**
Balloch. *High* . . . 4A **48**
Balloch. *N Lan* . . . 1C **18**
Balloch. *Per* . . . 2H **25**
Balloch. *W Dun* . . . 5C **24**
Ballochan. *Abers* . . . 4A **42**
Ballochgoy. *Arg* . . . 2D **16**
Ballochmyle. *E Ayr* . . . 1C **10**
Ballochroy. *Arg* . . . 3A **16**
Ballygown. *Arg* . . . 4F **29**
Ballygrant. *Arg* . . . 2E **15**
Ballymichael. *N Ayr* . . . 5C **16**
Balmacara. *High* . . . 1H **37**
Balmaclellan. *Dum* . . . 1H **5**
Balmacqueen. *High* . . . 1D **44**
Balmaha. *Stir* . . . 4D **24**
Balmalcolm. *Fife* . . . 3E **27**
Balmalloch. *N Lan* . . . 1C **18**
Balmeanach. *High* . . . 5E **45**
Balmedie. *Abers* . . . 2E **43**
Balmerino. *Fife* . . . 1E **27**
Balmore. *E Dun* . . . 1B **18**
Balmore. *High* . . . 4B **44**
Balmuir. *Ang* . . . 5B **34**
Balmullo. *Fife* . . . 1F **27**
Balmurrie. *Dum* . . . 2D **4**
Balnaboth. *Ang* . . . 2A **34**
Balnabruaich. *High* . . . 1A **48**
Balnabruich. *High* . . . 5E **59**
Balnacoil. *High* . . . 2F **55**
Balnacra. *High* . . . 4A **46**
Balnacroft. *Abers* . . . 4F **41**
Balnageith. *Mor* . . . 3D **48**
Balnaglaic. *High* . . . 5F **47**
Balnagrantach. *High* . . . 5F **47**
Balnaguard. *Per* . . . 3E **33**
Balnahard. *Arg* . . . 4B **22**
Balnain. *High* . . . 5F **47**
Balnakeil. *High* . . . 2E **57**
Balnaknock. *High* . . . 2D **44**
Balnamoon. *Abers* . . . 3E **51**
Balnamoon. *Ang* . . . 2C **34**
Balnapaling. *High* . . . 2A **48**
Balornock. *Glas* . . . 2B **18**
Balquhidder. *Stir* . . . 1E **25**
Baltasound. *Shet* . . . 2K **67**
Balterson. *Dum* . . . 2F **5**
Balthangie. *Abers* . . . 3D **50**
Balvaird. *High* . . . 3G **47**
Balvaird. *Per* . . . 2C **26**
Balvenie. *Mor* . . . 4G **49**
Balvicar. *Arg* . . . 2E **23**
Balvraid. *High* . . . 2H **37**
Balvraid Lodge. *High* . . . 5B **48**
Banavie. *High* . . . 1E **31**
Banchory. *Abers* . . . 4B **42**
Banchory-Devenick. *Abers* . . . 3E **43**
Banff. *Abers* . . . 2B **50**
Bankend. *Dum* . . . 2D **6**
Bankfoot. *Per* . . . 5F **33**
Bankglen. *E Ayr* . . . 2C **10**
Bankhead. *Aber* . . . 2D **42**
Bankhead. *Abers* . . . 3B **42**
Bankhead. *S Lan* . . . 4E **19**
Banknock. *Falk* . . . 1C **18**
Bankshill. *Dum* . . . 5A **12**
Banniskirk. *High* . . . 3E **59**
Bannockburn. *Stir* . . . 4H **25**
Banton. *N Lan* . . . 1C **18**
Barabhas. *W Isl* . . . 2H **63**
Barabhas Iarach. *W Isl* . . . 3H **63**
Baramore. *High* . . . 1H **29**
Barassie. *S Ayr* . . . 5G **17**
Baravullin. *Arg* . . . 4C **30**
Barbaraville. *High* . . . 1A **48**
Barbhas Uarach. *W Isl* . . . 2H **63**
Barbieston. *S Ayr* . . . 2B **10**
Barcaldine. *Arg* . . . 4C **30**
Barclose. *Cumb* . . . 2H **7**
Bardister. *Shet* . . . 5G **67**
Bardnabeinne. *High* . . . 4E **55**
Bardowie. *E Dun* . . . 1A **18**
Bardrainney. *Inv* . . . 1G **17**
Barelees. *Nmbd* . . . 5F **21**
Bargeddie. *N Lan* . . . 2C **18**
Bargrennan. *Dum* . . . 1E **5**
Barharrow. *Dum* . . . 3H **5**
Barlanark. *Glas* . . . 2B **18**
Barmoor. *Nmbd* . . . 5H **21**
Barmulloch. *Glas* . . . 2B **18**
Barnbarroch. *Dum* . . . 3B **6**
Barnhead. *Ang* . . . 3D **34**
Barnhill. *D'dee* . . . 5B **34**
Barnhill. *Mor* . . . 3E **49**
Barnhill. *Per* . . . 1C **26**
Barnhills. *Dum* . . . 1A **4**
Barony, The. *Orkn* . . . 2B **64**
Barr. *Dum* . . . 3E **11**
Barr. *S Ayr* . . . 4H **9**
Barra Airport. *W Isl* . . . 4C **60**
Barrachan. *Dum* . . . 4E **5**

Barraglom—Ceallan

Barraglom. *W Isl* 1C 62
Barrahormid. *Arg* 5E 23
Barrapol. *Arg* 4A 28
Barravullin. *Arg* 3F 23
Barrhead. *E Ren* 3A 18
Barrhill. *S Ayr* 5H 9
Barrmill. *N Ayr* 3G 17
Barrock. *High* 1F 59
Barrowburn. *Nmbd* 2H 13
Barry. *Ang* 5C 34
Barthol Chapel. *Abers* 5D 50
Barton. *Cumb* 5H 7
Bassendean. *Bord* 4D 20
Bassenthwaite. *Cumb* 5F 7
Basta. *Shet* 3J 67
Bathgate. *W Lot* 2E 19
Bathville. *W Lot* 2E 19
Bauds of Cullen. *Mor* 2H 49
Baugh. *Arg* 4B 28
Beacrabhaicg. *W Isl* 5C 62
Beal. *Nmbd* 4H 21
Beaquoy. *Orkn* 2C 64
Bearsden. *E Dun* 1A 18
Beattock. *Dum* 3H 11
Beauly. *High* 4G 47
Beaumont. *Cumb* 3G 7
Beckfoot. *Cumb* 4D 6
Bedrule. *Bord* 2F 13
Beeswing. *Dum* 2B 6
Beinn Casgro. *W Isl* 5J 63
Beith. *N Ayr* 3G 17
Belfatton. *Abers* 3F 51
Belford. *Nmbd* 5H 21
Belhaven. *E Lot* 1D 20
Belhelvie. *Abers* 2E 43
Belhinnie. *Abers* 1H 41
Bellabeg. *Abers* 2G 41
Belladrum. *High* 4G 47
Bellamore. *S Ayr* 5H 9
Bellanoch. *Arg* 4F 23
Belleheiglash. *Mor* 5E 49
Belle Vue. *Cumb* 5E 7
Bellfield. *S Lan* 5D 18
Belliehill. *Ang* 2C 34
Bellingham. *Nmbd* 5H 13
Bellochantuy. *Arg* 5H 15
Bellsbank. *E Ayr* 3B 10
Bellside. *N Lan* 3D 18
Bellspool. *Bord* 5G 19
Bellsquarry. *W Lot* 2F 19
Belmaduthy. *High* 3H 47
Belmont. *Shet* 2J 67
Belmont. *S Ayr* 2A 10
Belnacraig. *Abers* 2G 41
Belston. *S Ayr* 1A 10
Belts of Collonach. *Abers* 4B 42
Bemersyde. *Bord* 5C 20
Ben Alder Lodge. *High* 1A 32
Ben Armine Lodge. *High* 2E 55
Benbecula Airport. *W Isl* 5H 61
Benbuie. *Dum* 4E 11
Benderloch. *Arg* 5C 30
Bendronaig Lodge. *High* 5B 46
Benera. *High* 1H 37
Benholm. *Abers* 2F 35
Benmore Lodge. *High* 2A 54
Bennecarngan. *N Ayr* 1E 9
Benston. *Shet* 1D 66
Benstonhall. *Orkn* 1E 64
Bent. *Abers* 1D 34
Benthoul. *Aber* 3D 42
Bentpath. *Dum* 4C 12
Bents. *W Lot* 2E 19
Benvie. *D'dee* 5A 34
Beoraidbeg. *High* 4F 37
Bernice. *Arg* 4A 24
Bernisdale. *High* 3D 44
Berriedale. *High* 1H 55
Berrier. *Cumb* 5H 7
Berrington. *Nmbd* 4H 21
Berrington Law. *Nmbd* 4G 21
Berryhillock. *Mor* 2A 50
Berryscaur. *Dum* 4A 12
Berwick-upon-Tweed. *Nmbd* 3H 21
Betishill. *N Lan* 2C 18
Bettyhill. *High* 2A 58
Beul an Atha. *Arg* 2E 15
Bewaldeth. *Cumb* 5F 7
Bhalton. *W Isl* 1B 62
Bhatarsaigh. *W Isl* 5B 60
Bieldside. *Aber* 3D 42
Biggar. *S Lan* 5F 19
Biggings. *Shet* 1A 66
Bighouse. *High* 2B 58
Biglands. *Cumb* 3F 7
Big Sand. *High* 1G 45
Bigton. *Shet* 4C 66
Bilbster. *High* 3F 59
Bilston. *Midl* 2H 19
Bimbister. *Orkn* 3C 64
Bindal. *High* 5G 55
Binniehill. *Falk* 1D 18
Birchburn. *N Ayr* 1E 9
Birchview. *Mor* 5E 49
Birdston. *E Dun* 1B 18
Birgham. *Bord* 5E 21
Birichen. *High* 4E 55
Birkby. *Cumb* 5D 6
Birkenhills. *Abers* 4C 50
Birkenshaw. *N Lan* 2B 18
Birkhall. *Abers* 4G 41
Birkhill. *Ang* 5A 34
Birnam. *Per* 4F 33
Birsay. *Orkn* 2B 64
Birse. *Abers* 4A 42
Birsemore. *Abers* 4A 42
Birtley. *Nmbd* 5H 13
Bishopbriggs. *E Dun* 1B 18
Bishopmill. *Mor* 2F 49
Bishopton. *Dum* 4F 5
Bishopton. *Ren* 1H 17
Bixter. *Shet* 1C 66
Blackburn. *Abers* 2D 42
Blackburn. *W Lot* 2E 19
Black Clauchrie. *S Ayr* 5H 9
Black Corries. *High* 3F 31
Black Crofts. *Arg* 5C 30
Blackdog. *Abers* 2E 43
Blackdyke. *Cumb* 3E 7
Blackford. *Cumb* 2G 7
Blackford. *Per* 3H 25
Blackhall. *Edin* 1H 19
Blackhall. *Ren* 2H 17
Blackhill. *Abers* 4F 51
Blackhill. *High* 3C 44
Blackhills. *Abers* 2E 51
Blackhills. *High* 3C 48
Blacklunans. *Per* 2G 33
Black Mount. *Arg* 4F 31
Blackness. *Falk* 1F 19
Blackpool Gate. *Cumb* 5E 13
Blackridge. *W Lot* 2E 19
Blackrock. *Arg* 2E 15
Blackshaw. *Dum* 2D 6
Blacktop. *Aber* 3D 42
Blackwaterfoot. *N Ayr* 1D 8
Blackwood. *Dum* 5G 11
Blackwood. *S Lan* 4C 18
Bladnoch. *Dum* 3F 5
Blaich. *High* 1D 30
Blain. *High* 2H 29
Blair Atholl. *Per* 2D 32
Blair Drummond. *Stir* 4G 25
Blairgowrie. *Per* 4G 33
Blairhall. *Fife* 5B 26
Blairingone. *Per* 4A 26
Blairlogie. *Stir* 4H 25
Blairmore. *Abers* 5H 49
Blairmore. *Arg* 5A 24
Blairmore. *High* 3C 56
Blairquhanan. *W Dun* 5D 24
Blandy. *High* 3H 57
Blanefield. *Stir* 1A 18
Blantyre. *S Lan* 3B 18
Blarmachfoldach. *High* 2D 30
Blarnalearoch. *High* 4G 53
Blathaisbhal. *W Isl* 3J 61
Blebocraigs. *Fife* 2F 27
Blencogo. *Cumb* 4E 7
Blennerhasset. *Cumb* 4E 7
Blindburn. *Nmbd* 2H 13
Blindcrake. *Cumb* 5E 7
Blitterlees. *Cumb* 3E 7
Bloomfield. *Bord* 1E 13
Blyth. *Bord* 4G 19
Blyth Bank. *Bord* 4G 19
Blyth Bridge. *Bord* 4G 19
Boarhills. *Fife* 2G 27
Boath. *High* 1G 47
Boat of Garten. *High* 2C 40
Boddam. *Abers* 4G 51
Boddam. *Shet* 5C 66
Bogallan. *High* 3H 47
Bogbrae Croft. *Abers* 5F 51
Bogend. *S Ayr* 5G 17
Boghall. *Midl* 2H 19
Boghall. *W Lot* 2E 19
Boghead. *S Lan* 4C 18
Bogindollo. *Ang* 3B 34
Bogmoor. *Mor* 2G 49
Bogniebrae. *Abers* 4A 50
Bograxie. *Abers* 2C 42
Bogside. *N Lan* 3D 18
Bogton. *Abers* 3B 50
Bogue. *Dum* 5D 10
Bohenie. *High* 5D 38
Boirseam. *W Isl* 6B 62
Boleside. *Bord* 5B 20
Bolshan. *Ang* 3D 34
Boltachan. *Per* 3D 32
Bolton. *E Lot* 1C 20
Boltonfellend. *Cumb* 2H 7
Boltongate. *Cumb* 4F 7
Bolton Low Houses. *Cumb* 4F 7
Bolton New Houses. *Cumb* 4F 7
Bolton Wood Lane. *Cumb* 4F 7
Bonar Bridge. *High* 4D 54
Bonawe. *Arg* 5D 30
Bonchester Bridge. *Bord* 2E 13
Bo'ness. *Falk* 5A 26
Bonhill. *W Dun* 1G 17
Bonjedward. *Bord* 1F 13
Bonkle. *N Lan* 3D 18
Bonnington. *Ang* 5C 34
Bonnington. *Edin* 2G 19
Bonnybank. *Fife* 3E 27
Bonnybridge. *Falk* 5H 25
Bonnykelly. *Abers* 3D 50
Bonnyrigg. *Midl* 2A 20
Bonnyton. *Ang* 5A 34
Bonnytown. *Fife* 2G 27
Booth of Toft. *Shet* 5H 67
Boquhan. *Stir* 5E 25
Bordlands. *Bord* 4G 19
Boreland. *Dum* 4A 12
Borestone Brae. *Stir* 4H 25
Borgh. *W Isl* 4B 60 (on Barra)
Borgh. *W Isl* 5H 61 (on Benbecula)
Borgh. *W Isl* 2K 61 (on Berneray)
Borgh. *W Isl* 2J 63 (on Isle of Lewis)
Borghasdal. *W Isl* 6B 62
Borghastan. *W Isl* 3F 63
Borgh na Sgiotaig. *High* 1C 44
Borgie. *High* 3H 57
Borgue. *Dum* 4H 5
Borgue. *High* 5E 59
Borlum. *High* 1G 39
Bornais. *W Isl* 2C 60
Bornesketaig. *High* 1C 44
Borreraig. *High* 3A 44
Borrobol Lodge. *High* 1F 55
Borrodale. *High* 4A 44
Borrowston. *High* 4G 59
Borrowstonehill. *Orkn* 4D 64
Borrowstoun. *Falk* 5A 26
Borthwick. *Midl* 3A 20
Borve. *High* 4D 44
Bostadh. *W Isl* 3F 63
Bothel. *Cumb* 5E 7
Bothwell. *S Lan* 3B 18
Bottacks. *High* 2F 47
Bottomcraig. *Fife* 1E 27
Bousd. *Arg* 2D 28
Bousta. *Shet* 1B 66
Boustead Hill. *Cumb* 3F 7
Bowden. *Bord* 5C 20
Bower. *Nmbd* 5G 13
Bowermadden. *High* 2F 59
Bowershall. *Fife* 4B 26
Bowertower. *High* 2F 59
Bowhousebog. *N Lan* 3D 18
Bowling. *W Dun* 1H 17
Bowmore. *Arg* 3E 15
Bowness-on-Solway. *Cumb* 2F 7
Bow of Fife. *Fife* 2E 27
Bowriefauld. *Ang* 4C 34
Bowscale. *Cumb* 5G 7
Bowsden. *Nmbd* 4G 21
Bowside Lodge. *High* 2B 58
Boyndlie. *Abers* 2E 51
Boyndie. *Abers* 2B 50
Braal Castle. *High* 2E 59
Brabster. *High* 2G 59
Bracadale. *High* 5C 44
Bracara. *High* 4G 37
Brackenlands. *Cumb* 4F 7
Brackenthwaite. *Cumb* 4F 7
Brackla. *High* 3B 48
Brackletter. *High* 5C 38
Brackloch. *High* 1G 53
Braco. *Per* 3H 25
Bracobrae. *Mor* 3A 50
Brae. *High* 2A 48
Brae. *Shet* 6G 67
Braeantra. *High* 1G 47
Braefield. *High* 5F 47
Braefindon. *High* 3H 47
Braegrum. *Per* 1B 26
Braehead. *Ang* 3D 34
Braehead. *Dum* 3F 5
Braehead. *Mor* 4F 49
Braehead. *Orkn* 3G 65
Braehead. *S Lan* 5D 18 (nr. Coalburn)
Braehead. *S Lan* 3E 19 (nr. Forth)
Braehoulland. *Shet* 5F 67
Braemar. *Abers* 4E 41
Braemore. *High* 5D 58 (nr. Dunbeath)
Braemore. *High* 1C 46 (nr. Ullapool)
Brae of Achnahaird. *High* 2F 53
Brae Roy Lodge. *High* 4E 39
Braeside. *Abers* 5E 51
Braeside. *Inv* 1F 17
Braes of Coul. *Ang* 3H 33
Braeswick. *Orkn* 4J 65
Braetongue. *High* 3G 57
Braeval. *Stir* 3E 25
Braevallich. *Arg* 3G 23
Braewick. *Shet* 1C 66
Bragar. *W Isl* 3G 63
Bragleenbeg. *Arg* 1G 23
Braidwood. *S Lan* 4D 18
Braigo. *Arg* 2D 14
Brampton. *Cumb* 2H 7
Branault. *High* 2G 29
Branchill. *Mor* 3D 48
Branderburgh. *Mor* 1F 49
Branthwaite. *Cumb* 5G 7
Branxholme. *Bord* 2D 12
Branxton. *Nmbd* 5F 21
Brathens. *Abers* 4B 42
Braulen Lodge. *High* 5D 46
Brawl. *High* 2B 58
Brawlbin. *High* 3D 58
Breacleit. *W Isl* 1C 62
Breakachy. *High* 4F 47
Breakish. *High* 1F 37
Breanais. *W Isl* 2A 62
Breascleit. *W Isl* 1D 62
Brecais Àrd. *High* 1F 37
Brecais Iosal. *High* 1F 37
Brechin. *Ang* 3D 34
Breibhig. *W Isl* 5B 60 (on Barra)
Breibhig. *W Isl* 4J 63 (on Isle of Lewis)
Breich. *W Lot* 2E 19
Breiwick. *Shet* 2D 66
Brenachie. *High* 1A 48
Brettabister. *Shet* 1D 66
Brewlands Bridge. *Ang* 2G 33
Bridekirk. *Cumb* 5E 7
Brideswell. *Abers* 5A 50
Bridge End. *Cumb* 4G 7
Bridge End. *Shet* 3C 66
Bridgefoot. *Ang* 5A 34
Bridgefoot. *Cumb* 5D 6
Bridgend. *Abers* 5A 50 (nr. Huntly)
Bridgend. *Abers* 5F 51 (nr. Peterhead)
Bridgend. *Ang* 2C 34 (nr. Brechin)
Bridgend. *Ang* 4A 34 (nr. Kirriemuir)
Bridgend. *Arg* 4F 23 (nr. Lochgilphead)
Bridgend. *Arg* 2E 15 (on Islay)
Bridgend. *Fife* 2E 27
Bridgend. *High* 3E 47
Bridgend. *Mor* 5G 49
Bridgend. *Per* 1C 26
Bridgend. *W Lot* 1F 19
Bridgend of Lintrathen. *Ang* 3H 33
Bridgeness. *Falk* 5B 26
Bridge of Alford. *Abers* 2A 42
Bridge of Allan. *Stir* 4G 25
Bridge of Avon. *Mor* 5E 49
Bridge of Awe. *Arg* 1H 23
Bridge of Balgie. *Per* 4A 32
Bridge of Brown. *High* 1E 41
Bridge of Cally. *Per* 3G 33
Bridge of Canny. *Abers* 4B 42
Bridge of Dee. *Dum* 2A 6
Bridge of Don. *Aber* 2E 43
Bridge of Dun. *Ang* 3D 34
Bridge of Dye. *Abers* 5B 42
Bridge of Earn. *Per* 2C 26
Bridge of Ericht. *Per* 3A 32
Bridge of Feugh. *Abers* 4C 42
Bridge of Forss. *High* 2D 58
Bridge of Gairn. *Abers* 4G 41
Bridge of Gaur. *Per* 3A 32
Bridge of Muchalls. *Abers* 4D 42
Bridge of Oich. *High* 3E 39
Bridge of Orchy. *Arg* 5G 31
Bridge of Walls. *Shet* 1B 66
Bridge of Weir. *Ren* 2G 17
Bridister. *Shet* 1B 66
Brigham. *Cumb* 5D 6
Brightons. *Falk* 1E 19
Brig o'Turk. *Stir* 3E 25
Brims. *Orkn* 6B 64
Brindister. *Shet* 3D 66
Brinian. *Orkn* 2D 64
Brisco. *Cumb* 3H 7
Broadfield. *Inv* 1G 17
Broadford. *High* 1F 37
Broadhaven. *High* 3G 59
Broadley. *Mor* 2G 49
Broadrashes. *Mor* 3H 49
Broadsea. *Abers* 2E 51
Broadwath. *Cumb* 3H 7
Broallan. *High* 4F 47
Brochel. *High* 4E 45
Brocketsbrae. *S Lan* 5D 18
Brockhill. *Bord* 1C 12
Brockleymoor. *Cumb* 5H 7
Brodick. *N Ayr* 5D 16
Brodie. *Mor* 3C 48
Brodiesord. *Abers* 3A 50
Brogaig. *High* 2D 44
Bromfield. *Cumb* 4E 7
Brookfield. *Ren* 2H 17
Broom. *Fife* 3E 27
Broomend. *Abers* 2C 42
Broomfield. *Abers* 5E 51
Broomhill. *High* 1C 40 (nr. Grantown-on-Spey)
Broomhill. *High* 1A 48 (nr. Invergordon)
Broomhillbank. *Dum* 4A 12
Broomlands. *Dum* 3H 11
Broom of Moy. *Mor* 3D 48
Brora. *High* 3G 55
Broubster. *High* 2D 58
Brough. *High* 1F 59
Brough. *Orkn* 3C 64 (nr. Finstown)
Brough. *Orkn* 6D 64 (nr. St Margaret's Hope)
Brough. *Shet* 1D 66 (nr. Benston)
Brough. *Shet* 5H 67 (nr. Booth of Toft)
Brough. *Shet* 2E 66 (on Bressay)
Brough. *Shet* 6J 67 (on Whalsay)
Brough Lodge. *Shet* 3J 67
Broughton. *Orkn* 3G 65
Broughton. *Bord* 5G 19
Broughton Cross. *Cumb* 5D 6
Broughton Moor. *Cumb* 5D 6
Broughtown. *Orkn* 3J 65
Broughty Ferry. *D'dee* 5B 34
Browland. *Shet* 1B 66
Broxburn. *E Lot* 1D 20
Broxburn. *W Lot* 1F 19
Brù. *W Isl* 3H 63
Bruach Mairi. *W Isl* 4J 63
Bruairnis. *W Isl* 4C 60
Bruan. *High* 5G 59
Bruar Lodge. *Per* 1D 32
Brucehill. *W Dun* 1G 17
Brucklay. *Abers* 3E 51
Bruichladdich. *Arg* 2D 14
Brunery. *High* 1A 30
Brunton. *Fife* 1E 27
Brusta. *W Isl* 2K 61
Brydekirk. *Dum* 1E 7
Buaile nam Bodach. *W Isl* 4C 60
Bualintur. *High* 1D 36
Buccleuch. *Bord* 3C 12
Buchanan Smithy. *Stir* 5D 24
Buchanhaven. *Abers* 4G 51
Buchanty. *Per* 1A 26
Buchany. *Stir* 3G 25
Buchley. *E Dun* 1A 18
Buchlyvie. *Stir* 4E 25
Buckabank. *Cumb* 4G 7
Buckhaven. *Fife* 4E 27
Buckholm. *Bord* 5B 20
Buckie. *Mor* 2H 49
Buckpool. *Mor* 2H 49
Bucksburn. *Aber* 3D 42
Buckton. *Nmbd* 5H 21
Buldoo. *High* 2C 58
Bullgill. *Cumb* 5D 6
Bullwood. *Arg* 1E 17
Bulwark. *Abers* 4E 51
Bun Abhainn Eadarra. *W Isl* 4C 62
Bunacaimb. *High* 5F 37
Bun a' Mhuillinn. *W Isl* 3C 60
Bunarkaig. *High* 5C 38
Bunchrew. *High* 4H 47
Bundalloch. *High* 1H 37
Buness. *Shet* 2K 67
Bunessan. *Arg* 1A 22
Bunkegivie. *High* 2G 39
Bunloit. *High* 1G 39
Bunnahabhain. *Arg* 1F 15
Bunoich. *High* 3E 39
Bunree. *High* 2D 30
Bunroy. *High* 5D 38
Buntait. *High* 5E 47
Burg. *Arg* 4E 29
Burgh by Sands. *Cumb* 3G 7
Burghead. *Mor* 2E 49
Burgh Muir. *Abers* 2C 42
Burgie. *Mor* 3D 48
Burland. *Shet* 3C 66
Burness. *Orkn* 3J 65
Burnfoot. *E Ayr* 3B 10
Burnfoot. *Per* 3A 26
Burnfoot. *Bord* 2E 13 (nr. Hawick)
Burnfoot. *Bord* 2D 12 (nr. Roberton)
Burnhaven. *Abers* 4G 51
Burnhead. *Dum* 4F 11
Burnhervie. *Abers* 2C 42
Burnhouse. *N Ayr* 3G 17
Burnmouth. *Bord* 2G 21
Burn of Cambus. *Stir* 3G 25
Burnside. *Ang* 3C 34
Burnside. *E Ayr* 2C 10
Burnside. *Per* 3C 26
Burnside. *Shet* 5F 67
Burnside. *S Lan* 3B 18
Burnside. *W Lot* 1F 19 (nr. Broxburn)
Burnside. *W Lot* 1F 19 (nr. Winchburgh)
Burntisland. *Fife* 5D 26
Burnton. *E Ayr* 3B 10
Burnwynd. *Edin* 2G 19
Burrafirth. *Shet* 1K 67
Burragarth. *Shet* 2J 67
Burravoe. *Shet* 4J 67 (nr. North Roe)
Burravoe. *Shet* 6G 67 (on Mainland)
Burravoe. *Shet* 5J 67 (on Yell)
Burray Village. *Orkn* 5D 64
Burrelton. *Per* 5G 33
Burrigill. *High* 5F 59
Burroughston. *Orkn* 2E 64
Burthwaite. *Cumb* 4H 7
Burwick. *Orkn* 6D 64
Busby. *E Ren* 3A 18
Busby. *Per* 1B 26
Busta. *Shet* 6G 67
Butterstone. *Per* 4F 33
Butteryhaugh. *Nmbd* 4F 13
Byrness. *Nmbd* 3G 13

C

Cabharstadh. *W Isl* 3E 62
Cabrach. *Arg* 2F 15
Cabrach. *Mor* 1G 41
Cadder. *E Dun* 1B 18
Caddonfoot. *Bord* 5B 20
Cadham. *Fife* 3D 26
Caenn-na-Cleithe. *W Isl* 5C 62
Caerlaverock. *Per* 2H 25
Cairinis. *W Isl* 4J 61
Cairisiadar. *W Isl* 1C 62
Cairminis. *W Isl* 6B 62
Cairnbaan. *Arg* 4F 23
Cairnbulg. *Abers* 2F 51
Cairncross. *Ang* 1B 34
Cairndow. *Arg* 2A 24
Cairness. *Abers* 2F 51
Cairneyhill. *Fife* 5B 26
Cairngarroch. *Dum* 4B 4
Cairngorms. *High* 3C 40
Cairnhill. *Abers* 5B 50
Cairnie. *Abers* 4H 49
Cairnorrie. *Abers* 4D 50
Cairnryan. *Dum* 2B 4
Cairston. *Orkn* 3B 64
Calanais. *W Isl* 1D 62
Calbost. *W Isl* 6J 63
Caldback. *Shet* 2K 67
Caldbeck. *Cumb* 5G 7
Calderbank. *N Lan* 2C 18
Caldercruix. *N Lan* 2D 18
Calder Mains. *High* 3D 58
Caldermill. *S Lan* 4B 18
Calderwood. *S Lan* 3B 18
Calfsound. *Orkn* 1E 64
Calgary. *Arg* 3E 29
Califer. *Mor* 3D 48
California. *Falk* 1E 19
Callakille. *High* 3F 45
Callander. *Stir* 3F 25
Callendoun. *Arg* 5C 24
Calligarry. *High* 3F 37
Calthwaite. *Cumb* 4H 7
Calvine. *Per* 2D 32
Calvo. *Cumb* 3E 7
Camaghael. *High* 1E 31
Camas-luinie. *High* 1A 38
Camasnacroise. *High* 3B 30
Camastianavaig. *High* 5E 45
Camasunary. *High* 2E 37
Camault Muir. *High* 4G 47
Camb. *Shet* 3J 67
Cambus. *Clac* 4H 25
Cambusbarron. *Stir* 4G 25
Cambuskenneth. *Stir* 4H 25
Cambuslang. *S Lan* 2B 18
Cambusnethan. *N Lan* 3D 18
Cambus o'May. *Abers* 4H 41
Camelon. *Falk* 5H 25
Camerton. *Cumb* 5D 6
Camghouran. *Per* 3A 32
Cammachmore. *Abers* 4E 43
Camore. *High* 4E 55
Campbelton. *N Ayr* 3E 17
Campbeltown. *Arg* 1C 8
Campbeltown Airport. *Arg* 1B 8
Cample. *Dum* 4G 11
Campmuir. *Per* 5H 33
Camptoun. *E Lot* 1C 20
Camptown. *Bord* 2F 13
Camserney. *Per* 4D 32
Camster. *High* 4F 59
Camus Croise. *High* 2F 37
Camuscross. *High* 2F 37
Camusdarach. *High* 4F 37
Camusnagaul. *High* 1D 30 (nr. Fort William)
Camusnagaul. *High* 5F 53 (nr. Little Loch Broom)
Camusteel. *High* 4G 45
Camusterrach. *High* 4G 45
Camusvrachan. *Per* 4B 32
Candy Mill. *S Lan* 4F 19
Canisbay. *High* 1G 59
Cannich. *High* 5E 47
Canonbie. *Dum* 1G 7
Cantray. *High* 4A 48
Cantraybruich. *High* 4A 48
Cantraywood. *High* 4A 48
Cantsdam. *Fife* 4C 26
Caol. *High* 1E 31
Caolas. *W Isl* 5B 60
Caolas Liubharsaigh. *W Isl* 6J 61
Caolas Scalpaigh. *W Isl* 5D 62
Caolas Stocinis. *W Isl* 5C 62
Caoles. *Arg* 4B 28
Caol Ila. *Arg* 2F 15
Caol Loch Ailse. *High* 1G 37
Caol Reatha. *High* 1G 37
Cappercleuch. *Bord* 1B 12
Capplegill. *Dum* 3A 12
Caputh. *Per* 5F 33
Carbost. *High* 5C 44 (nr. Loch Harport)
Carbost. *High* 4D 44 (nr. Portree)
Carcluie. *S Ayr* 2A 10
Cardenden. *Fife* 4D 26
Cardewlees. *Cumb* 3G 7
Cardno. *Abers* 2E 51
Cardow. *Mor* 4E 49
Cardross. *Arg* 1G 17
Cardurnock. *Cumb* 3E 7
Careston. *Ang* 2C 34
Carfin. *N Lan* 3C 18
Carfrae. *Bord* 3C 20
Cargenbridge. *Dum* 1C 6
Cargill. *Per* 5G 33
Cargo. *Cumb* 3G 7
Carham. *Nmbd* 5E 21
Carie. *Per* 3B 32 (nr. Loch Rannah)
Carie. *Per* 5B 32 (nr. Loch Tay)
Carlabhagh. *W Isl* 3G 63
Carleton. *Cumb* 3H 7
Carlisle. *Cumb* 3H 7
Carloonan. *Arg* 2H 23
Carlops. *Bord* 3G 19
Carluke. *S Lan* 3D 18
Carmichael. *S Lan* 5E 19
Carmunnock. *Glas* 3B 18
Carmyle. *S Lan* 2B 18
Carmyllie. *Ang* 4C 34
Carnach. *High* 1B 38 (nr. Lochcarron)
Carnach. *High* 4F 53 (nr. Ullapool)
Carnach. *Mor* 4D 48
Carnach. *W Isl* 5D 62
Carnachy. *High* 3A 58
Carnain. *Arg* 2E 15
Carnais. *W Isl* 1B 62
Carnan. *Arg* 4B 28
Carnan. *W Isl* 6H 61
Carnbee. *Fife* 3G 27
Carnbo. *Per* 3B 26
Carndu. *High* 1H 37
Carnell. *S Ayr* 5H 17
Carn-gorm. *High* 1A 38
Carnie. *Abers* 3D 42
Carnock. *Fife* 5B 26
Carnoustie. *Ang* 5C 34
Carntyne. *Glas* 2B 18
Carnwath. *S Lan* 4E 19
Carradale. *Arg* 5B 16
Carragraich. *W Isl* 5C 62
Carrbridge. *High* 1C 40
Carrick Castle. *Arg* 4A 24
Carrick Ho. *Orkn* 1E 64
Carriden. *Falk* 5B 26
Carrington. *Midl* 2A 20
Carron. *Falk* 5H 25
Carron. *Mor* 4F 49
Carronbridge. *Dum* 4F 11
Carronshore. *Falk* 5H 25
Carrutherstown. *Dum* 1E 7
Carsaig. *Arg* 1C 22
Carscreugh. *Dum* 2D 4
Carsegowan. *Dum* 3F 5
Carse House. *Arg* 2A 16
Carseriggan. *Dum* 2E 5
Carsethorn. *Dum* 3C 6
Carskiey. *Arg* 3B 8
Carsluith. *Dum* 3F 5
Carsphairn. *Dum* 4C 10
Carstairs. *S Lan* 4E 19
Carstairs Junction. *S Lan* 4E 19
Carterhaugh. *Ang* 4B 34
Cartland. *S Lan* 4D 18
Carwath. *Cumb* 4G 7
Carwinley. *Cumb* 1H 7
Cash Feus. *Fife* 3D 26
Cashlie. *Per* 4H 31
Castlebay. *W Isl* 5B 60
Castlecary. *N Lan* 1C 18
Castlecraig. *High* 2B 48
Castle Douglas. *Dum* 2A 6
Castle Heaton. *Nmbd* 4G 21
Castlehill. *Per* 5H 33
Castlehill. *S Lan* 3D 18
Castlehill. *W Dun* 1G 17
Castle Kennedy. *Dum* 3C 4
Castle Lachlan. *Arg* 4H 23
Castlemilk. *Glas* 3B 18
Castle O'er. *Dum* 4B 12
Castleton. *Abers* 4E 41
Castleton. *Arg* 5F 23
Castleton. *Mor* 1E 41
Castleton. *Per* 2A 26
Castletown. *Cumb* 5H 7
Castletown. *High* 2E 59
Catacol. *N Ayr* 4C 16
Catcleugh. *Nmbd* 3G 13
Catfirth. *Shet* 1D 66
Cathcart. *Glas* 2A 18
Catlodge. *High* 4H 39
Catlowdy. *Cumb* 1H 7
Catrine. *E Ayr* 1C 10
Catterlen. *Cumb* 5H 7
Catterline. *Abers* 1F 35
Cauldhame. *Stir* 4F 25
Cauldmill. *Bord* 2E 13
Cauldwells. *Abers* 3C 50
Caulkerbush. *Dum* 3C 6
Caulside. *Dum* 5D 12
Causewayend. *S Lan* 5F 19
Causewayhead. *Stir* 4H 25
Cawdor. *High* 4B 48
Ceallan. *W Isl* 5J 61

Ceann a Bhàigh—Drumgley

Ceann a Bhàigh. W Isl 6B 62 (on Harris)
Ceann a Bhaigh. W Isl 4H 61 (on North Uist)
Ceann a Bhaigh. W Isl 5D 62 (on Scalpay)
Ceann a Bhaigh. W Isl 5C 62 (on South Harris)
Ceannacroc Lodge. High 2D 38
Ceann a Deas Loch Baghasdail. W Isl 3C 60
Ceann an Leothaid. High 5F 37
Ceann a Tuath Loch Baghasdail. W Isl 2C 60
Ceann Loch Ailleart. High 5G 37
Ceann Loch Muideirt. High 1A 30
Ceann Shiphoirt. W Isl 3D 62
Ceann Tarabhaigh. W Isl 3D 62
Cearsiadar. W Isl 2E 62
Ceathramh Meadhanach. W Isl 3H 61
Cellardyke. Fife 3G 27
Ceos. W Isl 2E 62
Ceres. Fife 2F 27
Cessford. Bord 1G 13
Challister. Shet 6J 67
Challoch. Dum 2E 5
Champany. Falk 1F 19
Chance Inn. Fife 2E 27
Chanlockfoot. Dum 3E 11
Channerwick. Shet 4D 66
Chapel. Cumb 5F 7
Chapel. Fife 4D 26
Chapelfield. Abers 2E 35
Chapelhall. N Lan 2C 18
Chapel Hill. Abers 5F 51
Chapelhill. Per 1D 26 (nr. Glencarse)
Chapelhill. Per 5F 33 (nr. Harrietfield)
Chapelknowe. Dum 1G 7
Chapel of Garioch. Abers 1C 42
Chapelton. Ang 4D 34
Chapelton. High 2C 40 (nr. Grantown-on-Spey)
Chapelton. High 3G 47 (nr. Inverness)
Chapelton. S Lan 4B 18
Chapeltown. Mor 1F 41
Charlesfield. Dum 2E 7
Charleston. Ang 4A 34
Charleston. Ren 2H 17
Charlestown. Aber 3E 43
Charlestown. Abers 2F 51
Charlestown. Fife 5B 26
Charlestown. High 1H 45 (nr. Gairloch)
Charlestown. High 4H 47 (nr. Inverness)
Charlestown of Aberlour. Mor 4F 49
Charlton. Nmbd 5H 13
Chatton. Nmbd 5H 21
Cherrybank. Per 1C 26
Chesterhope. Nmbd 5H 13
Chesters. Bord 2F 13
Cheswick. Nmbd 4H 21
Chillingham. Nmbd 5H 21
Chirmorie. S Ayr 1D 4
Chirnside. Bord 3F 21
Chirnsidebridge. Bord 3F 21
Chryston. N Lan 1B 18
Churchtown. Cumb 4G 7
Churnsike Lodge. Nmbd 5F 13
Cill Amhlaidh. W Isl 6H 61
Cill Donnain. High 1G 55
Cill Donnain. W Isl 2C 60
Cille a' Bhacstair. High 2C 44
Cille Bhrighde. W Isl 3C 60
Cille Pheadair. W Isl 3C 60
Cirbhig. W Isl 3F 63
Circebost. W Isl 1C 62
Clabhach. Arg 3C 28
Clachaig. Arg 5A 24
Clachaig. High 3E 31 (nr. Kinlochleven)
Clachaig. High 2D 40 (nr. Nethy Bridge)
Clachamish. High 3C 44
Clachan. Arg 3A 16 (on Kintyre)
Clachan. Arg 4B 30 (on Lismore)
Clachan. High 2A 58 (nr. Bettyhill)
Clachan. High 2D 44 (nr. Staffin)
Clachan. High 1C 44 (nr. Uig)
Clachan. High 5E 45 (on Raasay)
Clachan Farm. Arg 2A 24
Clachan na Luib. W Isl 4J 61
Clachan of Campsie. E Dun 1B 18
Clachan of Glendaruel. Arg 5G 23
Clachan-Seil. Arg 2E 23
Clachan Shannda. W Isl 3J 61
Clachan Strachur. Arg 3H 23
Clachbreck. Arg 1A 16
Clachnaharry. High 4H 47
Clachtoll. High 1F 53
Clackmannan. Clac 4A 26
Clackmannanshire Bridge. Falk 5A 26
Clackmarras. Mor 3F 49
Cladach a Chaolais. W Isl 4H 61
Cladach Chairinis. W Isl 5J 61
Cladach Chircebost. W Isl 4H 61
Cladach Iolaraigh. W Isl 4H 61
Cladich. Arg 1H 23
Claggan. High 1E 31 (nr. Fort William)
Claggan. High 4H 29 (nr. Lochaline)
Claigan. High 3B 44
Claonaig. Arg 3B 16
Clappers. Bord 3G 21
Clapphoull. Shet 4D 66
Clarebrand. Dum 2A 6
Clarencefield. Dum 2D 6
Clarilaw. Bord 2E 13
Clarkston. E Ren 3A 18
Clashedy. High 2H 57
Clashindarroch. Abers 5H 49
Clashmore. High 5E 55 (nr. Dornoch)
Clashmore. High 5B 56 (nr. Stoer)
Clashnessie. High 5B 56
Clashnoir. Mor 1F 41
Clate. Shet 6J 67
Clathick. Per 1H 25
Clathy. Per 2A 26
Clatt. Abers 1A 42
Claygate. Dum 1G 7
Clayholes. Ang 5C 34
Claylock. High 3E 59
Cleadale. High 5D 36
Cleat. Orkn 3G 65 (nr. Braehead)
Cleat. Orkn 6D 64 (nr. St Margaret's Hope)
Cleekhimin. N Lan 3C 18
Cleigh. Arg 1F 23
Cleish. Per 4B 26
Cleland. N Lan 3D 18
Clephanton. High 3B 48
Clerkhill. High 2A 58
Clestrain. Orkn 4C 64
Cliaid. W Isl 4B 60
Cliasmol. W Isl 4B 62
Clibberswick. Shet 1K 67
Cliffburn. Ang 4D 34
Clifton. Stir 5G 31
Climpy. S Lan 3E 19
Clintmains. Bord 5D 20
Cliobh. W Isl 1B 62
Cliuthar. W Isl 5C 62
Clivocast. Shet 2K 67
Clochan. Mor 2H 49
Clochforbie. Abers 3D 50
Cloddymoss. Mor 2C 48
Clola. Abers 4F 51
Closeburn. Dum 4F 11
Clousta. Shet 1C 66
Clouston. Orkn 3B 64
Clova. Abers 1H 41
Clova. Ang 1A 34
Clovenfords. Bord 5B 20
Clovenstone. Abers 2C 42
Clovullin. High 2D 30
Cluanie Inn. High 2B 38
Cluanie Lodge. High 2B 38
Clunas. High 4B 48
Clune. High 1A 40
Clunes. High 5D 38
Clunie. Per 4G 33
Cluny. Fife 4D 26
Clydebank. W Dun 1A 18
Clynder. Arg 5B 24
Clynelish. High 3F 55
Clyth. High 5F 59
Cnip. W Isl 1B 62
Cnoc Amhlaigh. W Isl 4K 63
Coalburn. S Lan 5D 18
Coalford. Abers 4D 42
Coalhall. E Ayr 2B 10
Coalsnaughton. Clac 4A 26
Coaltown of Balgonie. Fife 4E 27
Coaltown of Wemyss. Fife 4E 27
Coatbridge. N Lan 2C 18
Coatdyke. N Lan 2C 18
Cock Bridge. Abers 3F 41
Cockburnspath. Bord 1E 21
Cockenzie and Port Seton. E Lot 1B 20
Cockermouth. Cumb 5E 7
Cocklaw. Abers 4F 51
Cockmuir. Abers 3E 51
Coignafearn Lodge. High 2H 39
Coig Peighinnean. W Isl 1K 63
Coig Peighinnean Bhuirgh. W Isl 2J 63
Coilleag. W Isl 3C 60
Coilliemore. High 1H 47
Coillore. High 5C 44
Coire an Fhuarain. W Isl 1D 62
Col. W Isl 3J 63
Colaboll. High 2C 54
Colbost. High 4B 44
Coldbackie. High 3H 57
Coldingham. Bord 2G 21
Coldrain. Per 3B 26
Coldstream. Bord 4F 21
Coldwells. Abers 5G 51
Coldwells Croft. Abers 1A 42
Cole. Shet 6G 67
Coleburn. Mor 3F 49
Colinsburgh. Fife 3F 27
Colinton. Edin 2H 19
Colintraive. Arg 1D 16
Collace. Per 5H 33
Collam. W Isl 5C 62
College of Roseisle. Mor 2E 49
Collessie. Fife 2D 26
Collieston. Abers 1F 43
Collin. Dum 1D 6
Collistan. Ang 4D 34
Collydean. Fife 3D 26
Colmonell. S Ayr 5G 9
Colpy. Abers 5B 50
Colstoun House. E Lot 1C 20
Coltfield. Mor 2E 49
Coltness. N Lan 3C 18
Col Uarach. W Isl 4J 63
Colvend. Dum 3B 6
Colvister. Shet 3J 67
Comers. Abers 3B 42
Comrie. Fife 5B 26
Comrie. Per 1G 25
Conaglen. High 2D 30
Conchra. Arg 5H 23
Conchra. High 1H 37
Condorrat. N Lan 1C 18
Conicavel. Mor 3C 48
Conisby. Arg 2D 14
Connel. Arg 5C 30
Connel Park. E Ayr 2D 10
Connista. High 1D 44
Conon Bridge. High 3G 47
Cononsyth. Ang 4C 34
Conordan. High 5E 45
Contin. High 3F 47
Contullich. High 1H 47
Cookney. Abers 4D 42
Copister. Shet 5H 67
Cordon. N Ayr 5D 16
Corgarff. Abers 3F 41
Corlae. Dum 4D 10
Cormiston. S Lan 5F 19
Cornaigbeg. Arg 4A 28
Cornaigmore. Arg 2D 28 (on Coll)
Cornaigmore. Arg 4A 28 (on Tiree)
Cornhill. Abers 3A 50
Cornhill. High 4C 54
Cornhill-on-Tweed. Nmbd 5F 21
Cornquoy. Orkn 4E 64
Corntown. High 3G 47
Corpach. High 1D 30
Corra. Dum 2B 6
Corran. High 2D 30 (nr. Arnisdale)
Corran. High 3H 37 (nr. Fort William)
Corribeg. High 1C 30
Corrie. N Ayr 4D 16
Corrie Common. Dum 5B 12
Corriecravie. N Ayr 1E 9
Corriekinloch. High 1A 54
Corriemoillie. High 2E 47
Corrievarkie Lodge. Per 1A 32
Corrievorrie. High 1A 40
Corrigall. Orkn 3C 64
Corrimony. High 5E 47
Corrour Shooting Lodge. High 2H 31
Corry. High 1F 37
Corrybrough. High 1B 40
Corrygills. N Ayr 5D 16
Corry of Ardnagrask. High 4G 47
Corsback. High 1F 59 (nr. Dunnet)
Corsback. High 3F 59 (nr. Halkirk)
Corse. Abers 4B 50
Corsehill. Abers 3E 51
Corse of Kinnoir. Abers 4A 50
Corsock. Dum 1A 6
Corstorphine. Edin 1H 19
Cortachy. Ang 3A 34
Corwar House. S Ayr 5H 9
Costa. Orkn 2C 64
Cotehill. Cumb 3H 7
Cothall. Abers 2D 42
Cott. Orkn 5J 65
Cottartown. High 5D 48
Cottown. Abers 4D 50
Coulags. High 4A 46
Coulin Lodge. High 3B 46
Coull. Abers 3A 42
Coulport. Arg 5B 24
Coulter. S Lan 5F 19
Coupar Angus. Per 4H 33
Coupland. Nmbd 5G 21
Cour. Arg 4B 16
Courance. Dum 4H 11
Courteachan. High 4F 37
Cousland. Midl 2A 20
Coustonn. Arg 1D 16
Cove. Arg 5B 24
Cove. High 4D 52
Cove. Bord 1E 21
Cove Bay. Aber 3E 43
Covesea. Mor 1E 49
Covington. S Lan 5E 19
Cowdenbeath. Fife 4C 26
Cowdenburn. Bord 3H 19
Cowdenend. Fife 4C 26
Cowfords. Mor 3G 49
Cowie. Abers 5D 42
Cowie. Stir 5H 25
Cowstrandburn. Fife 4B 26
Coylton. S Ayr 2B 10
Coylumbridge. High 2C 40
Coynach. Abers 3H 41
Coynachie. Abers 5H 49
Crackaig. High 2G 55
Cradhlastadh. W Isl 1B 62
Cragabus. Arg 4E 15
Craggan. High 1D 40
Cragganmore. Mor 5E 49
Cragganvallie. High 5G 47
Craggie. High 1F 55
Craggiemore. High 5A 48
Craibstone. Aber 2D 42
Craichie. Ang 4C 34
Craig. Arg 5D 30
Craig. Dum 1H 5
Craig. High 4B 46 (nr. Achnashellach)
Craig. High 2G 45 (nr. Lower Diabaig)
Craig. High 5H 45 (nr. Stromeferry)
Craiganour Lodge. Per 3B 32
Craigbrack. Arg 4A 24
Craigdallie. Per 1D 26
Craigdam. Abers 5D 50
Craigdarroch. E Ayr 3D 10
Craigdarroch. High 3F 47
Craigdhu. High 4F 47
Craigearn. Abers 2C 42
Craigellachie. Mor 4F 49
Craigend. Per 1C 26
Craigendoran. Arg 5C 24
Craigends. Ren 2H 17
Craigenputtock. Dum 5E 11
Craigens. E Ayr 2C 10
Craighall. Edin 1G 19
Craighead. Fife 2H 27
Craighouse. Arg 2G 15
Craigie. Abers 2E 43
Craigie. D'dee 5B 34
Craigie. Per 4G 33 (nr. Blairgowrie)
Craigie. Per 1C 26 (nr. Perth)
Craigie. S Ayr 5H 17
Craigielaw. E Lot 1B 20
Craiglemine. Dum 5F 5
Craiglockhart. Edin 1H 19
Craig Lodge. Arg 1D 16
Craigmalloch. E Ayr 4B 10
Craigmaud. Abers 3D 50
Craigmill. Stir 4H 25
Craigmillar. Edin 1H 19
Craigmore. Arg 2E 17
Craigmuie. Dum 5E 11
Craignair. Dum 2B 6
Craigneuk. N Lan 2C 18 (nr. Airdrie)
Craigneuk. N Lan 3C 18 (nr. Motherwell)
Craignure. Arg 5A 30
Craigo. Abers 2D 34
Craigrory. High 4H 47
Craigrothie. Fife 2E 27
Craigs. Dum 1F 7
Craigshill. W Lot 2F 19
Craigs, The. High 4B 54
Craigton. Aber 3D 42
Craigton. Abers 3C 42
Craigton. Ang 5C 34 (nr. Carnoustie)
Craigton. Ang 3A 34 (nr. Kirriemuir)
Craigton. High 4H 47
Craigtown. High 3B 58
Craigyloch. Ang 3H 33
Craik. Bord 3C 12
Crail. Fife 3H 27
Crailing. Bord 1F 13
Crailinghall. Bord 1F 13
Cramond. Edin 1G 19
Cramond Bridge. Edin 1G 19
Cranloch. Mor 3F 49
Crannich. Arg 4G 29
Crannoch. Mor 3H 49
Cranshaws. Bord 2D 20
Craobh Haven. Arg 3E 23
Craobhnaclag. High 4F 47
Crarae. Arg 4G 23
Crask. High 2A 58
Crask Inn. High 1C 54
Crask of Aigas. High 4F 47
Crathes. Abers 4C 42
Crathie. Abers 4F 41
Crathie. High 4G 39
Crawford. S Lan 1G 11
Crawforddyke. S Lan 3D 18
Crawfordjohn. S Lan 1F 11
Crawick. Dum 2E 11
Crawton. Abers 5D 42
Cray. Per 2G 33
Creagan. Arg 4C 30
Creag Aoil. High 1E 31
Creag Ghoraidh. W Isl 6H 61
Creaguaineach Lodge. High 2G 31
Creca. Dum 1F 7
Creebridge. Dum 2F 5
Creetown. Dum 3F 5
Creggans. Arg 3H 23
Creich. Arg 1A 22
Creich. Fife 1E 27
Crepkill. High 4D 44
Crianlarich. Stir 1C 24
Crichton. Midl 2A 20
Crieff. Per 1H 25
Crimond. Abers 3F 51
Crimonmogate. Abers 3F 51
Crinan. Arg 4E 23
Crocketford. Dum 1B 6
Croftamie. Stir 5D 24
Croftfoot. Glas 2A 18
Croftmill. Per 5D 32
Crofton. Cumb 3G 7
Crofts. Dum 1A 6
Crofts of Benachielt. High 5E 59
Crofts of Dipple. Mor 3G 49
Croggan. Arg 1E 23
Croich. High 4B 54
Croick. High 3B 58
Croig. Arg 3E 29
Cromarty. High 2A 48
Crombie. Fife 5B 26
Cromdale. High 1D 40
Cromor. W Isl 5J 63
Cromra. High 5G 39
Cronberry. E Ayr 1D 10
Crookdake. Cumb 4E 7
Crookedholm. E Ayr 5H 17
Crookham. Nmbd 5G 21
Crook of Devon. Per 3B 26
Crookston. Ren 2A 18
Cros. W Isl 1K 63
Crosbie. N Ayr 4F 17
Crosbost. W Isl 2E 62
Crosby. Cumb 5D 6
Crosby Villa. Cumb 5D 6
Crossaig. Arg 3B 16
Crossapol. Arg 4A 28
Crosscanonby. Cumb 5D 6
Crossford. Fife 5B 26
Crossford. S Lan 4D 18
Crossgate. Orkn 3D 64
Crossgatehall. E Lot 2A 20
Crossgates. Fife 5C 26
Crosshands. E Ayr 5H 17
Crosshill. E Ayr 1B 10
Crosshill. Fife 4C 26
Crosshill. S Ayr 3A 10
Crosshills. High 1H 47
Crosshouse. E Ayr 5G 17
Crossings. Cumb 1H 7
Crosskirk. High 2D 58
Crosslee. Ren 2H 17
Crossmichael. Dum 2A 6
Cross of Jackston. Abers 5C 50
Crossroads. Abers 3E 43 (nr. Aberdeen)
Crossroads. Abers 4C 42 (nr. Banchory)
Crossroads. E Ayr 5H 17
Crosston. Ang 3C 34
Crothair. W Isl 1C 62
Crovie. Abers 2D 50
Croy. High 4A 48
Croy. N Lan 1C 18
Crubenbeg. High 4H 39
Crubenmore Lodge. High 4H 39
Cruden Bay. Abers 5F 51
Crudie. Abers 3C 50
Crulabhig. W Isl 1C 62
Cuaich. High 5H 39
Cuaig. High 3G 45
Cuan. Arg 2E 23
Cuckron. Shet 1D 66
Cuidhir. W Isl 4B 60
Cuidhsiadar. W Isl 2K 63
Cuidhtinis. W Isl 6B 62
Culbo. High 2H 47
Culbokie. High 3H 47
Culburnie. High 4F 47
Culcabock. High 4H 47
Culcharry. High 3B 48
Culduie. High 4G 45
Culeave. High 4C 54
Culkein. High 5B 56
Culkein Drumbeg. High 5C 56
Cullen. Mor 2A 50
Cullicudden. High 2H 47
Cullipool. Arg 2E 23
Cullivoe. Shet 2J 67
Culloch. Per 2G 25
Culloden. High 4A 48
Cul na Caepaich. High 5F 37
Culnacnoc. High 2E 45
Culnacraig. High 3F 53
Culrain. High 4C 54
Culross. Fife 5A 26
Culroy. S Ayr 2A 10
Culswick. Shet 2B 66
Cults. Aber 3D 42
Cults. Abers 5A 50
Cults. Fife 3E 27
Cultybraggan Camp. Per 1G 25
Culzie Lodge. High 1G 47
Cumbernauld. N Lan 1C 18
Cumbernauld Village. N Lan 1C 18
Cumdivock. Cumb 4G 7
Cuminestown. Abers 3D 50
Cumledge Mill. Bord 3E 21
Cumlewick. Shet 4D 66
Cummersdale. Cumb 3G 7
Cummertrees. Dum 2E 7
Cummingstown. Mor 2E 49
Cumnock. E Ayr 2C 10
Cumwhinton. Cumb 3H 7
Cumwhitton. Cumb 3H 7
Cunninghamhead. N Ayr 4G 17
Cunning Park. S Ayr 2A 10
Cunningsburgh. Shet 4D 66
Cunnister. Shet 3J 67
Cupar. Fife 2E 27
Cupar Muir. Fife 2E 27
Currie. Edin 2G 19
Cuthill. E Lot 1A 20
Cutts. Shet 3D 66
Cuttyhill. Abers 3F 51

D

Dacre. Cumb 5H 7
Dail. Arg 5D 30
Dail Beag. W Isl 3G 63
Dail bho Dheas. W Isl 1J 63
Dailly. S Ayr 3H 9
Dail Mor. W Isl 3G 63
Dairsie. Fife 2F 27
Dalabrog. W Isl 2C 60
Dalavich. Arg 2G 23
Dalbeattie. Dum 2B 6
Dalblair. E Ayr 2D 10
Dalchalm. High 3G 55
Dalcharn. High 3H 57
Dalchork. High 2C 54
Dalchreichart. High 2D 38
Dalchruin. Per 2G 25
Dalcross. High 4A 48
Dalelia. High 2A 30
Dale of Walls. Shet 1A 66
Dalgarven. N Ayr 4F 17
Dalgety Bay. Fife 5C 26
Dalginross. Per 1G 25
Dalguise. Per 4E 33
Dalhalvaig. High 3B 58
Dalintart. Arg 1F 23
Dalkeith. Midl 2A 20
Dallas. Mor 3E 49
Dalleagles. E Ayr 2C 10
Dall House. Per 3A 32
Dalmally. Arg 1A 24
Dalmarnock. Glas 2B 18
Dalmellington. E Ayr 3B 10
Dalmeny. Edin 1G 19
Dalmigavie. High 2A 40
Dalmilling. S Ayr 2A 10
Dalmore. High 2H 47 (nr. Alness)
Dalmore. High 3E 55 (nr. Rogart)
Dalmuir. W Dun 1H 17
Dalmunach. Mor 4F 49
Dalnabreck. High 2A 30
Dalnacardoch Lodge. Per 1C 32
Dalnamein Lodge. Per 2C 32
Dalnaspidal Lodge. Per 1B 32
Dalnatrat. High 3C 30
Dalnavie. High 1H 47
Dalnawillan Lodge. High 4D 58
Dalness. High 3E 31
Dalnessie. High 2D 54
Dalqueich. Per 3B 26
Dalquhairn. S Ayr 4A 10
Dalreavoch. High 3E 55
Dalreoch. Per 2B 26
Dalry. Edin 1H 19
Dalry. N Ayr 4F 17
Dalrymple. E Ayr 2A 10
Dalserf. S Lan 3C 18
Dalsmirren. Arg 2B 8
Dalston. Cumb 3G 7
Dalswinton. Dum 5G 11
Dalton. Dum 1E 7
Dalton. S Lan 3B 18
Daltot. Arg 5E 23
Dalvey. High 5E 49
Dalwhinnie. High 5H 39
Damhead. Mor 3D 48
Danderhall. Midl 2A 20
Danestone. Aber 2E 43
Dargill. Per 2H 25
Darnford. Abers 4C 42
Darnick. Bord 5C 20
Darra. Abers 4C 50
Dartfield. Abers 3F 51
Darvel. E Ayr 5A 18
Dava. Mor 5D 48
Davidson's Mains. Edin 1H 19
Davidston. High 2A 48
Davington. Dum 3B 12
Daviot. Abers 1C 42
Daviot. High 5A 48
Deadwater. Nmbd 4F 13
Dean. Cumb 5D 6
Deanburnhaugh. Bord 2C 12
Deanich Lodge. High 5A 54
Deans. W Lot 2F 19
Deanscales. Cumb 5D 6
Deanston. Stir 3G 25
Dearham. Cumb 5D 6
Dechmont. W Lot 1F 19
Deebank. Abers 4B 42
Deerhill. Mor 3H 49
Deerness. Orkn 4E 64
Delfour. High 3B 40
Dellieture. High 5D 48
Delny. High 1A 48
Denbeath. Fife 4E 27
Denhead. Abers 5E 51 (nr. Ellon)
Denhead. Abers 3E 51 (nr. Strichen)
Denhead. Fife 2F 27
Denholm. Bord 2E 13
Denny. Falk 5H 25
Dennyloanhead. Falk 5H 25
Den of Lindores. Fife 2D 26
Denside. Abers 4D 42
Den, The. N Ayr 3G 17
Derculich. Per 3D 32
Derryguaig. Arg 5F 29
Dervaig. Arg 3F 29
Detchant. Nmbd 5H 21
Deuchar. Ang 2B 34
Devonside. Clac 4A 26
Dewartown. Midl 2A 20
Digg. High 2D 44
Dillarburn. S Lan 4D 18
Dingleton. Bord 5C 20
Dingwall. High 3G 47
Dinnet. Abers 4H 41
Dippen. Arg 5A 16
Dippin. N Ayr 1F 9
Dipple. S Ayr 3H 9
Dirleton. E Lot 5G 27
Dishes. Orkn 5J 65
Divach. High 1F 39
Dixonfield. High 2E 59
Dochgarroch. High 4H 47
Doddington. Nmbd 5G 21
Doll. High 3F 55
Dollar. Clac 4A 26
Dolphingstone. E Lot 1A 20
Dolphinton. S Lan 4G 19
Doonfoot. S Ayr 2A 10
Doonholm. S Ayr 2A 10
Dorback Lodge. High 2D 40
Dores. High 5G 47
Dornie. High 1H 37
Dornoch. High 5E 55
Dornock. Dum 2F 7
Dorrery. High 3D 58
Dougarie. N Ayr 5B 16
Douglas. S Lan 5D 18
Douglastown. Ang 4B 34
Douglas Water. S Lan 5D 18
Dounby. Orkn 2B 64
Doune. High 3B 40 (nr. Kingussie)
Doune. High 3B 54 (nr. Lairg)
Doune. Stir 3G 25
Dounie. High 4C 54 (nr. Bonar Bridge)
Dounie. High 5D 54 (nr. Tain)
Dounreay. High 2C 58
Doura. N Ayr 4G 17
Dovenby. Cumb 5D 6
Dowally. Per 4F 33
Downfield. D'dee 5A 34
Downham. Nmbd 5F 21
Downies. Abers 4E 43
Draffan. S Lan 4C 18
Drakemyre. N Ayr 3F 17
Dreghorn. N Ayr 5G 17
Drem. E Lot 1C 20
Dreumasdal. W Isl 1C 60
Drimnin. High 3G 29
Drinisiadar. W Isl 5C 62
Droman. High 3C 56
Dron. Per 2C 26
Drongan. E Ayr 2B 10
Dronley. Ang 5A 34
Druim. High 3C 48
Druimarbin. High 1D 30
Druim Fhearna. High 2F 37
Druimindarroch. High 5F 37
Druim Saighdinis. W Isl 4J 61
Drum. Per 3B 26
Drumbeg. High 5C 56
Drumblade. Abers 4A 50
Drumbuie. Dum 5C 10
Drumbuie. High 5G 45
Drumburgh. Cumb 3F 7
Drumburn. Dum 2C 6
Drumchapel. Glas 1A 18
Drumchardine. High 4G 47
Drumchork. High 5D 52
Drumclog. S Lan 5B 18
Drumeldrie. Fife 3F 27
Drumelzier. Bord 5G 19
Drumfearn. High 2F 37
Drumgask. High 4H 39
Drumgelloch. N Lan 2C 18
Drumgley. Ang 3B 34

Drumguish—Gorgie

Drumguish. *High* 4A 40
Drumin. *Mor* 5E 49
Drumindorsair. *High* 4F 47
Drumlamford House. *S Ayr* 1D 4
Drumlasie. *Abers* 3B 42
Drumlemble. *Arg* 2B 8
Drumlithie. *Abers* 5C 42
Drummoddie. *Dum* 4E 5
Drummond. *High* 2H 47
Drummore. *Dum* 5C 4
Drummuir. *Mor* 4G 49
Drumnadrochit. *High* 5G 47
Drumnagorrach. *Mor* 3A 50
Drumoak. *Abers* 4C 42
Drumrunie. *High* 3G 53
Drumry. *W Dun* 1A 18
Drums. *Abers* 1E 43
Drumsleet. *Dum* 1C 6
Drumsmittal. *High* 4H 47
Drums of Park. *Abers* 3A 50
Drumsturdy. *Ang* 5B 34
Drumtochty Castle. *Abers* 5B 42
Drumuie. *High* 4D 44
Drumuillie. *High* 1C 40
Drumvaich. *Stir* 3F 25
Drumwhindle. *Abers* 5E 51
Drunkendub. *Ang* 4D 34
Drybridge. *Mor* 2H 49
Drybridge. *N Ayr* 5G 17
Dryburgh. *Bord* 5C 20
Drymen. *Stir* 5D 24
Drymuir. *Abers* 4E 51
Drynachan Lodge. *High* 5B 48
Drynie Park. *High* 3G 47
Drynoch. *High* 5D 44
Dubford. *Abers* 2C 50
Dubiton. *Abers* 3B 50
Dubton. *Ang* 3C 34
Duchally. *High* 2A 54
Duddingston. *Edin* 1H 19
Duddo. *Nmbd* 4G 21
Dufftown. *Mor* 4G 49
Duffus. *Mor* 2E 49
Duirinish. *High* 5G 45
Duisdalemore. *High* 2F 37
Duisdeil Mòr. *High* 2F 37
Duisky. *High* 1D 30
Dull. *Per* 4D 32
Dullatur. *N Lan* 1C 18
Dulnain Bridge. *High* 1C 40
Dumbarton. *W Dun* 1H 17
Dumfin. *Arg* 5C 24
Dumfries. *Dum* 1C 6 & 71
Dumgoyne. *Stir* 5E 25
Dun. *Ang* 2D 34
Dunagoil. *Arg* 3D 16
Dunalastair. *Per* 3C 32
Dunan. *High* 1E 37
Dunbar. *E Lot* 1D 20
Dunbeath. *High* 5E 59
Dunbeg. *Arg* 5B 30
Dunblane. *Stir* 3G 25
Dunbog. *Fife* 2D 26
Duncanston. *Abers* 1A 42
Duncanston. *High* 3G 47
Dun Charlabhaigh. *W Isl* 3F 63
Duncow. *Dum* 5G 11
Duncrievie. *Per* 3C 26
Dundee. *D'dee* 5B 34 & 72
Dundee Airport. *D'dee* 1E 27
Dundonald. *S Ayr* 5G 17
Dundonnell. *High* 5F 53
Dundraw. *Cumb* 4F 7
Dundreggan. *High* 2E 39
Dundrennan. *Dum* 4A 6
Dunecht. *Abers* 3C 42
Dunfermline. *Fife* 5B 26 & 73
Dunino. *Fife* 2G 27
Dunipace. *Falk* 5H 25
Dunira. *Per* 1G 25
Dunkeld. *Per* 4F 33
Dunlappie. *Ang* 2C 34
Dunlichity Lodge. *High* 5H 47
Dunlop. *E Ayr* 4H 17
Dunmaglass Lodge. *High* 1G 39
Dunmore. *Arg* 2A 16
Dunmore. *Falk* 5H 25
Dunmore. *High* 4G 47
Dunnet. *High* 1F 59
Dunnichen. *Ang* 4C 34
Dunning. *Per* 2B 26
Dunoon. *Arg* 1E 17
Dunphail. *Mor* 4D 48
Dunragit. *Dum* 3C 4
Dunrostan. *Arg* 5E 23
Duns. *Bord* 3E 21
Dunscore. *Dum* 5F 11
Dunshalt. *Fife* 2D 26
Dunshillock. *Abers* 4E 51
Dunsyre. *S Lan* 4F 19
Duntocher. *W Dun* 1H 17
Duntulm. *High* 1D 44
Dunure. *S Ayr* 2H 9
Dunvegan. *High* 4B 44
Durdar. *Cumb* 3H 7
Durisdeer. *Dum* 3F 11
Durisdeermill. *Dum* 3F 11
Durnamuck. *High* 4F 53
Durness. *High* 2F 57
Durno. *Abers* 1C 42
Duror. *High* 3C 30
Durran. *Arg* 3G 23
Durran. *High* 2E 59
Dury. *Shet* 1D 66
Duthil. *High* 1C 40
Dyce. *Aber* 2D 42
Dyke. *Mor* 3C 48
Dykehead. *Ang* 2A 34
Dykehead. *N Lan* 2D 18
Dykehead. *Stir* 4E 25
Dykend. *Ang* 3H 33
Dykesfield. *Cumb* 3G 7
Dysart. *Fife* 4E 27

E

Eadar Dha Fhadhail. *W Isl* 1B 62
Eaglesfield. *Cumb* 5D 6
Eaglesfield. *Dum* 1F 7
Eaglesham. *E Ren* 3A 18
Eallabus. *Arg* 2E 15
Earlais. *High* 2C 44
Earle. *Nmbd* 5G 21
Earlish. *High* 2C 44
Earlsferry. *Fife* 3F 27
Earlsford. *Abers* 5D 50
Earlston. *E Ayr* 5H 17
Earlston. *Bord* 5C 20
Earlstoun. *Dum* 5D 10
Earlyvale. *Bord* 3H 19
Earsairidh. *W Isl* 5C 60
Easdale. *Arg* 2E 23
Easington. *Nmbd* 5H 21
Eassie. *Ang* 4A 34
Eassie and Nevay. *Ang* 4A 34
East Barns. *E Lot* 1E 21
East Bennan. *N Ayr* 1E 9
East Burrafirth. *Shet* 1C 66
East Calder. *W Lot* 2F 19
East Clyne. *High* 3F 55
East Clyth. *High* 5F 59
East Croachy. *High* 1H 39
Easter Ardross. *High* 1H 47
Easter Balgedie. *Per* 3C 26
Easter Balmoral. *Abers* 4F 41
Easter Brae. *High* 2H 47
Easter Buckieburn. *Stir* 5G 25
Easter Bush. *Midl* 2H 19
Easter Fearn. *High* 5D 54
Easter Galcantray. *High* 4B 48
Easterhouse. *Glas* 2B 18
Easter Howgate. *Midl* 2H 19
Easter Kinkell. *High* 3G 47
Easter Lednathie. *Ang* 2A 34
Easter Ogil. *Ang* 2B 34
Easter Ord. *Abers* 3D 42
Easter Quarff. *Shet* 3D 66
Easter Rhynd. *Per* 2C 26
Easter Skeld. *Shet* 2C 66
Easter Suddie. *High* 3H 47
Easter Tulloch. *Abers* 1E 35
Eastfield. *N Lan*
(nr. Caldercruix)
Eastfield. *N Lan* 2D 18
(nr. Harthill)
Eastfield. *S Lan* 2B 18
East Fortune. *E Lot* 1C 20
East Haven. *Ang* 5C 34
East Helmsdale. *High* 2H 55
East Horton. *Nmbd* 6H 21
Easthouses. *Midl* 2A 20
East Kilbride. *S Lan* 3B 18
East Kyloe. *Nmbd* 5H 21
East Langwell. *High* 3E 55
East Learmouth. *Nmbd* 5F 21
East Linton. *E Lot* 1C 20
East Mains. *Abers* 4B 42
East Mey. *High* 1G 59
Easton. *Cumb* 3F 7
(nr. Burgh by Sands)
Easton. *Cumb* 1H 7
(nr. Longtown)
East Ord. *Nmbd* 3G 21
East Pitcorthie. *Fife* 3G 27
East Rhidorroch Lodge. *High* 4H 53
Eastriggs. *Dum* 3E 7
East Saltoun. *E Lot* 2B 20
Eastshore. *Shet* 5C 66
East Wemyss. *Fife* 4E 27
East Whitburn. *W Lot* 2E 19
Eastwick. *Shet* 5G 67
East Woodburn. *Nmbd* 5H 13
Ecclefechan. *Dum* 1E 7
Eccles. *Bord* 4E 21
Ecclesmachan. *W Lot* 1F 19
Echt. *Abers* 3C 42
Eckford. *Bord* 1G 13
Eday Airport. *Orkn* 1E 64
Edderside. *Cumb* 4E 7
Edderton. *High* 5E 55
Eddleston. *Bord* 4H 19
Eddlewood. *S Lan* 3C 18
Edendonich. *Arg* 1A 24
Edentaggart. *Arg* 4C 24
Edgehead. *Midl* 2A 20
Edinbane. *High* 3C 44
Edinburgh. *Edin* 1H 19 & 74-75
Edinburgh Airport. *Edin* 1G 19
Edmonstone. *Orkn* 2E 64
Ednam. *Bord* 5E 21
Edrom. *Bord* 3F 21
Edzell. *Ang* 2D 34
Effirth. *Shet* 1C 66
Efstigarth. *Shet* 3H 67
Eight Mile Burn. *Midl* 3G 19
Eignaig. *High* 4A 30
Eilanreach. *High* 2H 37
Eildon. *Bord* 5C 20
Eileanach Lodge. *High* 2G 47
Eilean Fhlodaigh. *W Isl* 5J 61
Eilean Iarmain. *High* 2G 37
Einacleit. *W Isl* 2C 62
Eisgein. *W Isl* 3E 62
Elcho. *Per* 1C 26
Elderslie. *Ren* 2H 17
Elgin. *Mor* 2F 49
Elgol. *High* 2E 37
Elie. *Fife* 3F 27
Elishaw. *Nmbd* 4H 13
Elizafield. *Dum* 1D 6
Ellan. *High* 1B 40
Ellary. *Arg* 1A 16
Ellemford. *Bord* 2E 21
Ellenabeich. *Arg* 2E 23
Ellenborough. *Cumb* 5D 6
Elleric. *Arg* 4D 30
Elliot. *Ang* 5D 34
Ellishadder. *High* 2E 45
Ellon. *Abers* 5E 51
Ellonby. *Cumb* 5H 7
Elphin. *High* 2H 53
Elphinstone. *E Lot* 1A 20
Elrick. *Abers* 3D 42
Elrick. *Mor* 1H 41
Elrig. *Dum* 4E 5
Elsrickle. *S Lan* 4F 19
Elvanfoot. *S Lan* 2G 11
Elvingston. *E Lot* 1B 20
Elwick. *Nmbd* 5H 21
Embleton. *Cumb* 5E 7
Embo. *High* 4F 55
Embo Street. *High* 4F 55
Enoch. *Dum* 3F 11
Enochdhu. *Per* 2F 33
Ensay. *Arg* 4E 29
Enterkinfoot. *Dum* 3F 11
Eolaigearraidh. *W Isl* 4C 60
Eorabus. *Arg* 1A 22
Eoropaidh. *W Isl* 1K 63
Erbusaig. *High* 1G 37
Erchless Castle. *High* 4F 47
Eredine. *Arg* 3G 23
Eriboll. *High* 3F 57
Ericstane. *Dum* 2H 11
Erines. *Arg* 1B 16
Errogie. *High* 1G 39
Errol. *Per* 1D 26
Errol Station. *Per* 1D 26
Erskine. *Ren* 1H 17
Erskine Bridge. *Ren* 1H 17
Ervie. *Dum* 2B 4
Eskadale. *High* 5F 47
Eskbank. *Midl* 2A 20
Eskdalemuir. *Dum* 4B 12
Esknish. *Arg* 2E 15
Essich. *High* 5H 47
Eswick. *Shet* 1D 66
Etal. *Nmbd* 5G 21
Ethie Haven. *Ang* 4D 34
Etteridge. *High* 4H 39
Ettrick. *Bord* 2B 12
Ettrickbridge. *Bord* 1C 12
Evanton. *High* 2H 47
Evelix. *High* 4E 55
Everbay. *Orkn* 5J 65
Evertown. *Dum* 1G 7
Ewes. *Dum* 4C 12
Exnaboe. *Shet* 5C 66
Eyemouth. *Bord* 2G 21
Eynort. *High* 1C 36
Eyre. *High* 3D 44
(on Isle of Skye)
Eyre. *High* 5E 45
(on Raasay)

F

Faichem. *High* 3D 38
Faifley. *W Dun* 1A 18
Fail. *S Ayr* 1B 10
Failford. *S Ayr* 1B 10
Fair Hill. *Cumb* 5H 7
Fairhill. *S Lan* 3C 18
Fair Isle Airport. *Shet* 1J 65
Fairlie. *N Ayr* 3F 17
Fairmilehead. *Edin* 2H 19
Fala. *Midl* 2B 20
Fala Dam. *Midl* 2B 20
Falkirk. *Falk* 1D 18 & 81
Falkland. *Fife* 3D 26
Fallin. *Stir* 4H 25
Falstone. *Nmbd* 5G 13
Fanagmore. *High* 4C 56
Fanellan. *High* 4F 47
Fankerton. *Falk* 5G 25
Fanmore. *Arg* 4F 29
Fannich Lodge. *High* 2D 46
Fans. *Bord* 4D 20
Farley. *High* 4F 47
Farmtown. *Mor* 3A 50
Farnell. *Ang* 3D 34
Farr. *High* 2A 58
(nr. Bettyhill)
Farr. *High* 5H 47
(nr. Inverness)
Farr. *High* 3B 40
(nr. Kingussie)
Farraline. *High* 1G 39
Fasag. *High* 3H 45
Fascadale. *High* 1G 29
Fasnacloich. *Arg* 4D 30
Fassfern. *High* 1D 30
Fauldhouse. *W Lot* 2E 19
Feagour. *High* 4G 39
Fearann Dhomhnaill. *High* 3F 37
Fearn. *High* 1B 48
Fearnan. *Per* 4C 32
Fearnbeg. *High* 3G 45
Fearnmore. *High* 2G 45
Felkington. *Nmbd* 4G 21
Fell Side. *Cumb* 5G 7
Fenham. *Nmbd* 4H 21
Fenton. *Cumb* 3H 7
Fenton. *Nmbd* 5G 21
Fenton Barns. *E Lot* 5G 27
Fenwick. *E Ayr* 4H 17
Fenwick. *Nmbd* 4H 21
Feochaig. *Arg* 2C 8
Feolin Ferry. *Arg* 2F 15
Feorlan. *Arg* 3B 8
Ferindonald. *High* 3F 37
Feriniquarrie. *High* 3A 44
Fern. *Ang* 2B 34
Ferness. *High* 4C 48
Fernieflatt. *Abers* 1F 35
Ferniegair. *S Lan* 3C 18
Fernilea. *High* 5C 44
Ferryden. *Ang* 3E 35
Ferryhill. *Aber* 3E 43
Ferryton. *High* 2H 47
Fersit. *High* 1G 31
Feshiebridge. *High* 3B 40
Fetterangus. *Abers* 3E 51
Fettercairn. *Abers* 1D 34
Fiag Lodge. *High* 1B 54
Fidden. *Arg* 1A 22
Fieldhead. *Cumb* 5H 7
Fife Keith. *Mor* 3H 49
Finavon. *Ang* 3B 34
Fincharn. *Arg* 3G 23
Findhorn. *Mor* 2D 48
Findhorn Bridge. *High* 1B 40
Findochty. *Mor* 2H 49
Findo Gask. *Per* 1B 26
Findon. *Abers* 4E 43
Findon Mains. *High* 2H 47
Fingland. *Cumb* 3F 7
Fingland. *Dum* 2E 11
Finiskaig. *High* 4H 37
Finnart. *Per* 3A 32
Finnygaud. *Abers* 3B 50
Finstown. *Orkn* 3C 64
Fintry. *Abers* 3C 50
Fintry. *D'dee* 5B 34
Fintry. *Stir* 5F 25
Finzean. *Abers* 4B 42
Fionnphort. *Arg* 1A 22
Fionnsabhagh. *W Isl* 6B 62
First Coast. *High* 4E 53
Firth. *Shet* 5H 67
Fishcross. *Clac* 4A 26
Fisherford. *Abers* 5B 50
Fisherrow. *E Lot* 1A 20
Fisherton. *High* 3A 48
Fisherton. *S Ayr* 2H 9
Fishnish. *Arg* 4H 29
Fishwick. *Bord* 3G 21
Fiskavaig. *High* 5C 44
Fitch. *Shet* 2C 66
Fiunary. *High* 4H 29
Fladda. *Shet* 4G 67
Fladdabister. *Shet* 3D 66
Flashader. *High* 3C 44
Flatt, The. *Cumb* 5E 13
Fleck. *Shet* 5C 66
Fleisirin. *W Isl* 4K 63
Flemington. *S Lan* 2B 18
(nr. Glasgow)
Flemington. *S Lan* 4C 18
(nr. Strathaven)
Fleoideabhagh. *W Isl* 6B 62
Fletchertown. *Cumb* 4F 7
Fleuchary. *High* 4E 55
Flimby. *Cumb* 5D 6
Flodden. *Nmbd* 5G 21
Flodigarry. *High* 1D 44
Flushing. *Abers* 4F 51
Fochabers. *Mor* 3G 49
Fodderty. *High* 3G 47
Foffarty. *Ang* 4B 34
Fogo. *Bord* 4E 21
Fogorig. *Bord* 4E 21
Foindle. *High* 4C 56
Folda. *Ang* 2G 33
Folla Rule. *Abers* 5C 50
Foodieash. *Fife* 2E 27
Footdee. *Aber* 3E 43
Forbestown. *Abers* 2G 41
Ford. *Arg* 3F 23
Ford. *Nmbd* 5G 21
Fordell. *Fife* 5C 26
Fordie. *Per* 1G 25
Fordoun. *Abers* 1E 35
Fordyce. *Abers* 2A 50
Foresterseat. *Mor* 3E 49
Forest Lodge. *Per* 1E 33
Forest Mill. *Clac* 4A 26
Forfar. *Ang* 3B 34
Forgandenny. *Per* 2B 26
Forgewood. *N Lan* 3C 18
Forgie. *Mor* 3G 49
Forgue. *Abers* 4B 50
Forneth. *Per* 4F 33
Forres. *Mor* 3D 48
Forrestfield. *N Lan* 2D 18
Forrest Lodge. *Dum* 5C 10
Forse. *High* 5F 59
Forsinard. *High* 4B 58
Forss. *High* 2D 58
Fort Augustus. *High* 3E 39
Forteviot. *Per* 2B 26
Fort George. *High* 3A 48
Forth. *S Lan* 3E 19
Forth Road Bridge. *Fife* 1G 19
Fortingall. *Per* 4C 32
Fort Matilda. *Inv* 1F 17
Fortrie. *Abers* 4B 50
Fortrose. *High* 3A 48
Fort William. *High* 1E 31 & 81
Foss. *Per* 3C 32
Fothergill. *Cumb* 5D 6
Foubister. *Orkn* 4E 64
Foula Airport. *Shet* 5A 66
Foulbridge. *Cumb* 4H 7
Foulden. *Bord* 3G 21
Fountainhall. *Bord* 4B 20
Foveran. *Abers* 1E 43
Fowlershill. *Abers* 2E 43
Fowlis. *Ang* 5A 34
Fowlis Wester. *Per* 1A 26
Foyers. *High* 1F 39
Foynesfield. *High* 3B 48
Fraserburgh. *Abers* 2E 51
Freester. *Shet* 1D 66
Frenich. *Stir* 3D 24
Fresgoe. *High* 2C 58
Freswick. *High* 2G 59
Freuchie. *Fife* 3D 26
Friockheim. *Ang* 4C 34
Frobost. *W Isl* 2C 60
Frotoft. *Orkn* 2D 64
Fullwood. *E Ayr* 3H 17
Funzie. *Shet* 3K 67
Furnace. *Arg* 3H 23
Fyvie. *Abers* 5C 50

G

Gabhsann bho Dheas. *W Isl* 2J 63
Gabhsann bho Thuath. *W Isl* 2J 63
Gabroc Hill. *E Ayr* 3H 17
Gadgirth. *S Ayr* 1B 10
Gaick Lodge. *High* 5A 40
Gairletter. *Arg* 5A 24
Gairloch. *Abers* 3C 42
Gairloch. *High* 1H 45
Gairlochy. *High* 5C 38
Gairney Bank. *Per* 4C 26
Gairnshiel Lodge. *Abers* 3F 41
Gaitsgill. *Cumb* 4G 7
Galashiels. *Bord* 5B 20
Gallatown. *Fife* 4D 26
Gallin. *Per* 4A 32
Gallowfauld. *Ang* 4B 34
Gallowhill. *E Dun* 1B 18
Gallowhill. *Per* 5G 33
Gallowhill. *Ren* 2H 17
Gallowhills. *Abers* 3F 51
Galltair. *High* 1H 37
Galmisdale. *High* 5D 36
Galston. *E Ayr* 5H 17
Galtrigill. *High* 3A 44
Gamelsby. *Cumb* 3F 7
Ganavan. *Arg* 5B 30
Gannochy. *Ang* 1C 34
Gannochy. *Per* 1C 26
Gansclet. *High* 4G 59
Garafad. *High* 2D 44
Gardenstown. *Abers* 2D 50
Garderhouse. *Shet* 2C 66
Gardie. *Shet* 1A 66
(on Papa Stour)
Gardie. *Shet* 1K 67
(on Unst)
Gardie Ho. *Shet* 2D 66
Garelochhead. *Arg* 4B 24
Gargunnock. *Stir* 4G 25
Garleffin. *S Ayr* 5F 9
Garlieston. *Dum* 5F 5
Garlogie. *Abers* 3C 42
Garmond. *Abers* 3D 50
Garmony. *Arg* 4H 29
Garmouth. *Mor* 2G 49
Garnkirk. *N Lan* 2B 18
Garrabost. *W Isl* 4K 63
Garrallan. *E Ayr* 2C 10
Garrogie Lodge. *High* 2G 39
Garros. *High* 2D 44
Garrow. *Per* 4D 32
Gartcosh. *N Lan* 2B 18
Garth. *Shet* 1B 66
(nr. Sandness)
Garth. *Shet* 1D 66
(nr. Skellister)
Garthamlock. *Glas* 2B 18
Gartly. *Abers* 5A 50
Gartmore. *Stir* 4E 25
Gartness. *N Lan* 2C 18
Gartness. *Stir* 5E 25
Gartocharn. *W Dun* 5D 24
Gartsherrie. *N Lan* 2C 18
Gartymore. *High* 2H 55
Garvald. *E Lot* 1C 20
Garvamore. *High* 4G 39
Garvard. *Arg* 4A 22
Garvault. *High* 5A 58
Garve. *High* 2E 47
Garvie. *Arg* 4H 23
Garvock. *Abers* 1E 35
Garvock. *Inv* 1F 17
Gaskan. *High* 1B 30
Gatehead. *E Ayr* 5G 17
Gatehouse. *Nmbd* 5G 13
Gatehouse of Fleet. *Dum* 3H 5
Gatelawbridge. *Dum* 4G 11
Gateside. *Ang* 4B 34
(nr. Forfar)
Gateside. *Ang* 4A 34
(nr. Kirriemuir)
Gateside. *Fife* 3C 26
Gateside. *N Ayr* 3G 17
Gattonside. *Bord* 5C 20
Gauldry. *Fife* 1E 27
Gavinton. *Bord* 3E 21
Gayfield. *Orkn* 2G 65
Geanies. *High* 1B 48
Gearraidh Bhailteas. *W Isl* 2C 60
Gearraidh Bhaird. *W Isl* 3E 62
Gearraidh na Monadh. *W Isl* 3C 60
Gearraidh na h-Aibhne. *W Isl* 1D 62
Geary. *High* 2B 44
Geddes. *High* 3B 48
Gedintailor. *High* 5E 45
Geilston. *Arg* 1G 17
Geirinis. *W Isl* 6H 61
Geise. *High* 2E 59
Geisiadar. *W Isl* 1C 62
Gelder Shiel. *Abers* 5F 41
Gellyburn. *Per* 5F 33
Gelston. *Dum* 3A 6
Geocrab. *W Isl* 5C 62
Georgetown. *Ren* 2H 17
Georth. *Orkn* 2C 64
Gerston. *High* 3E 59
Giffnock. *E Ren* 3A 18
Gifford. *E Lot* 2C 20
Giffordtown. *Fife* 2D 26
Gilchriston. *E Lot* 2B 20
Gilcrux. *Cumb* 5E 7
Gillen. *High* 3B 44
Gillock. *High* 3F 59
Gills. *High* 1G 59
Gilmanscleuch. *Bord* 1C 12
Gilmerton. *Edin* 2H 19
Gilmerton. *Per* 1H 25
Gilston. *Midl* 3B 20
Giosla. *W Isl* 2C 62
Girdle Toll. *N Ayr* 4G 17
Girlsta. *Shet* 1D 66
Girthon. *Dum* 3H 5
Girvan. *S Ayr* 4G 9
Gladsmuir. *E Lot* 1B 20
Glaichbea. *High* 5G 47
Glame. *High* 4E 45
Glamis. *Ang* 4A 34
Glamisdale. *High* 5D 36
Glas Aird. *Arg* 4A 22
Glas-allt Shiel. *Abers* 5F 41
Glaschoil. *Mor* 5D 48
Glasgow. *Glas* 2A 18 & 78-79
Glasgow Airport. *Ren* 2H 17
Glasgow Prestwick Airport. *S Ayr* 1A 10
Glashvin. *High* 2D 44
Glas na Cardaich. *High* 4F 37
Glasnacardoch. *High* 4F 37
Glasnakille. *High* 2E 37
Glassburn. *High* 5E 47
Glasserton. *Dum* 5F 5
Glassford. *S Lan* 4C 18
Glassgreen. *Mor* 2F 49
Glasson. *Cumb* 2F 7
Glasterlaw. *Ang* 3C 34
Gleann Dail bho Dheas. *W Isl* 3C 60
Gleann Tholastaidh. *W Isl* 3K 63
Gleann Uige. *High* 1H 29
Glecknabae. *Arg* 2D 16
Glen. *Dum* 3G 5
Glenancross. *High* 4F 37
Glenbarr. *Arg* 5H 15
Glenbeg. *High* 2G 29
Glen Bernisdale. *High* 4D 44
Glenbervie. *Abers* 5C 42
Glenboig. *N Lan* 2C 18
Glenborrodale. *High* 2H 29
Glenbranter. *Arg* 4A 24
Glenbreck. *Bord* 1H 11
Glenbrein Lodge. *High* 2F 39
Glenbrittle. *High* 1D 36
Glenbuchat Lodge. *Abers* 2G 41
Glenbuck. *E Ayr* 1E 11
Glenburn. *Ren* 2H 17
Glencalvie Lodge. *High* 5B 54
Glencaple. *Dum* 2C 6
Glencarron Lodge. *High* 3B 46
Glencarse. *Per* 1C 26
Glencassley Castle. *High* 3B 54
Glencat. *Abers* 4A 42
Glencoe. *High* 3E 31
Glen Cottage. *High* 5F 37
Glencraig. *Fife* 4C 26
Glendale. *High* 4A 44
Glendevon. *Per* 3A 26
Glendoebeg. *High* 3F 39
Glendoick. *Per* 1D 26
Glendoune. *S Ayr* 4G 9
Glenduckie. *Fife* 2D 26
Gleneagles. *Per* 3A 26
Glenegedale. *Arg* 3E 15
Glenegedale Lots. *Arg* 3E 15
Glenelg. *High* 2H 37
Glenernie. *Mor* 4D 48
Glenesslin. *Dum* 5F 11
Glenfarg. *Per* 2C 26
Glenfarquhar Lodge. *Abers* 5C 42
Glenferness Mains. *High* 4C 48
Glenfeshie Lodge. *High* 4B 40
Glenfiddich Lodge. *Mor* 5G 49
Glenfinnan. *High* 5A 38
Glenfintaig Lodge. *High* 5D 38
Glenfoot. *Per* 2C 26
Glenfyne Lodge. *Arg* 2B 24
Glengap. *Dum* 3H 5
Glengarnock. *N Ayr* 3G 17
Glengolly. *High* 2E 59
Glengorm Castle. *Arg* 3F 29
Glengrasco. *High* 4D 44
Glenhead Farm. *Ang* 2H 33
Glenholm. *Bord* 5G 19
Glen House. *Bord* 5H 19
Glenhurich. *High* 2B 30
Glenkerry. *Bord* 2B 12
Glenkiln. *Dum* 1B 6
Glenkindie. *Abers* 2H 41
Glenkinglass Lodge. *Arg* 5E 31
Glenkirk. *Bord* 1E 11
Glenlean. *Arg* 5H 23
Glenlee. *Dum* 5D 10
Glenleraig. *High* 5C 56
Glenlichorn. *Per* 2G 25
Glenlivet. *Mor* 1E 41
Glenlochar. *Dum* 2A 6
Glenlochsie Lodge. *Per* 1F 33
Glenluce. *Dum* 3C 4
Glenmarskie. *High* 3E 47
Glenmassan. *Arg* 5A 24
Glenmavis. *N Lan* 2C 18
Glenmazeran Lodge. *High* 1A 40
Glenmidge. *Dum* 5F 11
Glenmore. *High* 2G 29
(nr. Glenborrodale)
Glenmore. *High* 3C 40
(nr. Kingussie)
Glenmore. *High* 4D 44
(on Isle of Skye)
Glenmoy. *Ang* 2B 34
Glennoe. *Arg* 5D 30
Glen of Coachford. *Abers* 4H 49
Glenogil. *Ang* 2B 34
Glenprosen Village. *Ang* 2A 34
Glenree. *N Ayr* 1E 9
Glenrosa. *N Ayr* 5D 16
Glenrothes. *Fife* 3D 26
Glensanda. *High* 4B 30
Glensaugh. *Abers* 1D 34
Glenshero Lodge. *High* 4G 39
Glensluain. *Arg* 4H 23
Glenstockadale. *Dum* 2B 4
Glenstriven. *Arg* 1D 16
Glen Tanar House. *Abers* 4H 41
Glenton. *Abers* 1B 42
Glentress. *Bord* 5H 19
Glentromie Lodge. *High* 4A 40
Glentrool Lodge. *Dum* 5B 10
Glentrool Village. *Dum* 1E 5
Glentruim House. *High* 4H 39
Glenuig. *High* 1H 29
Glen Village. *Falk* 1D 18
Glenwhilly. *Dum* 1C 4
Glenzierfoot. *Dum* 1G 7
Glespin. *S Lan* 1F 11
Gletness. *Shet* 1D 66
Glib Cheois. *W Isl* 2E 62
Gloup. *Shet* 2J 67
Glutt Lodge. *High* 5C 58
Gobernuisgach Lodge. *High* 4F 57
Gobernuisgeach. *High* 5C 58
Gobhaig. *W Isl* 4B 62
Gogar. *Edin* 1G 19
Gollanfield. *High* 3B 48
Golspie. *High* 4F 55
Gometra House. *Arg* 4E 29
Gonfirth. *Shet* 6G 67
Gord. *Shet* 4D 66
Gordon. *Bord* 4D 20
Gordonbush. *High* 3F 55
Gordonstown. *Abers* 3A 50
(nr. Cornhill)
Gordonstown. *Abers* 5C 50
(nr. Fyvie)
Gorebridge. *Midl* 2A 20
Gorgie. *Edin* 1H 19

Gorseness—Kintessack

Gorseness. Orkn 3D 64
Gorstan. High 2E 47
Gortantaoid. Arg 1E 15
Gorteneorn. High 2H 29
Gortenfern. High 2H 29
Gossabrough. Shet 4J 67
Goswick. Nmbd 4H 21
Gott. Arg 4B 28
Gott. Shet 2D 66
Gourdon. Abers 1F 35
Gourock. Inv 1F 17
Govan. Glas 2A 18
Govanhill. Glas 2A 18
Gowanhill. Abers 2F 51
Gowkhall. Fife 5B 26
Grabhair. W Isl 3E 62
Gramasdail. W Isl 5J 61
Grandtully. Per 3E 33
Grange. E Ayr 5H 17
Grange. Per 1D 26
Grange Crossroads. Mor 3H 49
Grangemouth. Falk 5A 26
Grange of Lindores. Fife 2D 26
Grangepans. Falk 5B 26
Granish. High 2B 40
Grantlodge. Abers 2C 42
Granton. Edin 1H 19
Grantown-on-Spey. High 1D 40
Grantshouse. Bord 2F 21
Grassgarth. Cumb 4G 7
Graven. Shet 5H 67
Grealin. High 2E 45
Great Blencow. Cumb 5H 7
Great Broughton. Cumb 5D 6
Great Clifton. Cumb 5D 6
Great Corby. Cumb 3H 7
Great Orton. Cumb 3G 7
Greenbank. Shet 2J 67
Greenburn. W Lot 2E 19
Greendykes. Nmbd 5H 21
Greenfield. Arg 4B 24
Greenfoot. N Lan 2C 18
Greengairs. N Lan 1C 18
Greengill. Cumb 5E 7
Greenhaugh. Nmbd 5G 13
Greenhill. Dum 1E 7
Greenhill. Falk 1D 18
Greenhills. N Ayr 3G 17
Greenholm. E Ayr 5A 18
Greenigoe. Orkn 4D 64
Greenland. High 2F 59
Greenland Mains. High 2F 59
Greenlaw. Bord 4E 21
Greenlea. Dum 1D 6
Greenloaning. Per 3H 25
Greenmow. Shet 4D 66
Greenock. Inv 1F 17
Greenock Mains. E Ayr 1D 10
Greenrow. Cumb 3E 7
Greens. Abers 4D 50
Greenwall. Orkn 4E 64
Grein. W Isl 4B 60
Greinetobht. W Isl 3J 61
Gremista. Shet 2D 66
Greosabhagh. W Isl 5C 62
Greshornish. High 3C 44
Gretna. Dum 2G 7
Gretna Green. Dum 2G 7
Greysouthen. Cumb 5D 6
Greystoke. Cumb 5H 7
Greystoke Gill. Cumb 5H 7
Greystone. Ang 4C 34
Griais. W Isl 3J 63
Grianan. W Isl 4J 63
Gribun. Arg 5F 29
Grimbister. Orkn 3C 64
Grimeston. Orkn 3C 64
Griminis. W Isl 5H 61 (on Benbecula)
Griminis. W Isl 3H 61 (on North Uist)
Grimister. Shet 3H 67
Grimness. Orkn 5D 64
Grindiscol. Shet 3D 66
Grindon. Nmbd 4G 21
Grinsdale. Cumb 3G 7
Griomsidar. W Isl 5J 63
Grishipoll. Arg 3C 28
Gritley. Orkn 4E 64
Grobister. Orkn 5J 65
Grobsness. Shet 6G 67
Grogport. Arg 4B 16
Groigearraidh. W Isl 6H 61
Grove, The. Dum 1C 6
Grudie. High 2E 47
Gruids. High 3C 54
Gruinard House. High 4E 53
Gruinart. Arg 2D 14
Grulinbeg. Arg 2D 14
Gruline. Arg 4G 29
Grummore. High 5H 57
Gruting. Shet 2B 66
Grutness. Shet 6D 66
Gualachulain. High 4E 31
Gualin House. High 3E 57
Guardbridge. Fife 2F 27
Guay. Per 4F 33
Guildtown. Per 5G 33
Gulberwick. Shet 3D 66
Gullane. E Lot 5F 27
Gunnerton. Nmbd 5H 13
Gunnista. Shet 2D 66
Gunsgreenhill. Bord 2G 21
Gutcher. Shet 3J 67
Guthrie. Ang 3C 34

H

Haa of Houlland. Shet 2J 67
Hackland. Orkn 2C 64
Hackness. Orkn 5C 64
Haclait. W Isl 6J 61
Hadden. Bord 5E 21
Haddington. E Lot 1C 20
Haddo. Abers 5D 50
Haggbeck. Cumb 1H 7
Haggersta. Shet 2C 66
Haggerston. Nmbd 4H 21
Haggrister. Shet 5G 67
Halbeath. Fife 5C 26
Halcro. High 2F 59
Halistra. High 3B 44
Halket. E Ayr 3H 17
Halkirk. High 3E 59
Hall. E Ren 3H 17
Halliburton. Bord 4D 20
Hallin. High 3B 44
Hallyne. Bord 4G 19
Haltcliff Bridge. Cumb 5G 7
Ham. High 1F 59
Ham. Shet 5A 66
Hamilton. S Lan 3C 18 & 82
Hamister. Shet 6J 67
Hamnavoe. Shet 4F 67 (nr. Braehoulland)
Hamnavoe. Shet 3C 66 (nr. Burland)
Hamnavoe. Shet 5H 67 (nr. Lunna)
Hamnavoe. Shet 4H 67 (on Yell)
Happas. Ang 4B 34
Happendon. S Lan 5D 18
Hardgate. Abers 3C 42
Hardgate. Dum 2B 6
Harelaw. Dum 1H 7
Hareshaw. N Lan 2D 18
Harker. Cumb 2G 7
Harkland. Shet 4H 67
Harlosh. High 4B 44
Haroldswick. Shet 1K 67
Harpsdale. High 3E 59
Harraby. Cumb 3H 7
Harrapool. High 1F 37
Harrapul. High 1F 37
Harrietfield. Per 1A 26
Harrington. Cumb 5C 6
Harriston. Cumb 4E 7
Harthill. N Lan 2E 19
Hartmount. High 1A 48
Hartwood. N Lan 3D 18
Hassendean. Bord 1E 13
Haster. High 3G 59
Hastigrow. High 2F 59
Hatton. Abers 5F 51
Hattoncrook. Abers 1D 42
Hatton of Fintray. Abers 2D 42
Haugh. E Ayr 1B 10
Haugh Head. Nmbd 5H 21
Haugh of Ballechin. Per 3E 33
Haugh of Glass. Mor 5H 49
Haugh of Urr. Dum 2B 6
Haunn. Arg 4E 29
Haunn. W Isl 3C 60
Hawick. Bord 2E 13
Hawksdale. Cumb 4G 7
Hayhill. E Ayr 2B 10
Hayshead. Ang 4D 34
Hayton. Aber 3E 43
Hayton. Cumb 4E 7 (nr. Aspatria)
Hayton. Cumb 3H 7 (nr. Brampton)
Haywood. S Lan 3E 19
Hazelbank. S Lan 4D 18
Hazelton Walls. Fife 1E 27
Head of Muir. Falk 5H 25
Heads Nook. Cumb 3H 7
Heanish. Arg 4B 28
Heaste. High 2F 37
Heatherfield. High 4D 44
Heathfield. Cumb 4E 7
Heathfield. Ren 2G 17
Heathhall. Dum 1C 6
Heck. Dum 5H 11
Heddle. Orkn 3C 64
Heglibister. Shet 1C 66
Heights of Brae. High 2G 47
Heights of Fodderty. High 2G 47
Heights of Kinlochewe. High 2B 46
Heiton. Bord 5E 21
Helensburgh. Arg 5B 24
Hellister. Shet 2C 66
Helmsdale. High 2H 55
Hempriggs. High 4G 59
Heogan. Shet 2D 66
Heribusta. High 1D 44
Heriot. Bord 3B 20
Hermiston. Edin 1G 19
Hermitage. Bord 4E 13
Heronsford. S Ayr 5G 9
Herra. Shet 3K 67
Herston. Orkn 5D 64
Hesket Newmarket. Cumb 5G 7
Hesleyside. Nmbd 5H 13
Hessilhead. N Ayr 3G 17
Hestaford. Shet 1B 66
Hestinsetter. Shet 2B 66
Hestwall. Orkn 3B 64
Hethersgill. Cumb 2H 7
Hetherside. Cumb 2H 7
Hethpool. Nmbd 1H 13
Hetton Steads. Nmbd 5H 21
Heugh-head. Abers 2G 41
Heylipol. Arg 4A 28
High Auldgirth. Dum 5G 11
High Banton. N Lan 5G 25
High Blantyre. S Lan 3B 18
High Bonnybridge. Falk 1D 18
Highbridge. Cumb 4G 7
Highbridge. High 5C 38
High Crosby. Cumb 3H 7
High Dougarie. N Ayr 5B 16
Highfield. N Ayr 3G 17
Highgate. N Ayr 3G 17
Highgreen Manor. Nmbd 4H 13
High Harrington. Cumb 5D 6
High Hesket. Cumb 4H 7
High Ireby. Cumb 5F 7
High Keil. Arg 3B 8
Highlaws. Cumb 4E 7
High Longthwaite. Cumb 4F 7
High Lorton. Cumb 5E 7
Highmoor. Cumb 4F 7
High Row. Cumb 5G 7
High Scales. Cumb 4E 7
High Side. Cumb 5F 7
Hightae. Dum 1D 6
High Valleyfield. Fife 5B 26
Hillbrae. Abers 4B 50 (nr. Aberchirder)
Hillbrae. Abers 1C 42 (nr. Inverurie)
Hillbrae. Abers 5D 50 (nr. Methlick)
Hillend. Fife 5C 26 (nr. Inverkeithing)
Hill End. Fife 4B 26 (nr. Saline)
Hillend. N Lan 2D 18
Hillhead. Abers 5A 50
Hillhead. S Ayr 2B 10
Hillhead of Auchentumb. Abers 3E 51
Hilliclay. High 2E 59
Hillington. Ren 2A 18
Hill of Beath. Fife 4C 26
Hill of Fearn. High 1B 48
Hill of Fiddes. Abers 1E 43
Hill of Keillor. Ang 4H 33
Hill of Overbrae. Abers 2D 50
Hillside. Abers 4E 43
Hillside. Ang 2E 35
Hillside. Orkn 2C 64
Hillside. Shet 6H 67
Hillside of Prieston. Ang 5A 34
Hillswick. Shet 5F 67
Hillwell. Shet 5C 66
Hillyland. Per 1B 26
Hilton. High 5E 55
Hilton of Cadboll. High 1B 48
Hirn. Abers 3C 42
Hirst. N Lan 2D 18
Hobbister. Orkn 4C 64
Hobkirk. Bord 2E 13
Hoddomcross. Dum 1E 7
Hogaland. Shet 5G 67
Hogha Gearraidh. W Isl 3H 61
Holburn. Nmbd 5H 21
Holland. Orkn 2G 65 (on Papa Westray)
Holland. Orkn 5J 65 (on Stronsay)
Hollandstoun. Orkn 2K 65
Hollows. Dum 1G 7
Hollybush. E Ayr 2A 10
Holmend. Dum 3H 11
Holme St Cuthbert. Cumb 4E 7
Holmhead. E Ayr 1C 10
Holmisdale. High 4A 44
Holm of Drumlanrig. Dum 4F 11
Holmsgarth. Shet 2D 66
Holmwrangle. Cumb 4H 7
Holytown. N Lan 2C 18
Holywood. Dum 5G 11
Hoove. Shet 2C 66
Hope. High 2F 57
Hopeman. Mor 2E 49
Horgabost. W Isl 5B 62
Horncliffe. Nmbd 4G 21
Horndean. Bord 4F 21
Hornsby. Cumb 3H 7
Hornsbygate. Cumb 3H 7
Horsbrugh Ford. Bord 5H 19
Horsley. Nmbd 4H 13
Horsleyhill. Bord 2E 13
Hosh. Per 1H 25
Hosta. W Isl 3H 61
Hoswick. Shet 4D 66
Houbie. Shet 3K 67
Hough. Arg 4A 28
Houghton. Cumb 3H 7
Houlland. Shet 1C 66 (on Mainland)
Houlland. Shet 5J 67 (on Yell)
Houndslow. Bord 4D 20
Houndwood. Bord 2F 21
Housabister. Shet 1D 66
Housay. Shet 5K 67
Househill. High 3B 48
Housetter. Shet 4F 67
Houss. Shet 3C 66
Houston. Ren 2H 17
Housty. High 5E 59
Houton. Orkn 4C 64
How. Cumb 3H 7
Howe. High 2G 59
Howe of Teuchar. Abers 4C 50
Howes. Dum 2E 7
Howgate. Midl 3H 19
Hownam. Bord 2G 13
Howtel. Nmbd 5F 21
Howwood. Ren 2G 17
Hughton. High 4F 47
Huisinis. W Isl 3A 62
Humbie. E Lot 2B 20
Humbleton. Nmbd 5G 21
Hume. Bord 4E 21
Huna. High 1G 59
Hungladder. High 1C 44
Hunspow. High 1F 59
Hunterfield. Midl 2A 20
Hunter's Quay. Arg 1E 17
Hunthill Lodge. Ang 1B 34
Huntington. E Lot 1B 20
Huntingtower. Per 1B 26
Huntly. Abers 4A 50
Huntlywood. Bord 4D 20
Hurlet. Glas 2A 18
Hurlford. E Ayr 5H 17
Hurliness. Orkn 6B 64
Hutton. Cumb 5H 7
Hutton. Bord 3G 21
Hutton End. Cumb 5H 7
Hutton Roof. Cumb 5G 7
Huxter. Shet 1A 66 (on Mainland)
Huxter. Shet 6J 67 (on Whalsay)
Hyndford Bridge. S Lan 4E 19
Hynish. Arg 5A 28
Hythie. Abers 3F 51

I

Ianstown. Mor 2H 49
Iarsiadar. W Isl 1C 62
Ibrox. Glas 2A 18
Ichrachan. Arg 5D 30
Idrigill. High 2C 44
Imachar. N Ayr 4B 16
Inchbae Lodge. High 2F 47
Inchbare. Ang 2D 34
Inchberry. Mor 3G 49
Inchbraoch. Ang 3E 35
Incheril. High 2B 46
Inchinnan. Ren 2H 17
Inchlaggan. High 3C 38
Inchmichael. Per 1D 26
Inchnadamph. High 1H 53
Inchree. High 2D 30
Inchture. Per 1D 26
Inchyra. Per 1C 26
Inkstack. High 1F 59
Innellan. Arg 2E 17
Innerleith. Fife 2D 26
Innerleithen. Bord 5A 20
Innerleven. Fife 3E 27
Innermessan. Dum 2B 4
Innerwick. E Lot 1E 21
Innerwick. Per 4A 32
Insch. Abers 1B 42
Insh. High 3B 40
Inshegra. High 3D 56
Inshore. High 1E 57
Inver. Abers 4F 41
Inver. High 5F 55
Inver. Per 4F 33
Inverailort. High 5G 37
Inveralligin. High 3H 45
Inverallochy. Abers 2F 51
Inveramsay. Abers 1C 42
Inveran. High 4C 54
Inveraray. Arg 3H 23
Inverarish. High 5E 45
Inverarity. Ang 4B 34
Inverarnan. Arg 2C 24
Inverarnie. High 5H 47
Inverbeg. Arg 4C 24
Inverbervie. Abers 1F 35
Inverboyndie. Abers 2B 50
Invercassley. High 3B 54
Invercharnan. High 4E 31
Inverchoran. High 3D 46
Invercreran. Arg 4D 30
Inverdruie. High 2C 40
Inverebrie. Abers 5E 51
Invereck. Arg 5A 24
Inveresk. E Lot 1A 20
Inveresragan. Arg 5C 30
Inverey. Abers 5D 40
Inverfarigaig. High 1G 39
Invergarry. High 3E 39
Invergeldie. Per 1G 25
Invergordon. High 2A 48
Invergowrie. Per 5A 34
Inverguseran. High 3G 37
Inverharroch. Mor 5G 49
Inverie. High 3G 37
Inverinan. Arg 2G 23
Inverinate. High 1A 38
Inverkeilor. Ang 4D 34
Inverkeithing. Fife 5C 26
Inverkeithny. Abers 4B 50
Inverkip. Inv 1F 17
Inverkirkaig. High 2F 53
Inverlael. High 5G 53
Inverliever Lodge. Arg 3F 23
Inverliver. Arg 5D 30
Inverloch. High 1E 31
Inverlochlarig. Stir 2D 24
Inverlussa. Arg 5D 22
Inver Mallie. High 5C 38
Invermarkie. Abers 5H 49
Invermoriston. High 2F 39
Invernaver. High 2A 58
Inverneil House. Arg 5F 23
Inverness. High 4H 47 & 82
Inverness Airport. High 3A 48
Invernettie. Abers 4G 51
Inverpolly Lodge. High 2F 53
Inverquhomery. Abers 4F 51
Inverroy. High 5D 38
Inversanda. High 3C 30
Invershiel. High 2A 38
Invershin. High 4C 54
Invershore. High 5F 59
Inversnaid. Stir 3C 24
Inverugie. Abers 4G 51
Inveruglas. Arg 3C 24
Inverurie. Abers 1C 42
Invervar. Per 4B 32
Inverythan. Abers 4C 50
Iochdar. W Isl 6H 61
Ireby. Cumb 5F 7
Ireland. Shet 4C 66
Irthington. Cumb 2H 7
Irvine. N Ayr 5G 17
Irvine Mains. N Ayr 5G 17
Isauld. High 2C 58
Isbister. Orkn 3C 64
Isbister. Shet 3G 67 (on Mainland)
Isbister. Shet 6J 67 (on Whalsay)
Islay Airport. Arg 3E 15
Isle of Whithorn. Dum 5F 5
Isleornsay. High 2G 37
Islesburgh. Shet 6G 67
Islesteps. Dum 1C 6
Islibhig. W Isl 2A 62
Itlaw. Abers 3B 50
Ivegill. Cumb 4H 7
Iverchaolain. Arg 1D 16

J

Jackton. S Lan 3A 18
Jamestown. Dum 4C 12
Jamestown. Fife 5C 26
Jamestown. High 3F 47
Jamestown. W Dun 5C 24
Janetstown. High 2D 58 (nr. Thurso)
Janetstown. High 3G 59 (nr. Wick)
Jedburgh. Bord 1F 13
Jemimaville. High 2A 48
Jenkins Park. High 3E 39
Johnby. Cumb 5H 7
John o' Groats. High 1G 59
Johnshaven. Abers 2E 35
Johnstone. Ren 2H 17
Johnstonebridge. Dum 4H 11
Joppa. Edin 1A 20
Joppa. S Ayr 2B 10
Juniper Green. Edin 2G 19

K

Kaimend. S Lan 4E 19
Kaimes. Edin 2H 19
Kaimrig End. Bord 4F 19
Kames. Arg 1C 16
Kames. E Ayr 1D 10
Kearvaig. High 1D 56
Kedlock Feus. Fife 2E 27
Keig. Abers 2B 42
Keilarsbrae. Clac 4H 25
Keilmore. Arg 5D 22
Keillor. Per 4H 33
Keillour. Per 1A 26
Keills. Arg 2F 15
Keiloch. Abers 4E 41
Keils. Arg 2G 15
Keir Mill. Dum 4F 11
Keiss. High 2G 59
Keith. Mor 3H 49
Keith Inch. Abers 4G 51
Kellan. Arg 4G 29
Kellas. Ang 5B 34
Kellas. Mor 3E 49
Kelloholm. Dum 2E 11
Kelsick. Cumb 3E 7
Kelso. Bord 5E 21
Keltneyburn. Per 4C 32
Kelton. Dum 1C 6
Kelton Hill. Dum 3A 6
Kelty. Fife 4C 26
Kelvinside. Glas 2A 18
Kemback. Fife 2F 27
Kemnay. Abers 2C 42
Kengharair. Arg 4F 29
Kennacraig. Arg 2B 16
Kennet. Clac 4A 26
Kennethmont. Abers 1A 42
Kennoway. Fife 3E 27
Kenovay. Arg 4A 28
Kensaleyre. High 3D 44
Kentallen. High 3D 30
Kentra. High 2H 29
Keoldale. High 2E 57
Keppoch. High 1A 38
Kerrow. High 5E 47
Kerrycroy. Arg 2E 17
Kerse. Ren 3G 17
Kershopefoot. Cumb 5D 12
Kettins. Per 5H 33
Kettlebridge. Fife 3E 27
Kettleholm. Dum 1E 7
Kettletoft. Orkn 4J 65
Keyhead. Abers 3F 51
Kiel Crofts. Arg 5C 30
Kielder. Nmbd 4F 13
Kilbagie. Fife 4A 26
Kilbarchan. Ren 2H 17
Kilbeg. High 3F 37
Kilberry. Arg 2A 16
Kilbirnie. N Ayr 3G 17
Kilbride. Arg 1F 23
Kilbride. High 1E 37
Kilbucho Place. Bord 5F 19
Kilchattan. Arg 4A 22 (on Colonsay)
Kilchattan. Arg 3E 17 (on Isle of Bute)
Kilchattan Bay. Arg 3D 16
Kilchenzie. Arg 1B 8
Kilcheran. Arg 5B 30
Kilchiaran. Arg 2D 14
Kilchoan. High 4G 37 (nr. Inverie)
Kilchoan. High 2F 29 (nr. Tobermory)
Kilchoman. Arg 2D 14
Kilchrenan. Arg 1H 23
Kilconquhar. Fife 3F 27
Kilcoy. High 3G 47
Kilcreggan. Arg 5B 24
Kildary. High 1A 48
Kildermorie Lodge. High 1G 47
Kildonan. Dum 3B 4
Kildonan. High 1G 55 (nr. Helmsdale)
Kildonan. High 3C 44 (on Isle of Skye)
Kildonan. N Ayr 1F 9
Kildonnan. High 5D 36
Kildrummy. Abers 2H 41
Kilfillan. Dum 3D 4
Kilfinan. Arg 1C 16
Kilfinnan. High 4D 38
Kilgour. Fife 3D 26
Kilgrammie. S Ayr 3H 9
Kilham. Nmbd 5F 21
Kilkenneth. Arg 4A 28
Killandrist. Arg 4B 30
Killean. Arg 4H 15
Killearn. Stir 5E 25
Killellan. Arg 2B 8
Killen. High 3H 47
Killichonan. Per 3A 32
Killiechronan. Arg 4G 29
Killiecrankie. Per 2E 33
Killilan. High 5A 46
Killimster. High 3G 59
Killin. Stir 5A 32
Killin Lodge. High 3G 39
Killinochonoch. Arg 4F 23
Killochyett. Bord 4B 20
Killundine. High 4G 29
Kilmacolm. Inv 1G 17
Kilmahog. Stir 3F 25
Kilmahumaig. Arg 4E 23
Kilmalieu. High 3B 30
Kilmaluag. High 1D 44
Kilmany. Fife 1E 27
Kilmarie. High 2E 37
Kilmarnock. E Ayr 5H 17 & 83
Kilmaron. Fife 2E 27
Kilmartin. Arg 4F 23
Kilmaurs. E Ayr 4H 17
Kilmelford. Arg 2F 23
Kilmeny. Arg 2E 15
Kilmichael Glassary. Arg 4F 23
Kilmichael of Inverlussa. Arg 5E 23
Kilmoluag. Arg 4A 28
Kilmorack. High 4F 47
Kilmore. Arg 1F 23
Kilmore. High 3F 37
Kilmory. Arg 1A 16
Kilmory. High 1G 29 (nr. Kilchoan)
Kilmory. High 3C 36 (on Rùm)
Kilmory. N Ayr 1E 9
Kilmory Lodge. Arg 3E 23
Kilmote. High 2G 55
Kilmuir. High 4B 44 (nr. Dunvegan)
Kilmuir. High 1A 48 (nr. Invergordon)
Kilmuir. High 4A 47 (nr. Inverness)
Kilmuir. High 1C 44 (nr. Uig)
Kilmun. Arg 5A 24
Kilnave. Arg 1D 14
Kilncadzow. S Lan 4D 18
Kilnhill. Cumb 5F 7
Kilninian. Arg 4E 29
Kilninver. Arg 1F 23
Kiloran. Arg 4A 22
Kilpatrick. N Ayr 1E 9
Kilrenny. Fife 3G 27
Kilspindie. Per 1D 26
Kilsyth. N Lan 1C 18
Kiltarlity. High 4G 47
Kilvaxter. High 2C 44
Kilwinning. N Ayr 4F 17
Kimmerston. Nmbd 5G 21
Kinbeachie. High 2H 47
Kinbrace. High 5B 58
Kinbuck. Stir 3G 25
Kincaple. Fife 2F 27
Kincardine. Fife 5A 26
Kincardine. High 5D 54
Kincardine Bridge. Fife 5A 26
Kincardine O'Neil. Abers 4A 42
Kinchrackine. Arg 1A 24
Kincorth. Aber 3E 43
Kincraig. High 3B 40
Kincraigie. Per 4E 33
Kindallachan. Per 3E 33
Kinfauns. Per 1C 26
Kingairloch. High 3B 30
Kingarth. Arg 3D 16
King Edward. Abers 3C 50
Kingholm Quay. Dum 1C 6
Kinghorn. Fife 5D 26
Kingie. High 3C 38
Kinglassie. Fife 4D 26
Kingledores. Bord 1A 12
Kingodie. Per 1E 27
King o' Muirs. Clac 4H 25
Kingsbarns. Fife 2G 27
Kingsburgh. High 3C 44
Kingscavil. W Lot 1F 19
Kingscross. N Ayr 1F 9
Kingseat. Fife 4C 26
Kingsford. E Ayr 4H 17
Kingshouse. High 3F 31
Kingshouse. Stir 1E 25
Kingskettle. Fife 3E 27
Kingsmuir. Ang 4B 34
Kingsmuir. Fife 3G 27
Kings Muir. Bord 5H 19
Kingsteps. High 3C 48
Kingston. E Lot 5G 27
Kingston. Mor 2G 49
Kingswells. Aber 3D 42
Kingswood. Per 5F 33
Kingussie. High 3A 40
Kinharrachie. Abers 5E 51
Kinhrive. High 1A 48
Kinkell Bridge. Per 2A 26
Kinknockie. Abers 4F 51
Kinkry Hill. Cumb 1H 7
Kinloch. High 1F 57 (nr. Loch More)
Kinloch. High 3H 29 (nr. Lochaline)
Kinloch. High 4D 36 (on Rùm)
Kinloch. Per 4G 33
Kinlochard. Stir 3D 24
Kinlochbervie. High 3D 56
Kinlocheil. High 1C 30
Kinlochewe. High 2B 46
Kinloch Hourn. High 3A 38
Kinloch Laggan. High 5G 39
Kinlochleven. High 2E 31
Kinloch Lodge. High 3G 57
Kinlochmoidart. High 1A 30
Kinlochmore. High 2E 31
Kinloch Rannoch. Per 3B 32
Kinlochspelve. Arg 1D 22
Kinloid. High 5F 37
Kinloss. Mor 2D 48
Kinmuck. Abers 2D 42
Kinnadie. Abers 4E 51
Kinnaird. Per 1D 26
Kinneff. Abers 1F 35
Kinnelhead. Dum 3B 11
Kinnell. Ang 3D 34
Kinnernie. Abers 2C 42
Kinnesswood. Per 3C 26
Kinnordy. Ang 3A 34
Kinross. Per 3C 26
Kinrossie. Per 5G 33
Kintessack. Mor 2D 48

Kintillo—Milltown of Aberdalgie

Kintillo. Per 2C 26
Kintore. Abers 2C 42
Kintour. Arg 3F 15
Kintra. Arg 1A 22
Kintraw. Arg 3F 23
Kinveachy. High 2C 40
Kippen. Stir 4F 25
Kippford. Dum 3B 6
Kirbister. Orkn 4C 64
(nr. Hobbister)
Kirbister. Orkn 3B 64
(nr. Quholm)
Kirbuster. Orkn 5J 65
Kirk. High 3F 59
Kirkabister. Shet 3D 66
(on Bressay)
Kirkabister. Shet 1D 66
(on Mainland)
Kirkandrews. Dum 4H 5
Kirkandrews-on-Eden. Cumb 3G 7
Kirkapol. Arg 4B 28
Kirkbampton. Cumb 3G 7
Kirkbean. Dum 3C 6
Kirkbride. Cumb 3F 7
Kirkbuddo. Ang 4C 34
Kirkcaldy. Fife 4D 26 & 83
Kirkcolm. Dum 2B 4
Kirkconnel. Dum 2E 11
Kirkconnell. Dum 2C 6
Kirkcowan. Dum 2E 5
Kirkcudbright. Dum 3H 5
Kirkfieldbank. S Lan 4D 18
Kirkforthar Feus. Fife 3D 26
Kirkgunzeon. Dum 2B 6
Kirkhill. Ang 2D 34
Kirkhill. High 4G 47
Kirkhope. S Lan 3G 11
Kirkhouse. Bord 5A 20
Kirkibost. High 2E 37
Kirkinch. Ang 4A 34
Kirkinner. Dum 3F 5
Kirkintilloch. E Dun 1B 18
Kirkland. Cumb 4F 7
Kirkland. Dum 2E 11
(nr. Kirkconnel)
Kirkland. Dum 1F 11
(nr. Moniaive)
Kirkland Guards. Cumb 4E 7
Kirklauchline. Dum 3B 4
Kirklinton. Cumb 2H 7
Kirkliston. Edin 1G 19
Kirkmabreck. Dum 3F 5
Kirkmaiden. Dum 5C 4
Kirkmichael. Per 2F 33
Kirkmichael. S Ayr 3A 10
Kirkmuirhill. S Lan 4C 18
Kirknewton. Nmbd 5G 21
Kirknewton. W Lot 2G 19
Kirkney. Abers 5A 50
Kirk of Shotts. N Lan 2D 18
Kirkoswald. S Ayr 3H 9
Kirkpatrick. Dum 4G 11
Kirkpatrick Durham. Dum 1A 6
Kirkpatrick-Fleming. Dum 1F 7
Kirkstile. Dum 4C 12
Kirkstyle. High 1G 59
Kirkton. Abers 2B 42
(nr. Alford)
Kirkton. Abers 1B 42
(nr. Insch)
Kirkton. Abers 4D 50
(nr. Turriff)
Kirkton. Ang 5B 34
(nr. Dundee)
Kirkton. Ang 4B 34
(nr. Forfar)
Kirkton. Ang 5H 41
(nr. Tarfside)
Kirkton. Dum 5G 11
Kirkton. Fife 1E 27
Kirkton. High 4E 55
(nr. Golspie)
Kirkton. High 1H 37
(nr. Kyle of Lochalsh)
Kirkton. High 4A 46
(nr. Lochcarron)
Kirkton. Bord 2E 13
Kirkton. S Lan 1G 11
Kirktonhill. W Dun 1G 17
Kirkton Manor. Bord 5H 19
Kirkton of Airlie. Ang 3A 34
Kirkton of Auchterhouse. Ang 5A 34
Kirkton of Bourtie. Abers 1D 42
Kirkton of Collace. Per 5G 33
Kirkton of Craig. Ang 3E 35
Kirkton of Culsalmond. Abers 5B 50
Kirkton of Durris. Abers 4C 42
Kirkton of Glenbuchat. Abers 2G 41
Kirkton of Glenisla. Ang 2H 33
Kirkton of Kingoldrum. Ang 3A 34
Kirkton of Largo. Fife 3F 27
Kirkton of Lethendy. Per 4G 33
Kirkton of Logie Buchan. Abers 1E 43
Kirkton of Maryculter. Abers 4D 42
Kirkton of Menmuir. Ang 2C 34
Kirkton of Monikie. Ang 5C 34
Kirkton of Oyne. Abers 1B 42
Kirkton of Rayne. Abers 5B 50
Kirkton of Skene. Abers 3D 42
Kirktown. Abers 2E 51
(nr. Fraserburgh)
Kirktown. Abers 3F 51
(nr. Peterhead)
Kirktown of Alvah. Abers 2B 50
Kirktown of Auchterless. Abers 4C 50
Kirktown of Deskford. Mor 2A 50
Kirktown of Fetteresso. Abers 5D 42
Kirktown of Mortlach. Mor 5G 49
Kirktown of Slains. Abers 1F 43
Kirkurd. Bord 4G 19
Kirkwall. Orkn 3D 64
Kirkwall Airport. Orkn 4D 64
Kirk Yetholm. Bord 1H 13
Kirn. Arg 1E 17
Kirriemuir. Ang 3A 34
Kirtlebridge. Dum 1F 7
Kirtleton. Dum 1F 7
Kirtomy. High 2A 58
Kishorn. High 4H 45
Kittybrowster. Aber 3E 43
Knapp. Per 5H 33
Knapperfield. High 3F 59
Knaven. Abers 4D 50
Knightswood. Glas 2A 18
Knock. Arg 5G 29
Knock. Mor 3A 50
Knockally. High 5E 69
Knockan. Arg 1B 22
Knockan. High 2H 53
Knockandhu. Mor 1F 41
Knockando. Mor 4E 49
Knockarthur. High 3E 55
Knockbain. High 3H 47
Knockbreck. High 2B 44
Knockdee. High 2E 59
Knockdolian. S Ayr 5G 9
Knockdon. S Ayr 2A 10
Knockenbaird. Abers 1B 42
Knockenkelly. N Ayr 1F 9
Knockentiber. E Ayr 5G 17
Knockfarrel. High 3G 47
Knockglass. High 2D 58
Knockie Lodge. High 2F 39
Knockinlaw. E Ayr 5H 17
Knockinnon. High 5E 59
Knockrome. Arg 1G 15
Knockshinnoch. E Ayr 2B 10
Knockvennie. Dum 1A 6
Knockvologan. Arg 2A 22
Knotts. High 3C 44
Knowe. Dum 1E 5
Knowefield. Cumb 3H 7
Knowehead. Dum 4D 10
Knowes. E Lot 1D 20
Knowside. S Ayr 2H 9
Knowles of Elrick. Abers 3B 50
Kyleakin. High 1G 37
Kyle of Lochalsh. High 1G 37
Kylerhea. High 1G 37
Kylesku. High 5D 56
Kyles Lodge. W Isl 2K 61
Kylesmorar. High 4H 37
Kylestrome. High 5D 56

L

Labost. W Isl 3G 63
Lacasaidh. W Isl 2E 62
Lacasdail. W Isl 4J 63
Lady. Orkn 3J 65
Ladybank. Fife 2E 27
Ladykirk. Bord 4F 21
Ladysford. Abers 2E 51
Laga. High 2H 29
Lagavulin. Arg 4F 15
Lagg. Arg 1G 15
Lagg. N Ayr 1E 9
Laggan. Arg 3D 14
Laggan. High 4D 38
(nr. Fort Augustus)
Laggan. High 4H 39
(nr. Newtonmore)
Laggan. Mor 5G 49
Lagganlia. High 3B 40
Lagganulva. Arg 4F 29
Laglingarten. Arg 3A 24
Laid. High 3F 57
Laide. High 4E 53
Laigh Fenwick. E Ayr 4H 17
Lairg. High 3C 54
Lairg Muir. High 3C 54
Laithes. Cumb 5H 7
Lamancha. Bord 3H 19
Lambden. Bord 4E 21
Lamberton. Bord 3G 21
Lambhill. Glas 2A 18
Lamington. Orkn 4J 65
Lamington. High 1A 48
Lamington. S Lan 5E 19
Lamlash. N Ayr 5D 16
Lamonby. Cumb 5H 7
Lanark. S Lan 4D 18
Landerberry. Abers 3C 42
Landhallow. High 5E 59
Lanehead. Nmbd 5G 13
Langais. W Isl 4J 61
Langal. High 2A 30
Langbank. Ren 1G 17
Langburnshiels. Bord 3E 13
Langdyke. Fife 3E 27
Langholm. Dum 5C 12
Langrigg. Cumb 4E 7
Langshaw. Bord 5C 20
Lanton. Nmbd 5G 21
Lanton. Bord 1F 13
Laphroaig. Arg 4E 15
Larachbeg. High 4H 29
Larbert. Falk 5H 25
Larel. High 3E 59
Largie. Abers 5B 50
Largiemore. Arg 5G 23
Largoward. Fife 3F 27
Largs. N Ayr 3F 17
Largue. Abers 4B 50
Largybeg. N Ayr 1F 9
Largymeanoch. N Ayr 1F 9
Largymore. N Ayr 1F 9
Larkfield. Inv 1F 17
Larkhall. S Lan 3C 18
Lary. Abers 3G 41
Lassodie. Fife 4C 26
Lasswade. Midl 2A 20
Latheron. High 5E 59
Latheronwheel. High 5E 59
Lathones. Fife 3F 27
Laudale House. High 3A 30
Lauder. Bord 4C 20
Laurencekirk. Abers 1E 35
Laurieston. Dum 2H 5
Laurieston. Falk 1E 19
Laverhay. Dum 4A 12
Laversdale. Cumb 2H 7
Law. S Lan 3D 18
Lawers. Per 5B 32
Laxfirth. Shet 1D 66
Laxo. Shet 6H 67
Leac a Li. W Isl 5C 62
Leachd. Arg 4H 23
Leachkin. High 4H 47
Leadburn. Midl 3H 19
Leaderfoot. Bord 5C 20
Leadhills. S Lan 2F 11
Lealt. Arg 4D 22
Lealt. High 2E 45
Leargybreck. Arg 1G 15
Leaths. Dum 2A 6
Leckfurin. High 3A 58
Leckgruinart. Arg 2D 14
Leckmelm. High 4G 53
Ledaig. Arg 5C 30
Ledgowan. High 3C 46
Ledmore. High 2H 53
Lednabirichen. High 4E 55
Lednagullin. High 2B 58
Leeans. Shet 2C 66
Leebotten. Shet 4D 66
Leetown. Per 1D 26
Legerwood. Bord 4C 20
Leirinmore. High 2F 57
Leishmore. High 4F 47
Leitfie. Per 4H 33
Leith. Edin 1H 19
Leitholm. Bord 4E 21
Lempitlaw. Bord 5E 21
Lenchie. Abers 5A 50
Lendalfoot. S Ayr 5G 9
Lendrick. Stir 3E 25
Lenimore. N Ayr 4B 16
Lennel. Bord 4F 21
Lennoxtown. E Dun 1B 18
Lentran. High 4G 47
Lenzie. E Dun 1B 18
Leochel Cushnie. Abers 2A 42
Leogh. Shet 1J 65
Lephenstrath. Arg 3B 8
Lephin. High 4A 44
Lephinchapel. Arg 4G 23
Lephinmore. Arg 4G 23
Lerwick. Shet 2D 66
Lerwick (Tingwall) Airport. Shet 2D 66
Leslie. Abers 1A 42
Leslie. Fife 3D 26
Lesmahagow. S Lan 5D 18
Lessonhall. Cumb 3F 7
Leswalt. Dum 2B 4
Letham. Ang 4C 34
Letham. Falk 5H 25
Letham. Fife 2E 27
Lethanhill. E Ayr 2B 10
Lethenty. Abers 4D 50
Lettan. Orkn 3K 65
Letter. Abers 2C 42
Letterewe. High 1A 46
Letterfearn. High 1H 37
Lettermore. Arg 4F 29
Letters. High 5G 53
Leuchars. Fife 1F 27
Leumrabhagh. W Isl 3E 62
Levaneap. Shet 6H 67
Leven. Fife 3E 27
Levencorroch. N Ayr 1F 9
Levenhall. E Lot 1A 20
Levenwick. Shet 4D 66
Leverburgh. W Isl 6B 62
Levishie. High 2F 39
Lewiston. High 1G 39
Leylodge. Abers 2C 42
Leys. Per 5H 33
Leysmill. Ang 4D 34
Lhanbryde. Mor 2F 49
Liatrie. High 5D 46
Libberton. S Lan 4E 19
Liberton. Edin 2H 19
Liceasto. W Isl 5C 62
Liddle. Orkn 6D 64
Lienassie. High 1B 38
Liff. Ang 5A 34
Lilliesleaf. Bord 1E 13
Lilybank. Inv 1G 17
Limekilnburn. S Lan 3C 18
Limekilns. Fife 5B 26
Limerigg. Falk 1D 18
Linburn. W Lot 2G 19
Lincluden. Dum 1C 6
Lindean. Bord 5B 20
Lindores. Fife 2D 26
Lingreabhagh. W Isl 6B 62
Lingy Close. Cumb 3G 7
Linicro. High 2C 44
Linklater. Orkn 6D 64
Linksness. Orkn 3E 64
Linktown. Fife 4D 26
Linkwood. Mor 2F 49
Linlithgow. W Lot 1E 19
Linlithgow Bridge. Falk 1E 19
Linneraineach. High 3G 53
Linshiels. Nmbd 3H 13
Linsiadar. W Isl 1D 62
Linsidemore. High 4C 54
Linstock. Cumb 3H 7
Lintlaw. Bord 3F 21
Lintmill. Mor 2A 50
Linton. Bord 1G 13
Linwood. Ren 2H 17
Lionacleit. W Isl 6H 61
Lionacro. High 2C 44
Lionacuidhe. W Isl 6H 61
Lional. W Isl 1K 63
Liquo. N Lan 3D 18
Litterty. Abers 3C 50
Little Ardo. Abers 5D 50
Little Ballinluig. Per 3E 33
Little Bampton. Cumb 3F 7
Little Blencow. Cumb 5H 7
Little Brechin. Ang 2C 34
Little Broughton. Cumb 5D 6
Little Clifton. Cumb 5D 6
Little Creich. High 5D 54
Little Dens. Abers 4F 51
Little Dunkeld. Per 4F 33
Littleferry. High 4F 55
Little Glenshee. Per 5E 33
Littlemill. Abers 4G 41
Littlemill. E Ayr 2B 10
Littlemill. High 4C 48
Little Orton. Cumb 3G 7
Little Rogart. High 3E 55
Little Scatwell. High 3E 47
Littlester. Shet 4J 67
Little Torboll. High 4E 55
Littletown. High 5E 55
Liurbost. W Isl 2E 62
Livingston. W Lot 2F 19
Livingston Village. W Lot 2F 19
Loan. Falk 1E 19
Loanend. Nmbd 3G 21
Loanhead. Midl 2H 19
Loaningfoot. Dum 3C 6
Loanreoch. High 1H 47
Loans. S Ayr 5G 17
Lochaber. Mor 3D 48
Loch a Charnain. W Isl 6J 61
Loch a Ghainmhich. W Isl 2D 62
Lochailort. High 5G 37
Lochaline. High 4H 29
Lochans. Dum 3B 4
Locharbriggs. Dum 5G 11
Lochardil. High 4H 47
Lochassynt Lodge. High 1G 53
Lochavich. Arg 2G 23
Lochawe. Arg 1A 24
Loch Baghasdail. W Isl 3C 60
Lochboisdale. W Isl 3C 60
Lochbuie. Arg 1D 22
Lochcarron. High 5H 45
Loch Choire Lodge. High 5H 57
Lochdar. W Isl 6H 61
Lochdochart House. Stir 1D 24
Lochdon. Arg 5A 30
Lochearnhead. Stir 1E 25
Lochee. D'dee 5A 34
Lochend. High 5G 47
(nr. Inverness)
Lochend. High 2F 59
(nr. Thurso)
Locherben. Dum 4G 11
Loch Euphort. W Isl 4J 61
Lochfoot. Dum 1B 6
Lochgair. Arg 4G 23
Lochgarthside. High 2G 39
Lochgelly. Fife 4C 26
Lochgilphead. Arg 5F 23
Lochgoilhead. Arg 3A 24
Loch Head. Dum 4E 5
Lochhill. Mor 2F 49
Lochindorb Lodge. High 5C 48
Lochinver. High 1F 53
Lochlane. Per 1H 25
Loch Lomond. Arg 3C 24
Loch Loyal Lodge. High 4H 57
Lochluichart. High 2E 47
Lochmaben. Dum 5H 11
Lochmaddy. W Isl 4K 61
Loch nam Madadh. W Isl 4K 61
Lochore. Fife 4C 26
Lochportain. W Isl 3K 61
Lochranza. N Ayr 3C 16
Loch Sgioport. W Isl 1D 60
Lochside. Abers 2E 35
Lochside. High 5B 58
(nr. Achentoul)
Lochside. High 3B 48
(nr. Nairn)
Lochslin. High 5F 55
Lochstack Lodge. High 4D 56
Lochton. Abers 4C 42
Lochty. Fife 3G 27
Lochuisge. High 3A 30
Lochussie. High 3F 47
Lochwinnoch. Ren 3G 17
Lochyside. High 1E 31
Lockerbie. Dum 5A 12
Lockhills. Cumb 4H 7
Logan. E Ayr 1C 10
Loganlea. W Lot 2E 19
Loggie. High 4G 53
Logie. Ang 2D 34
Logie. Fife 1F 27
Logie. Mor 3D 48
Logie Coldstone. Abers 3H 41
Logie Pert. Ang 2D 34
Logierait. Per 3E 33
Lonbain. High 3F 45
Londubh. High 5D 52
Lone. High 4E 57
Lonemore. High 5E 55
(nr. Dornoch)
Lonemore. High 1G 45
(nr. Gairloch)
Longbar. N Ayr 3G 17
Longburgh. Cumb 3G 7
Longcroft. Cumb 3F 7
Longcroft. Falk 1C 18
Longdales. Cumb 4H 7
Longfield. Shet 5C 66
Longforgan. Per 1E 27
Longformacus. Bord 3D 20
Longhill. Abers 3F 51
Longhope. Orkn 5C 64
Longlands. Cumb 5F 7
Longmanhill. Abers 2C 50
Longmorn. Mor 3F 49
Longnewton. Bord 1E 13
Longniddry. E Lot 1B 20
Longpark. Cumb 2H 7
Longridge. W Lot 2E 19
Longriggend. N Lan 1D 18
Longside. Abers 4F 51
Longtown. Cumb 2G 7
Longyester. E Lot 2C 20
Lonmore. High 4B 44
Losgaintir. W Isl 5B 62
Lossiemouth. Mor 2F 49
Lossit. Arg 3C 14
Lothbeg. High 2G 55
Lothianbridge. Midl 2A 20
Lothianburn. Edin 2H 19
Lothmore. High 2G 55
Low Ardwell. Dum 4B 4
Low Ballochdoan. S Ayr 1B 4
Low Braithwaite. Cumb 4H 7
Low Coylton. S Ayr 2B 10
Low Crosby. Cumb 3H 7
Lower Arboll. High 5F 55
Lower Auchenreath. Mor 2G 49
Lower Badcall. High 4C 56
Lower Breakish. High 1F 37
Lower Diabaig. High 2G 45
Lower Dounreay. High 2C 58
Lower Gledfield. High 4C 54
Lower Killeyan. Arg 4D 14
Lower Largo. Fife 3F 27
Lower Lenie. High 1G 39
Lower Milovaig. High 3A 44
Lower Oakfield. Fife 4C 26
Lower Ollach. High 5E 45
Lower Pitkerrie. High 1B 48
Lowertown. Orkn 5D 64
Low Hesket. Cumb 4H 7
Lowick. Nmbd 5H 21
Low Lorton. Cumb 5E 7
Lownie Moor. Ang 4B 34
Lowood. Bord 5C 20
Low Row. Cumb 4E 7
Low Torry. Fife 5B 26
Low Valleyfield. Fife 5A 26
Low Whinnow. Cumb 3G 7
Lubcroy. High 3A 54
Lubinvullin. High 2G 57
Lucklawhill. Fife 1F 27
Ludag. W Isl 3C 60
Lugar. E Ayr 1C 10
Luggate Burn. E Lot 1D 20
Luggiebank. N Lan 1C 18
Lugton. E Ayr 3H 17
Luib. High 1E 37
Luib. Stir 1D 24
Lumphanan. Abers 3A 42
Lumphinnans. Fife 4C 26
Lumsdaine. Bord 2F 21
Lumsden. Abers 1H 41
Lunan. Ang 3D 34
Lunanhead. Ang 3B 34
Luncarty. Per 1B 26
Lundie. Ang 5H 33
Lundin Links. Fife 3F 27
Lunna. Shet 6H 67
Lunning. Shet 6J 67
Luss. Arg 4C 24
Lussagiven. Arg 5D 22
Lusta. High 3B 44
Luthermuir. Abers 2D 34
Luthrie. Fife 2E 27
Lybster. High 5F 59
Lyham. Nmbd 5H 21
Lylestone. N Ayr 4G 17
Lynaberack Lodge. High 4A 40
Lynchat. High 3A 40
Lyne. Bord 4H 19
Lyneholmeford. Cumb 1H 7
Lyne of Gorthleck. High 1G 39
Lyne of Skene. Abers 2C 42
Lyness. Orkn 5C 64
Lynwilg. High 2B 40
Lyth. High 2F 59
Lythes. Orkn 6D 64
Lythmore. High 2D 58

M

Mabie. Dum 1C 6
Macbiehill. Bord 3G 19
Macduff. Abers 2C 50
Machan. S Lan 3C 18
Machariocn. Arg 3C 8
Machrie. N Ayr 5B 16
Machrihanish. Arg 1B 8
Macmerry. E Lot 1B 20
Madderty. Per 1A 26
Maddiston. Falk 1E 19
Maggieknockater. Mor 4G 49
Maidens. S Ayr 3H 9
Mail. Shet 4D 66
Mains of Auchindachy. Mor 4H 49
Mains of Auchnagatt. Abers 4E 51
Mains of Drum. Abers 4D 42
Mains of Edingight. Mor 3A 50
Mainsriddle. Dum 3C 6
Makerstoun. Bord 5D 20
Malacleit. W Isl 3H 61
Malaig. High 4F 37
Malaig Bheag. High 4F 37
Malcolmburn. Mor 3G 49
Maligar. High 2D 44
Mallaig. High 4F 37
Malleny Mills. Edin 2G 19
Malt Lane. Arg 3H 23
Manais. W Isl 6C 62
Mangurstadh. W Isl 1B 62
Mannal. Arg 4A 28
Mannerston. Falk 1F 19
Mannofield. Aber 3E 43
Mansewood. Glas 2A 18
Mansfield. E Ayr 2D 10
Maraig. W Isl 4D 62
Marbhig. W Isl 6J 63
Margnaheglish. N Ayr 5D 16
Marishader. High 2D 44
Marjoriebanks. Dum 5H 11
Mark. Dum 3C 4
Markethill. Per 5H 33
Markinch. Fife 3D 26
Mar Lodge. Abers 5D 40
Marnoch. Abers 3A 50
Marnock. N Lan 2C 18
Marrel. High 2H 55
Marrister. Shet 6J 67
Marshall Meadows. Nmbd 3G 21
Marwick. Orkn 2B 64
Marybank. High 3F 47
(nr. Dingwall)
Marybank. High 1A 48
(nr. Invergordon)
Maryburgh. High 3G 47
Maryhill. Glas 2A 18
Marykirk. Abers 2D 34
Marypark. Mor 5E 49
Maryport. Cumb 5D 6
Maryport. Dum 5C 4
Maryton. Ang 3A 34
(nr. Kirriemuir)
Maryton. Ang 3D 34
(nr. Montrose)
Marywell. Abers 4A 42
Marywell. Ang 4D 34
Masons Lodge. Abers 3D 42
Mastrick. Aber 3E 43
Mauchline. E Ayr 1B 10
Maud. Abers 4E 51
Mawbray. Cumb 4D 6
Maxton. Bord 5D 20
Maxwellheugh. Bord 5E 21
Maxwelltown. Dum 1C 6
Maybole. S Ayr 3A 10
Mayfield. Midl 2A 20
Mayfield. Per 1B 26
Maywick. Shet 4C 66
Meadowmill. E Lot 1B 20
Mealabost. W Isl 2J 63
(nr. Borgh)
Mealabost. W Isl 4J 63
(nr. Stornoway)
Mealasta. W Isl 2A 62
Mealrigg. Cumb 4E 7
Mealsgate. Cumb 4F 7
Meigle. Per 4H 33
Meikle Earnock. S Lan 3C 18
Meikle Kilchattan Butts. Arg 3D 16
Meikleour. Per 5G 33
Meikle Tarty. Abers 1E 43
Meikle Wartle. Abers 5C 50
Melby. Shet 1A 66
Melfort. Arg 2F 23
Melgarve. High 4F 39
Melkington. Nmbd 4F 21
Mellangaun. High 5D 52
Melldalloch. Arg 1C 16
Mellguards. Cumb 4H 7
Mellon Charles. High 4D 52
Mellon Udrigle. High 4D 52
Melrose. Bord 5C 20
Melsetter. Orkn 6B 64
Melvaig. High 5C 52
Melvich. High 2B 58
Memsie. Abers 2E 51
Memus. Ang 3B 34
Mennock. Dum 3F 11
Menstrie. Clac 4H 25
Merchiston. Edin 1H 19
Merkadale. High 5C 44
Merkland. S Ayr 4H 9
Merkland Lodge. High 1A 54
Methil. Fife 4E 27
Methilhill. Fife 4E 27
Methlick. Abers 5D 50
Methven. Per 1B 26
Mey. High 1F 59
Miabhag. W Isl 5C 62
Miabhaig. W Isl 4B 62
(nr. Cliasmol)
Miabhaig. W Isl 1B 62
(nr. Timsgearraidh)
Mial. High 1G 45
Micklethwaite. Cumb 3F 7
Mid Ardlaw. Abers 2E 51
Midbea. Orkn 3G 65
Mid Beltie. Abers 3B 42
Mid Calder. W Lot 2F 19
Mid Clyth. High 5F 59
Middlebie. Dum 1F 7
Middle Drums. Ang 3C 34
Middle Essie. Abers 3F 51
Middlemuir. Abers 4D 50
(nr. New Deer)
Middlemuir. Abers 3E 51
(nr. Strichen)
Middlesceugh. Cumb 4G 7
Middleton. Ang 4C 34
Middleton. Arg 4A 28
Middleton. Midl 3A 20
Middleton. Nmbd 5H 21
Middleton. Per 3C 26
Middleton Hall. Nmbd 5G 21
Midfield. High 2G 57
Mid Garrary. Dum 1G 5
Mid Ho. Shet 3J 67
Mid Kirkton. N Ayr 3E 17
Midland. Orkn 4C 64
Midlem. Bord 1E 13
Midton. Inv 1F 17
Midtown. High 5D 52
(nr. Poolewe)
Midtown. High 2G 57
(nr. Tongue)
Mid Walls. Shet 2A 66
Mid Yell. Shet 3J 67
Migdale. High 4D 54
Migvie. Abers 3H 41
Milesmark. Fife 5B 26
Milfield. Nmbd 5G 21
Millbank. High 2E 59
Millbeck. Cumb 5F 7
Millbounds. Orkn 1E 64
Millbreck. Abers 4F 51
Millden Lodge. Ang 1C 34
Milldens. Ang 3C 34
Millearn. Per 2A 26
Millerhill. Midl 2A 20
Millerston. N Lan 2B 18
Millfield. Abers 4H 41
Millhall. E Ren 3A 18
Millheugh. S Lan 3C 18
Millhouse. Arg 1C 16
Millhouse. Cumb 5G 7
Millhousebridge. Dum 5A 12
Millikenpark. Ren 2H 17
Mill Knowe. Arg 1C 8
Mill of Craigievar. Abers 2A 42
Mill of Fintray. Abers 2D 42
Mill of Haldane. W Dun 5D 24
Millport. N Ayr 3E 17
Milltimber. Aber 3D 42
Milltown. Abers 3F 41
(nr. Corgarff)
Milltown. Abers 2H 41
(nr. Lumsden)
Milltown. Dum 1G 7
Milltown. Mor 4A 50
Milltown of Aberdalgie. Per 1B 26

Milltown of Auchindoun—Quothquan

Milltown of Auchindoun. *Mor* 4G 49
Milltown of Campfield. *Abers* 3B 42
Milltown of Edinville. *Mor* 4F 49
Milltown of Towie. *Abers* 2H 41
Milnacraig. *Ang* 3H 33
Milnathort. *Per* 3C 26
Milngavie. *E Dun* 1A 18
Milnholm. *Stir* 5G 25
Milton. *Ang* 4A 34
Milton. *Dum* 1B 6 (nr. Crocketford)
Milton. *Dum* 3D 4 (nr. Glenluce)
Milton. *E Ayr* 1B 10
Milton. *Glas* 1A 18
Milton. *High* 3E 47 (nr. Achnasheen)
Milton. *High* 4G 45 (nr. Applecross)
Milton. *High* 5F 47 (nr. Drumnadrochit)
Milton. *High* 1A 48 (nr. Invergordon)
Milton. *High* 4G 47 (nr. Inverness)
Milton. *High* 3G 59 (nr. Wick)
Milton. *Mor* 2A 50 (nr. Cullen)
Milton. *Mor* 2E 41 (nr. Tomintoul)
Milton. *Stir* 3E 25 (nr. Aberfoyle)
Milton. *Stir* 4D 24 (nr. Drymen)
Milton. *W Dun* 1H 17
Milton Auchlossan. *Abers* 3A 42
Milton Bridge. *Midl* 2H 19
Milton Coldwells. *Abers* 5E 51
Miltonduff. *Mor* 2E 49
Milton Morenish. *Per* 5B 32
Milton of Auchinhove. *Abers* 3A 42
Milton of Balgonie. *Fife* 3E 27
Milton of Barras. *Abers* 1F 35
Milton of Campsie. *E Dun* 1B 18
Milton of Cultoquhey. *Per* 1H 25
Milton of Cushnie. *Abers* 2A 42
Milton of Finavon. *Ang* 3B 34
Milton of Gollanfield. *High* 3A 48
Milton of Lesmore. *Abers* 1H 41
Milton of Leys. *High* 4H 47
Milton of Tullich. *Abers* 4G 41
Minard. *Arg* 4G 23
Mindrum. *Nmbd* 5F 21
Mingarrypark. *High* 2H 29
Mingary. *High* 2G 29
Mingearraidh. *W Isl* 2C 60
Minishant. *S Ayr* 2A 10
Minnigaff. *Dum* 2F 5
Mintlaw. *Abers* 4F 51
Minto. *Bord* 1E 13
Miodar. *Arg* 4B 28
Mirbister. *Orkn* 2C 64
Mireland. *High* 2G 59
Moaness. *Orkn* 4B 64
Moarfield. *Shet* 2J 67
Moat. *Cumb* 1H 7
Mochrum. *Dum* 4E 5
Modsarie. *High* 2H 57
Moffat. *Dum* 3H 11
Mol-chlach. *High* 2D 36
Moll. *High* 5E 45
Mollinsburn. *N Lan* 1C 18
Monachyle. *Stir* 2D 24
Monar Lodge. *High* 4D 46
Moneydie. *Per* 1B 26
Moniaive. *Dum* 4E 11
Monifieth. *Ang* 5C 34
Monikie. *Ang* 5C 34
Monimail. *Fife* 2D 26
Monkhill. *Cumb* 3G 7
Monkshill. *Abers* 4C 50
Monkton. *S Ayr* 1A 10
Monktonhill. *S Ayr* 1A 10
Monreith. *Dum* 4E 5
Montford. *Arg* 2E 17
Montgarrie. *Abers* 2A 42
Montgarswood. *E Ayr* 1C 10
Montgreenan. *N Ayr* 4G 17
Montrave. *Fife* 3E 27
Montrose. *Ang* 3E 35
Monymusk. *Abers* 2B 42
Monzie. *Per* 1H 25
Moodiesburn. *N Lan* 1B 18
Moonzie. *Fife* 2E 27
Moorbrae. *Shet* 4H 67
Moorend. *Dum* 1F 7
Moorhouse. *Cumb* 3G 7 (nr. Carlisle)
Moorhouse. *Cumb* 3F 7 (nr. Wigton)
Moor of Granary. *Mor* 3D 48
Moor Row. *Cumb* 4F 7
Morangie. *High* 5E 55
Morar. *High* 4F 37
Morebattle. *Bord* 1G 13
Morefield. *High* 4G 53
Morenish. *Per* 5A 32
Morham. *E Lot* 1C 20
Morningside. *Edin* 1H 19
Morningside. *N Lan* 3D 18
Morrington. *Dum* 5F 11
Morton. *Cumb* 5H 7 (nr. Calthwaite)
Morton. *Cumb* 3G 7 (nr. Carlisle)
Morvich. *High* 3E 55 (nr. Golspie)
Morvich. *High* 1A 38 (nr. Shiel Bridge)
Moscow. *E Ayr* 4H 17
Mosedale. *Cumb* 5G 7
Moss. *Arg* 4A 28
Moss. *High* 2H 29
Mossatt. *Abers* 2H 41
Mossbank. *Shet* 5H 67
Mossblown. *S Ayr* 1B 10
Mossburnford. *Bord* 2F 13
Mossdale. *Dum* 1H 5
Mossedge. *Cumb* 2H 7
Mossend. *N Lan* 2C 18
Moss of Barmuckity. *Mor* 2F 49
Mosspark. *Glas* 2A 18
Mosspaul. *Bord* 4D 12
Moss Side. *Cumb* 3E 7
Moss-side. *High* 3B 48
Moss-side of Cairness. *Abers* 2F 51
Mosstodloch. *Mor* 2G 49
Motherby. *Cumb* 5H 7
Motherwell. *N Lan* 3C 18 & 84
Moulin. *Per* 3E 33
Mountain Cross. *Bord* 4G 19
Mountbenger. *Bord* 1C 12
Mountblow. *W Dun* 1H 17
Mountgerald. *High* 2G 47
Mount High. *High* 2H 47
Mount Lothian. *Midl* 3H 19
Mount Pleasant. *Fife* 2D 26
Mount Stuart. *Arg* 3E 17
Mouswald. *Dum* 1D 6
Mowhaugh. *Bord* 1H 13
Moy. *High* 5A 48
Moy Lodge. *High* 5F 39
Muasdale. *Arg* 4H 15
Muchalls. *Abers* 4E 43
Muchrachd. *High* 5D 46
Muckle Breck. *Shet* 6J 67
Mudale. *High* 5G 57
Mugdock. *Stir* 1A 18
Mugeary. *High* 5D 44
Muie. *High* 3D 54
Muirden. *Abers* 3C 50
Muirdrum. *Ang* 5C 34
Muiredge. *Per* 1D 26
Muirend. *Glas* 2A 18
Muirhead. *Ang* 5A 34
Muirhead. *Fife* 3D 26
Muirhead. *N Lan* 2B 18
Muirhouses. *Falk* 5B 26
Muirkirk. *E Ayr* 1D 10
Muir of Alford. *Abers* 2A 42
Muir of Fairburn. *High* 3F 47
Muir of Fowlis. *Abers* 2A 42
Muir of Miltonduff. *Mor* 3E 49
Muir of Ord. *High* 3G 47
Muir of Tarradale. *High* 3G 47
Muirshearlich. *High* 5C 38
Muirtack. *Abers* 5E 51
Muirton. *High* 2A 48
Muirton. *Per* 1C 26
Muirton of Ardblair. *Per* 4G 33
Muirtown. *Per* 2A 26
Muiryfold. *Abers* 3C 50
Mulben. *Mor* 3G 49
Mulindry. *Arg* 3E 15
Mulla. *Shet* 6H 67
Mullach Charlabhaigh. *W Isl* 3G 63
Munerigie. *High* 3D 38
Muness. *Shet* 2K 67
Mungasdale. *High* 4E 53
Mungrisdale. *Cumb* 5G 7
Munlochy. *High* 3H 47
Murieston. *W Lot* 2F 19
Murkle. *High* 2E 59
Murlaggan. *High* 4B 38
Murra. *Orkn* 4B 64
Murrayfield. *Edin* 1H 19
Murray, The. *S Lan* 3B 18
Murroes. *Ang* 5B 34
Murthly. *Per* 5F 33
Murton. *Nmbd* 4G 21
Musselburgh. *E Lot* 1A 20
Mutehill. *Dum* 4H 5
Muthill. *Per* 2H 25
Mybster. *High* 3E 59
Myrebird. *Abers* 4C 42
Myrelandhorn. *High* 3F 59

N

Naast. *High* 5D 52
Na Buirgh. *W Isl* 5B 62
Na Gearrannan. *W Isl* 3F 63
Nairn. *High* 3B 48
Navidale. *High* 2H 55
Nealhouse. *Cumb* 3G 7
Nedd. *High* 5C 56
Neilston. *E Ren* 3H 17
Nemphlar. *S Lan* 4D 18
Nenthorn. *Bord* 5D 20
Neribus. *Arg* 3D 14
Nerston. *S Lan* 3B 18
Nesbit. *Nmbd* 5G 21
Ness of Tenston. *Orkn* 3B 64
Nethanfoot. *S Lan* 4D 18
Nether Blainslie. *Bord* 4C 20
Netherbrae. *Abers* 3C 50
Netherbrough. *Orkn* 3C 64
Netherburn. *S Lan* 4D 18
Netherby. *Cumb* 1G 7
Nether Careston. *Ang* 3C 34
Nether Dallachy. *Mor* 2G 49
Nether Durdie. *Per* 1D 26
Nether Howcleugh. *Dum* 2H 11
Nether Kinmundy. *Abers* 4F 51
Netherlaw. *Dum* 4A 6
Netherley. *Abers* 4D 42
Nethermill. *Dum* 5H 11
Nethermills. *Mor* 3A 50
Netherplace. *E Ren* 3A 18
Netherthird. *E Ayr* 2C 10
Netherton. *Ang* 3C 34
Netherton. *Cumb* 5D 6
Netherton. *N Lan* 3C 18
Netherton. *Per* 3G 33
Netherton. *Stir* 1A 18
Nethertown. *High* 1G 59
Nether Urquhart. *Fife* 3C 26
Nether Welton. *Cumb* 4G 7
Nethy Bridge. *High* 1D 40
Neuk, The. *Abers* 4C 42
New Abbey. *Dum* 2C 6
New Aberdour. *Abers* 2D 50
New Alyth. *Per* 4H 33
Newark. *Orkn* 3K 65
Newarthill. *N Lan* 3C 18
Newbattle. *Midl* 2A 20
Newbie. *Dum* 2E 7
Newbiggin. *Cumb* 5H 7
Newbigging. *Ang* 5B 34 (nr. Monikie)
Newbigging. *Ang* 4H 33 (nr. Newtyle)
Newbigging. *Ang* 5B 34 (nr. Tealing)
Newbigging. *Edin* 1G 19
Newbigging. *S Lan* 4F 19
New Bridge. *Dum* 1C 6
Newbridge. *Edin* 1G 19
Newburgh. *Abers* 1E 43
Newburgh. *Fife* 2D 26
Newby East. *Cumb* 3H 7
New Byth. *Abers* 3D 50
Newby West. *Cumb* 3G 7
Newcastleton. *Bord* 5D 12
New Cowper. *Cumb* 4E 7
Newcraighall. *Edin* 1A 20
New Cumnock. *E Ayr* 2D 10
New Deer. *Abers* 4D 50
New Elgin. *Mor* 2F 49
New Galloway. *Dum* 1H 5
Newhaven. *Edin* 1H 19
Newhouse. *N Lan* 2C 18
Newington. *Edin* 1H 19
New Kelso. *High* 4A 46
New Lanark. *S Lan* 4D 18
Newlandrig. *Midl* 2A 20
Newlands. *Cumb* 5G 7
Newlands. *High* 4A 48
Newlands of Geise. *High* 2D 58
Newlands of Tynet. *Mor* 2G 49
New Langholm. *Dum* 5C 12
New Leeds. *Abers* 3E 51
Newlot. *Orkn* 3E 64
New Luce. *Dum* 2C 4
Newmachar. *Abers* 2D 42
Newmains. *N Lan* 3D 18
New Mains of Ury. *Abers* 5D 42
Newmarket. *W Isl* 4J 63
New Mill. *Abers* 4C 50
Newmill. *Mor* 3H 49
Newmill. *Bord* 2D 12
Newmills. *Fife* 5B 26
Newmills. *High* 2H 47
Newmiln. *Per* 5G 33
Newmilns. *E Ayr* 5A 18
Newmore. *High* 3G 47 (nr. Dingwall)
Newmore. *High* 1H 47 (nr. Invergordon)
Newpark. *Fife* 2F 27
New Pitsligo. *Abers* 3D 50
Newport-on-Tay. *Fife* 1F 27
New Prestwick. *S Ayr* 1A 10
New Rent. *Cumb* 5H 7
New Sauchie. *Clac* 4H 25
Newseat. *Abers* 5C 50
Newstead. *Bord* 5C 20
New Stevenston. *N Lan* 3C 18
Newton. *Arg* 4H 23
Newton. *Dum* 1F 7 (nr. Annan)
Newton. *Dum* 4A 12 (nr. Moffat)
Newton. *High* 2A 48 (nr. Cromarty)
Newton. *High* 4A 48 (nr. Inverness)
Newton. *High* 5D 56 (nr. Kylestrome)
Newton. *High* 4G 59 (nr. Wick)
Newton. *Mor* 2E 49
Newton. *Bord* 1F 13
Newton. *Shet* 3C 66
Newton. *S Lan* 2B 18 (nr. Glasgow)
Newton. *S Lan* 5E 19 (nr. Lanark)
Newton. *W Lot* 1F 19
Newtonairds. *Dum* 5F 11
Newton Arlosh. *Cumb* 3F 7
Newtongrange. *Midl* 2A 20
Newtonhill. *Abers* 4E 43
Newtonhill. *High* 4G 47
Newton Mearns. *E Ren* 3A 18
Newtonmore. *High* 4A 40
Newton of Ardtoe. *High* 1H 29
Newton of Balcanquhal. *Per* 2C 26
Newton of Beltrees. *Ren* 3G 17
Newton of Falkland. *Fife* 3D 26
Newton of Mountblairy. *Abers* 3C 50
Newton of Pitcairns. *Per* 2B 26
Newton Reigny. *Cumb* 5H 7
Newton Rigg. *Cumb* 5H 7
Newton Stewart. *Dum* 2F 5
Newton upon Ayr. *S Ayr* 1A 10
Newtown. *Abers* 2C 50
Newtown. *Cumb* 4D 6 (nr. Aspatria)
Newtown. *Cumb* 2H 7 (nr. Brampton)
New Town. *E Lot* 1B 20
Newtown. *Falk* 5A 26
Newtown. *High* 3E 39
Newtown. *Nmbd* 5H 21
Newtown. *Shet* 4H 67
Newtown St Boswells. *Bord* 5C 20
Newtyle. *Ang* 4H 33
New Winton. *E Lot* 1B 20
Niddrie. *Edin* 1H 19
Niddry. *Edin* 1F 19
Nigg. *Aber* 3E 43
Nigg. *High* 1B 48
Nigg Ferry. *High* 2A 48
Ninemile Bar. *Dum* 1B 6
Nine Mile Burn. *Midl* 3G 19
Nisbet. *Bord* 1F 13
Nisbet Hill. *Bord* 3E 21
Nitshill. *E Ren* 3A 18
Noness. *Shet* 4D 66
Nonikiln. *High* 1H 47
Nook. *Cumb* 1H 7
Noranside. *Ang* 2B 34
Norby. *Shet* 1A 66
Norham. *Nmbd* 4G 21
North Balfern. *Dum* 3F 5
North Ballachulish. *High* 2D 30
North Berwick. *E Lot* 5G 27
North Collafirth. *Shet* 4G 67
North Commonty. *Abers* 4D 50
North Craigo. *Ang* 2D 34
North Dronley. *Ang* 5A 34
Northdyke. *Orkn* 2B 64
North Erradale. *High* 5C 52
North Fearns. *High* 5E 45
North Feorline. *N Ayr* 1E 9
Northfield. *Aber* 3D 42
North Gluss. *Shet* 5G 67
North Hazelrigg. *Nmbd* 5H 21
North Kessock. *High* 4H 47
North Middleton. *Midl* 3A 20
Northmuir. *Ang* 3A 34
North Murie. *Per* 1D 26
North Ness. *Orkn* 5C 64
North Port. *Arg* 1H 23
North Queensferry. *Fife* 5C 26
North Roe. *Shet* 4G 67
North Ronaldsay Airport. *Orkn* 2K 65
North Row. *Cumb* 5F 7
North Sannox. *N Ayr* 4D 16
North Shian. *Arg* 4C 30
North Side. *Cumb* 5D 6
Northtown. *Orkn* 5D 64
North Town. *Shet* 5C 66
Northwall. *Orkn* 3K 65
North Water Bridge. *Ang* 2D 34
North Watten. *High* 3F 59
North Yardhope. *Nmbd* 3H 13
Norwick. *Shet* 1K 67
Noss. *Shet* 5C 66
Nostie. *High* 1H 37
Nunclose. *Cumb* 4H 7
Nunnerie. *S Lan* 2G 11
Nybster. *High* 2G 59

O

Oakbank. *Arg* 5A 30
Oakbank. *W Lot* 2F 19
Oakley. *Fife* 5B 26
Oakshaw Ford. *Cumb* 1H 7
Oape. *High* 3B 54
Oathlaw. *Ang* 3B 34
Oban. *Arg* 1F 23 & 84
Oban. *W Isl* 4C 62
Obsdale. *High* 2H 47
Ochiltree. *E Ayr* 1C 10
Ochtermuthill. *Per* 2H 25
Ochtertyre. *Per* 1H 25
Ockle. *High* 1G 29
Octofad. *Arg* 3D 14
Octomore. *Arg* 3D 14
Oddsta. *Shet* 3J 67
Odie. *Orkn* 5J 65
Okraquoy. *Shet* 3D 66
Old Aberdeen. *Aber* 3E 43
Oldany. *High* 5C 56
Old Blair. *Per* 2D 32
Old Bridge of Tilt. *Per* 2D 32
Old Bridge of Urr. *Dum* 2A 6
Old Dailly. *S Ayr* 4H 9
Old Deer. *Abers* 4E 51
Old Graitney. *Dum* 2G 7
Oldhall. *High* 3F 59
Oldhamstocks. *E Lot* 1E 21
Old Kilpatrick. *W Dun* 1H 17
Old Kinnernie. *Abers* 3C 42
Oldmeldrum. *Abers* 1D 42
Old Monkland. *N Lan* 2C 18
Old Pentland. *Midl* 2H 19
Old Philpstoun. *W Lot* 1F 19
Old Rayne. *Abers* 1B 42
Old Scone. *Per* 1C 26
Oldshore Beg. *High* 3C 56
Oldshoremore. *High* 3D 56
Old Town. *Cumb* 4H 7
Oldtown. *High* 5C 54
Old Town. *Nmbd* 4H 13
Oldtown of Ord. *Abers* 3B 50
Oldwall. *Cumb* 2H 7
Old Westhall. *Abers* 1B 42
Oldwhat. *Abers* 3D 50
Olgrinmore. *High* 3D 58
Ollaberry. *Shet* 4G 67
Olrig. *High* 2E 59
Omunsgarth. *Shet* 2C 66
Onich. *High* 2D 30
Onthank. *E Ayr* 5H 17
Opinan. *High* 1G 45 (nr. Gairloch)
Opinan. *High* 4D 52 (nr. Laide)
Orasaigh. *W Isl* 3E 62
Orbost. *High* 4B 44
Ord. *High* 2F 37
Ordale. *Shet* 2K 67
Ordhead. *Abers* 2B 42
Ordie. *Abers* 3H 41
Ordiquish. *Mor* 3G 49
Orgil. *Orkn* 4B 64
Ormacleit. *W Isl* 1C 60
Ormathwaite. *Cumb* 5F 7
Ormiscaig. *High* 4D 52
Ormiston. *E Lot* 2B 20
Ormsaigbeg. *High* 2F 29
Ormsaigmore. *High* 2F 29
Ormsary. *Arg* 1A 16
Orphir. *Orkn* 4C 64
Orthwaite. *Cumb* 5F 7
Orton. *Mor* 3G 49
Osclay. *High* 5F 59
Ose. *High* 4C 44
Oskaig. *High* 5E 45
Oskamull. *Arg* 4F 29
Osmondwall. *Orkn* 6C 64
Osnaburgh. *Fife* 2F 27
Ospisdale. *High* 5E 55
Otterburn. *Nmbd* 4H 13
Otterburn Camp. *Nmbd* 4H 13
Otterburn Hall. *Nmbd* 4H 13
Otter Ferry. *Arg* 5G 23
Otterswick. *Shet* 4J 67
Oughterby. *Cumb* 3F 7
Oughterside. *Cumb* 4E 7
Oulton. *Cumb* 3F 7
Ousdale. *High* 1H 55
Outertown. *Orkn* 3B 64
Overbister. *Orkn* 3J 65
Over Finlarg. *Ang* 4B 34
Overscaig. *High* 1B 54
Overton. *Aber* 2D 42
Overton. *High* 5F 59
Overtown. *N Lan* 3D 18
Oxgangs. *Edin* 2H 19
Oxnam. *Bord* 2G 13
Oxton. *Bord* 3B 20
Oykel Bridge. *High* 3A 54
Oyne. *Abers* 1B 42

P

Pabail Iarach. *W Isl* 4K 63
Pabail Uarach. *W Isl* 4K 63
Padanaram. *Ang* 3B 34
Paddockhole. *Dum* 5B 12
Paibeil. *W Isl* 4H 61 (on North Uist)
Paibeil. *W Isl* 5B 62 (on Taransay)
Paiblesgearraidh. *W Isl* 4H 61
Pairc Shiaboist. *W Isl* 3G 63
Paisley. *Ren* 2H 17 & 85
Palgowan. *Dum* 5A 10
Palnackie. *Dum* 3B 6
Palnure. *Dum* 2F 5
Panbride. *Ang* 5C 34
Pannanich. *Abers* 4G 41
Papa Stour Airport. *Shet* 1A 66
Papa Westray Airport. *Orkn* 2G 65
Papcastle. *Cumb* 5E 7
Papigoe. *High* 3G 59
Papil. *Shet* 3C 66
Papple. *E Lot* 1C 20
Park. *Abers* 4C 42
Park. *Arg* 4C 30
Park. *Dum* 4G 11
Parkburn. *Abers* 5C 50
Park End. *Nmbd* 5H 13
Parkgate. *Cumb* 4F 7
Parkgate. *Dum* 5H 11
Parkhall. *W Dun* 1H 17
Parkhead. *Cumb* 4G 7
Parkhead. *Glas* 2B 18
Parkneuk. *Abers* 1E 35
Parkside. *N Lan* 3D 18
Parsonby. *Cumb* 5E 7
Partick. *Glas* 2A 18
Parton. *Cumb* 3F 7
Parton. *Dum* 1H 5
Pathhead. *Abers* 2E 35
Pathhead. *E Ayr* 2D 10
Pathhead. *Fife* 4D 26
Pathhead. *Midl* 2A 20
Path of Condie. *Per* 2B 26
Pathstruie. *Per* 2B 26
Patna. *E Ayr* 2B 10
Pattiesmuir. *Fife* 5B 26
Pawston. *Nmbd* 5F 21
Paxton. *Bord* 3G 21
Pearsie. *Ang* 3A 34
Peaston. *E Lot* 2B 20
Peastonbank. *E Lot* 2B 20
Peathill. *Abers* 2E 51
Peat Inn. *Fife* 3F 27
Peaton. *Arg* 5B 24
Peebles. *Bord* 4H 19
Peel. *Bord* 5B 20
Peinchorran. *High* 5E 45
Peinlich. *High* 3D 44
Pelutho. *Cumb* 4E 7
Pencaitland. *E Lot* 2B 20
Penicuik. *Midl* 2H 19
Penifiler. *High* 4D 44
Peninver. *Arg* 1C 8
Penkill. *S Ayr* 4H 9
Pennan. *Abers* 2D 50
Pennyghael. *Arg* 1C 22
Pennyvenie. *E Ayr* 3B 10
Penpont. *Dum* 4F 11
Penrith. *Cumb* 5H 7
Penruddock. *Cumb* 5H 7
Penston. *E Lot* 1B 20
Perceton. *N Ayr* 4G 17
Percyhorner. *Abers* 2E 51
Perth. *Per* 1C 26 & 85
Peterburn. *High* 5C 52
Peterculter. *Aber* 3D 42
Peterhead. *Abers* 4G 51
Petertown. *Orkn* 4C 64
Pettinain. *S Lan* 4E 19
Pettycur. *Fife* 5D 26
Philiphaugh. *Bord* 1D 12
Philpstoun. *W Lot* 1F 19
Pickletillem. *Fife* 1F 27
Pierowall. *Orkn* 3G 65
Pilton. *Edin* 1H 19
Pinkerton. *E Lot* 1E 21
Pinmore. *S Ayr* 4H 9
Pinwherry. *S Ayr* 5G 9
Piperhill. *High* 3B 48
Pirnmill. *N Ayr* 4B 16
Pisgah. *Stir* 3G 25
Pitagowan. *Per* 2D 32
Pitcairn. *Per* 3D 32
Pitcairngreen. *Per* 1B 26
Pitcalnie. *High* 1B 48
Pitcaple. *Abers* 1C 42
Pitcox. *E Lot* 1D 20
Pitcur. *Per* 5H 33
Pitfichie. *Abers* 2B 42
Pitgrudy. *High* 4E 55
Pitkennedy. *Ang* 3C 34
Pitlessie. *Fife* 3E 27
Pitlochry. *Per* 3E 33
Pitmachie. *Abers* 1B 42
Pitmaduthy. *High* 1A 48
Pitmedden. *Abers* 1D 42
Pitnacree. *Per* 3E 33
Pitroddie. *Per* 1D 26
Pitscottie. *Fife* 2F 27
Pittentrail. *High* 3E 55
Pittenweem. *Fife* 3G 27
Pittulie. *Abers* 2E 51
Pitversie. *Per* 2C 26
Plaidy. *Abers* 3C 50
Plains. *N Lan* 2C 18
Plean. *Stir* 5H 25
Plockton. *High* 5H 45
Plocrapol. *W Isl* 5C 62
Plumbland. *Cumb* 5E 7
Plumpton. *Cumb* 5H 7
Plumpton Foot. *Cumb* 5H 7
Polbae. *Dum* 1D 4
Polbain. *High* 3F 53
Polbeth. *W Lot* 2F 19
Polchar. *High* 3B 40
Poles. *High* 4E 55
Polglass. *High* 3F 53
Polio. *High* 1A 48
Polla. *High* 3E 57
Polloch. *High* 2A 30
Pollok. *Glas* 2A 18
Pollokshaws. *Glas* 2A 18
Pollokshields. *Glas* 2A 18
Polmaily. *High* 5F 47
Polmont. *Falk* 1E 19
Polnessan. *E Ayr* 2B 10
Polnish. *High* 5G 37
Polskeoch. *Dum* 3D 10
Polton. *Midl* 2A 20
Polwarth. *Bord* 3E 21
Ponton. *Shet* 1C 66
Poolewe. *High* 5D 52
Pool o' Muckhart. *Clac* 3B 26
Porin. *High* 3E 47
Portachoillan. *Arg* 3A 16
Port Adhair Bheinn na Faoghla. *W Isl* 5H 61
Port Adhair Thirlodh. *Arg* 4B 28
Port Ann. *Arg* 5G 23
Port Appin. *Arg* 4C 30
Port Asgaig. *Arg* 2F 15
Port Askaig. *Arg* 2F 15
Portavadie. *Arg* 2C 16
Port Bannatyne. *Arg* 2D 16
Port Carlisle. *Cumb* 2F 7
Port Charlotte. *Arg* 3D 14
Port Driseach. *Arg* 1C 16
Port Dundas. *Glas* 2B 18
Port Ellen. *Arg* 4E 15
Port Elphinstone. *Abers* 1C 42
Portencalzie. *Dum* 1B 4
Portencross. *N Ayr* 4E 17
Port Erroll. *Abers* 5F 51
Portessie. *Mor* 2H 49
Port Glasgow. *Inv* 1G 17
Portgordon. *Mor* 2G 49
Portgower. *High* 2H 55
Porthalong. *High* 5C 44
Port Henderson. *High* 1G 45
Portincaple. *Arg* 4B 24
Portinnisherrich. *Arg* 2G 23
Portknockie. *Mor* 2H 49
Port Lamont. *Arg* 1D 16
Portlethen. *Abers* 4E 43
Portlethen Village. *Abers* 4E 43
Portling. *Dum* 3B 6
Port Logan. *Dum* 4B 4
Portmahomack. *High* 5G 55
Port Mholair. *W Isl* 4K 63
Port Mor. *High* 1F 29
Portnacroish. *Arg* 4C 30
Portnahaven. *Arg* 3C 14
Portnalong. *High* 5C 44
Portnaluchaig. *High* 5F 37
Portnancon. *High* 2F 57
Port Nan Giuran. *W Isl* 4K 63
Port nan Long. *W Isl* 3J 61
Port Nis. *W Isl* 1K 63
Portobello. *Edin* 1A 20
Port of Menteith. *Stir* 3E 25
Portormin. *High* 5E 59
Portpatrick. *Dum* 3B 4
Port Ramsay. *Arg* 4B 30
Portree. *High* 4D 44
Port Righ. *High* 4D 44
Portskerra. *High* 2B 58
Portsonachan. *Arg* 1H 23
Portsoy. *Abers* 2A 50
Porttannachy. *Mor* 2G 49
Portuairk. *High* 2F 29
Port Wemyss. *Arg* 3C 14
Port William. *Dum* 4E 5
Potarch. *Abers* 4B 42
Potterton. *Abers* 2E 43
Poundland. *S Ayr* 5G 9
Powfoot. *Dum* 2E 7
Powmill. *Per* 4B 26
Pressen. *Nmbd* 5F 21
Preston. *E Lot* 1C 20 (nr. East Linton)
Preston. *E Lot* 1A 20 (nr. Prestonpans)
Preston. *Bord* 3E 21
Prestonmill. *Dum* 3C 6
Prestonpans. *E Lot* 1A 20
Prestwick. *S Ayr* 1A 10
Priesthill. *Glas* 2A 18
Priestland. *E Ayr* 5A 18
Primsidemill. *Bord* 1H 13
Prior Muir. *Fife* 2G 27
Prospect. *Cumb* 4E 7
Provanmill. *Glas* 2B 18
Pulpit Hill. *Arg* 1F 23
Pumpherston. *W Lot* 2F 19

Q

Quarrier's Village. *Inv* 2G 17
Quarrywood. *Mor* 2E 49
Quartalehouse. *Abers* 4E 51
Quarter. *N Ayr* 2E 17
Quarter. *S Lan* 3C 18
Queenzieburn. *N Lan* 1B 18
Quendale. *Shet* 5C 66
Quholm. *Orkn* 3B 64
Quilquox. *Abers* 5E 51
Quindry. *Orkn* 5D 64
Quothquan. *S Lan* 5E 19

Quoyloo—Tarbrax

Quoyloo. *Orkn* 2B 64
Quoyness. *Orkn* 4B 64
Quoys. *Shet* 6H 67
(on Mainland)
Quoys. *Shet* 1K 67
(on Unst)

R

Raby. *Cumb* 3E 7
Rachan Mill. *Bord* 5G 19
Racks. *Dum* 1D 6
Rackwick. *Orkn* 5A 64
(on Hoy)
Rackwick. *Orkn* 3G 65
(on Westray)
Radernie. *Fife* 2F 27
Rafford. *Mor* 3D 48
Raggra. *High* 4G 59
Raigbeg. *High* 1B 40
Rait. *Per* 1D 26
Ralia. *High* 4A 40
Ramasaig. *High* 4A 44
Ramnageo. *Shet* 2K 67
Ramsburn. *Mor* 3A 50
Ramscraigs. *High* 5E 59
Ramstone. *Abers* 2B 42
Ranais. *W Isl* 5J 63
Ranfurly. *Ren* 2G 17
Rangag. *High* 4E 59
Rankinston. *E Ayr* 2B 10
Rannoch Station. *Per* 3H 31
Ranochan. *High* 5H 37
Raploch. *Stir* 4G 25
Rapness. *Orkn* 3H 65
Rascarrel. *Dum* 4A 6
Rashfield. *Arg* 5A 24
Ratagan. *High* 2A 38
Rathen. *Abers* 2F 51
Rathillet. *Fife* 1E 27
Ratho. *Edin* 1G 19
Ratho Station. *Edin* 1G 19
Rathven. *Mor* 2H 49
Rattar. *High* 1F 59
Ratten Row. *Cumb* 4G 7
Rattray. *Abers* 3F 51
Rattray. *Per* 4G 33
Raughton. *Cumb* 4G 7
Raughton Head. *Cumb* 4G 7
Ravenstruther. *S Lan* 4E 19
Rearquhar. *High* 4E 55
Reaster. *High* 2F 59
Reawick. *Shet* 2C 66
Reay. *High* 2C 58
Rechullin. *High* 3H 45
Redburn. *High* 4C 48
Redcastle. *High* 4G 47
Red Dial. *Cumb* 4F 7
Redding. *Falk* 1E 19
Reddingmuirhead. *Falk* 1E 19
Redesdale Camp.
Nmbd 4H 13
Redesmouth. *Nmbd* 5H 13
Redford. *Ang* 4C 34
Redfordgreen. *Bord* 2C 12
Redhill. *Abers* 3C 42
Redhouses. *Arg* 2E 15
Redland. *Orkn* 2C 64
Redmain. *Cumb* 5E 7
Redpath. *Bord* 5C 20
Redpoint. *High* 2G 45
Reemshill. *Abers* 4C 50
Regoul. *High* 3B 48
Reiff. *High* 2E 53
Reinigeadal. *W Isl* 4D 62
Reisque. *Abers* 1D 42
Reiss. *High* 3G 59
Relugas. *Mor* 4C 48
Renfrew. *Ren* 2A 18
Renton. *W Dun* 1G 17
Resaurie. *High* 4A 48
Rescobie. *Ang* 3C 34
Resipole. *High* 2A 30
Resolis. *High* 2H 47
Rest and be thankful. *Arg* 3B 24
Reston. *Bord* 2F 21
Rheindown. *High* 4G 47
Rhemore. *High* 3G 29
Rhenetra. *High* 3D 44
Rhian. *High* 2C 54
Rhian Breck. *High* 3C 54
Rhicarn. *High* 1F 53
Rhiconich. *High* 3D 56
Rhicullen. *High* 1H 47
Rhidorroch. *High* 4G 53
Rhifail. *High* 4A 58
Rhilochan. *High* 3E 55
Rhiroy. *High* 5G 53
Rhitongue. *High* 3H 57
Rhonehouse. *Dum* 3A 6
Rhu. *Arg* 5B 24
Rhubadach. *Arg* 1D 16
Rhubha Stoer. *High* 5B 56
Rhue. *High* 4F 53
Rhunahaorine. *Arg* 4A 16
Rhuvoult. *High* 3D 56
Rhynd. *Per* 1C 26
Rhynie. *Abers* 1H 41
Ribigill. *High* 3G 57
Riccarton. *E Ayr* 5H 17
Rickarton. *Abers* 5D 42
Rickerby. *Cumb* 3H 7
Ridsdale. *Nmbd* 5H 13
Riemore Lodge. *Per* 4F 33
Rigg. *Dum* 2F 7
Riggend. *N Lan* 1C 18
Rigside. *S Lan* 5D 18
Rimsdale. *High* 4A 58
Ringasta. *Shet* 5C 66
Ringford. *Dum* 3H 5
Rinmore. *Abers* 2H 41
Rinnigill. *Orkn* 5C 64
Riof. *W Isl* 1C 62
Rireavach. *High* 4F 53
Risabus. *Arg* 4E 15
Rispond. *High* 2F 57
Roadhead. *Cumb* 1H 7
Roadmeetings. *S Lan* 4D 18
Roadside. *High* 2E 59
Roadside of Catterline.
Abers 1F 35
Roadside of Kinneff. *Abers* 1F 35
Roag. *High* 4B 44
Roberton. *Bord* 2D 12
Roberton. *S Lan* 1G 11
Robertstown. *Mor* 4F 49
Rob Roy's House. *Arg* 2A 24
Rochester. *Nmbd* 4H 13
Rockcliffe. *Cumb* 2G 7
Rockcliffe. *Dum* 3B 6
Rockcliffe Cross. *Cumb* 2G 7
Rockfield. *High* 5G 55
Roddenloft. *E Ayr* 1B 10
Rodel. *W Isl* 6B 62
Roesound. *Shet* 6G 67
Rogart. *High* 3E 55
Roman Camp. *W Lot* 1F 19
Romannobridge. *Bord* 4G 19
Romesdal. *High* 3D 44
Ronaldsvoe. *Orkn* 5D 64
Rootfield. *High* 3G 47
Rootpark. *S Lan* 3E 19
Rora. *Abers* 3F 51
Rorandle. *Abers* 2B 42
Rosebank. *S Lan* 4D 18
Rosehall. *High* 3B 54
Rosehearty. *Abers* 2E 51
Roseisle. *Mor* 2E 49
Rosemarkie. *High* 3A 48
Rosemount. *Per* 4G 33
Rosewell. *Midl* 2H 19
Roshven. *High* 1A 30
Roskhill. *High* 4B 44
Rosley. *Cumb* 4G 7
Roslin. *Midl* 2H 19
Rosneath. *Arg* 5B 24
Ross. *Dum* 4H 5
Ross. *Per* 1G 25
Ross. *Bord* 2G 21
Rosskeen. *High* 2H 47
Rossland. *Ren* 1H 17
Roster. *High* 4F 59
Rosyth. *Fife* 5C 26
Rothes. *Mor* 4F 49
Rothesay. *Arg* 2D 16
Rothienorman. *Abers* 5C 50
Rothiesholm. *Orkn* 5J 65
Rottal. *Ang* 2A 34
Rough Haugh. *High* 4A 58
Roughsike. *Cumb* 1H 7
Roundyhill. *Ang* 3A 34
Rowanburn. *Dum* 1H 7
Rowanhill. *Abers* 3F 51
Rowardennan. *Stir* 4C 24
Roxburgh. *Bord* 5E 21
Roybridge. *High* 5D 38
Ruaig. *Arg* 4B 28
Ruarach. *High* 1A 38
Ruchazie. *Glas* 2B 18
Ruglen. *S Ayr* 3H 9
Ruilick. *High* 4G 47
Ruisaurie. *High* 4F 47
Ruisigearraidh. *W Isl* 2K 61
Rumbling Bridge. *Per* 4B 26
Rumford. *Falk* 1E 19
Runtaleave. *Ang* 2H 33
Ruskie. *Stir* 3F 25
Russland. *Orkn* 3C 64
Rutherglen. *S Lan* 2B 18
Ruthrieston. *Aber* 3E 43
Ruthven. *Abers* 4A 50
Ruthven. *Ang* 4H 33
Ruthven. *High* 5B 48
(nr. Inverness)
Ruthven. *High* 4A 40
(nr. Kingussie)
Ruthwaite. *Cumb* 5F 7
Ruthwell. *Dum* 2E 7
Rychraggan. *High* 5F 47

S

Saasaig. *High* 3F 37
Saddell. *Arg* 5A 16
Saighdinis. *W Isl* 4J 61
St Abbs. *Bord* 2G 21
St Andrews. *Fife* 2G 27 & 86
St Ann's. *Dum* 4H 11
St Boswells. *Bord* 5D 20
St Catherines. *Arg* 3A 24
St Colmac. *Arg* 2D 16
St Combs. *Abers* 2F 51
St Cyrus. *Abers* 2E 35
St David's. *Per* 1A 26
St Fergus. *Abers* 3F 51
St Fillans. *Per* 1F 25
St Helens. *Cumb* 5D 6
St John's Town of Dalry.
Dum 5D 10
St Katherines. *Abers* 5C 50
St Madoes. *Per* 1C 26
St Margaret's Hope. *Orkn* 5D 64
St Martins. *Per* 5G 33
St Mary's. *Orkn* 4D 64
St Monans. *Fife* 3G 27
St Ninians. *Stir* 4H 25
St Quivox. *S Ayr* 1A 10
St Vigeans. *Ang* 4D 34
Salen. *Arg* 4G 29
Salen. *High* 2H 29
Saligo. *Arg* 2D 14
Saline. *Fife* 4B 26
Sallachan. *High* 2C 30
Sallachy. *High* 3C 54
(nr. Lairg)
Sallachy. *High* 5A 46
(nr. Stromeferry)
Salmond's Muir. *Ang* 5C 34
Salsburgh. *N Lan* 2D 18
Salta. *Cumb* 4D 6
Saltburn. *High* 2A 48
Saltcoats. *N Ayr* 4F 17
Saltness. *Orkn* 6B 64
Saltness. *Shet* 2B 66
Salum. *Arg* 4B 28
Samalaman. *High* 1H 29
Samhia. *W Isl* 4H 61
Samsonlane. *Orkn* 5J 65
Samuelston. *E Lot* 1B 20
Sanaigmore. *Arg* 1D 14
Sand. *High* 4E 53
Sand. *Shet* 2C 66
Sandaig. *Arg* 4A 28
Sandaig. *High* 3G 37
Sandale. *Cumb* 4F 7
Sandavore. *High* 5D 36
Sanday Airport. *Orkn* 3J 65
Sandbank. *Arg* 5A 24
Sandend. *Abers* 2A 50
Sandford. *S Lan* 4C 18
Sandfordhill. *Abers* 4G 51
Sandgreen. *Dum* 3G 5
Sandhaven. *Abers* 2E 51
Sandhead. *Dum* 3B 4
Sandness. *Shet* 1A 66
Sandsound. *Shet* 2C 66
Sandvoe. *Shet* 3G 67
Sandwick. *Orkn* 3B 64
(on Mainland)
Sandwick. *Orkn* 6D 64
(on South Ronaldsay)
Sandwick. *Shet* 4D 66
(on Mainland)
Sandwick. *Shet* 5G 67
(on Whalsay)
Sandyhills. *Dum* 3B 6
Sandystones. *Bord* 1E 13
Sangobeg. *High* 2F 57
Sangomore. *High* 2F 57
Sanna. *High* 2F 29
Sanndabhaig. *W Isl* 4J 63
(on Isle of Lewis)
Sanndabhaig. *W Isl* 6J 61
(on South Uist)
Sannox. *N Ayr* 4D 16
Sanquhar. *Dum* 2E 11
Sarclet. *High* 4G 59
Sauchen. *Abers* 2B 42
Saucher. *Per* 5G 33
Saughtree. *Bord* 4E 13
Saval. *High* 3C 54
Scadabhagh. *W Isl* 5C 62
Scaladal. *W Isl* 3C 62
Scalasaig. *Arg* 4A 22
Scaleby. *Cumb* 2H 7
Scaleby Hill. *Cumb* 2H 7
Scales. *Cumb* 5G 7
Scalloway. *Shet* 3C 66
Scalpaigh. *W Isl* 5D 62
Scalpay House. *High* 1F 37
Scamodale. *High* 1B 30
Scaniport. *High* 5H 47
Scapa. *Orkn* 4D 64
Scar. *Orkn* 3J 65
Scarasta. *W Isl* 5B 62
Scardroy. *High* 3D 46
Scarfskerry. *High* 1F 59
Scarinish. *Arg* 4B 28
Scarvister. *Shet* 2C 66
Scatness. *Shet* 6C 66
Scatwell. *High* 3E 47
Scaur. *Dum* 3B 6
Scolpaig. *W Isl* 3H 61
Scone. *Per* 1C 26
Sconser. *High* 5E 45
Scoonie. *Fife* 3E 27
Scoraig. *High* 4F 53
Scotbheinn. *W Isl* 5J 61
Scotby. *Cumb* 3H 7
Scotlandwell. *Per* 3C 26
Scotsburn. *High* 1A 48
Scotsburn. *Mor* 2F 49
Scotsdike. *Cumb* 1G 7
Scotstoun. *Glas* 2A 18
Scotstown. *High* 2B 30
Scottas. *High* 3G 37
Scourie. *High* 4C 56
Scourie More. *High* 4C 56
Scousburgh. *Shet* 5C 66
Scrabster. *High* 1D 58
Scremerston. *Nmbd* 4H 21
Scuggate. *Cumb* 1H 7
Sculamus. *High* 1F 37
Seafield. *High* 5G 55
Seafield. *Midl* 2H 19
Seafield. *S Ayr* 1A 10
Seafield. *W Lot* 2F 19
Seamill. *N Ayr* 4E 17
Seaside. *Per* 1D 26
Seater. *High* 1G 59
Seaton. *Cumb* 5D 6
Seatown. *Abers* 2A 50
Seatown. *Mor* 2A 50
(nr. Cullen)
Seatown. *Mor* 1F 49
(nr. Lossiemouth)
Seaville. *Cumb* 3E 7
Sebergham. *Cumb* 4G 7
Second Coast. *High* 4E 53
Sefster. *Shet* 1C 66
Seggat. *Abers* 4C 50
Seilebost. *W Isl* 5B 62
Seisiadar. *W Isl* 4K 63
Selkirk. *Bord* 1D 12
Sellafirth. *Shet* 3J 67
Semblister. *Shet* 1C 66
Setter. *Shet* 4H 67
Settiscarth. *Orkn* 3C 64
Sgallairidh. *W Isl* 5B 60
Sgarasta Mhor. *W Isl* 5B 62
Sgiogarstaigh. *W Isl* 1K 63
Sgreadan. *Arg* 4A 22
Shandon. *Arg* 5B 24
Shandwick. *High* 1B 48
Shawhead. *Dum* 1B 6
Shawwood. *E Ayr* 1C 10
Shearington. *Dum* 2D 6
Shebster. *High* 2D 58
Sheddocksley. *Aber* 3D 42
Shedog. *N Ayr* 5C 16
Sheigra. *High* 2C 56
Shennanton. *Dum* 2E 5
Shenval. *Mor* 1F 41
Sheppardstown. *High* 4E 59
Sheriffston. *Mor* 2F 49
Shettleston. *Glas* 2B 18
Shiel Bridge. *High* 2A 38
Shieldaig. *High* 1H 45
(nr. Charlestown)
Shieldaig. *High* 3H 45
(nr. Torridon)
Shieldhill. *Dum* 5H 11
Shieldhill. *Falk* 1D 18
Shieldhill. *S Lan* 4F 19
Shieldmuir. *N Lan* 3C 18
Shielfoot. *High* 2H 29
Shielhill. *Abers* 3F 51
Shielhill. *Ang* 3B 34
Shillford. *E Ren* 3H 17
Shillmoor. *Nmbd* 3H 13
Shinness. *High* 2C 54
Shires Mill. *Fife* 5A 26
Shiskine. *N Ayr* 1E 9
Shoresdean. *Nmbd* 4G 21
Shoreswood. *Nmbd* 4G 21
Shore, The. *Fife* 2D 26
Shotton. *Nmbd* 5F 21
Shotts. *N Lan* 2D 18
Shulishadermor. *High* 4D 44
Shulista. *High* 1D 44
Shurrery. *High* 3D 58
Siabost. *W Isl* 3G 63
Siabost bho Dheas. *W Isl* 3G 63
Siabost bho Thuath. *W Isl* 3G 63
Siadar. *W Isl* 2H 63
Siadar Uarach. *W Isl* 2H 63
Sibbaldbie. *Dum* 5A 12
Sibster. *High* 3G 59
Siddick. *Cumb* 5D 6
Sighthill. *Edin* 1G 19
Sildinis. *W Isl* 3D 62
Silloth. *Cumb* 3E 7
Sills. *Nmbd* 3H 13
Sillyearn. *Mor* 3A 50
Silverbank. *Abers* 4C 42
Silverburn. *Midl* 2H 19
Silverhillocks. *Abers* 2C 50
Silverton. *W Dun* 1H 17
Simprim. *Bord* 4F 21
Sinclairston. *E Ayr* 2B 10
Sinclairtown. *Fife* 4D 26
Sinnahard. *Abers* 2H 41
Skail. *High* 4A 58
Skaill. *Orkn* 3B 64
Skaills. *Orkn* 4E 64
Skares. *E Ayr* 2C 10
Skateraw. *E Lot* 1E 21
Skaw. *Shet* 6J 67
Skeabost. *High* 4D 44
Skeabrae. *Orkn* 2B 64
Skelberry. *Shet* 5C 66
(nr. Boddam)
Skelberry. *Shet* 4G 67
(nr. Housetter)
Skelbo. *High* 4E 55
Skelbo Street. *High* 4E 55
Skelfhill. *Bord* 3D 12
Skellister. *Shet* 1D 66
Skelmorlie. *N Ayr* 2E 17
Skelpick. *High* 3A 58
Skelton. *Cumb* 5H 7
Skelwick. *Orkn* 3G 65
Skeroblingarry. *Arg* 1C 8
Skerray. *High* 2H 57
Skerricha. *High* 3D 56
Skerries Airport. *Shet* 5K 67
Skiall. *High* 2D 58
Skinburness. *Cumb* 3E 7
Skinflats. *Falk* 5A 26
Skinidin. *High* 4B 44
Skinnet. *High* 2G 57
Skipness. *Arg* 3B 16
Skiprigg. *Cumb* 4G 7
Skirling. *Bord* 5F 19
Skirza. *High* 2G 59
Skitby. *Cumb* 2H 7
Skroo. *Shet* 1J 65
Skulamus. *High* 1F 37
Skullomie. *High* 2H 57
Skye of Curr. *High* 1C 40
Slackhead. *Mor* 2H 49
Slacks of Cairnbanno.
Abers 4D 50
Slamannan. *Falk* 1D 18
Slickly. *High* 2F 59
Sliddery. *N Ayr* 1E 9
Sligachan. *High* 1D 36
Slochd. *High* 1B 40
Slockavullin. *Arg* 4F 23
Sluggan. *High* 1B 40
Smailholm. *Bord* 5D 20
Smallholm. *E Ayr* 1D 10
Smallholm. *Dum* 1E 7
Smerclett. *W Isl* 3C 60
Smerral. *High* 5E 59
Smirisary. *High* 1H 29
Smithfield. *Cumb* 2H 7
Smithstown. *High* 1G 45
Smithton. *High* 4A 48
Smoogro. *Orkn* 4C 64
Snaigow House. *Per* 4F 33
Sniseabhal. *W Isl* 1C 60
Sockbridge. *Cumb* 5H 7
Sodom. *Shet* 6J 67
Solas. *W Isl* 3J 61
Sorbie. *Dum* 4F 5
Sordale. *High* 2E 59
Sorisdale. *Arg* 2D 28
Sorn. *E Ayr* 1C 10
Sornhill. *E Ayr* 5A 18
Sortat. *High* 2F 59
Soulby. *Cumb* 5H 7
Sound. *Shet* 2D 66
(nr. Lerwick)
Sound. *Shet* 1C 66
(nr. Tresta)
Sourhope. *Bord* 1H 13
Sourin. *Orkn* 1D 64
Sour Nook. *Cumb* 4G 7
South Alloa. *Falk* 4H 25
Southannan. *N Ayr* 3F 17
South Balfern. *Dum* 3F 5
South Ballachulish. *High* 3D 30
South Broomage. *Falk* 5H 25
South Clunes. *High* 4G 47
South Creagan. *Arg* 4C 30
Southdean. *Bord* 3F 13
Southend. *Arg* 3B 8
Southerfield. *Cumb* 4E 7
Southerhouse. *Shet* 3C 66
Southerness. *Dum* 3C 6
South Erradale. *High* 1G 45
South Feorline. *N Ayr* 1E 9
South Garvan. *High* 1C 30
South Gluss. *Shet* 5G 67
South Hazelrigg. *Nmbd* 5H 21
South Kessock. *High* 4H 47
South Kirkton. *Abers* 3C 42
South Ledaig. *Arg* 5C 30
South Newton. *N Ayr* 3C 16
South Port. *Arg* 1H 23
Southpunds. *Shet* 5D 66
South Queensferry.
Edin 1G 19
Southside. *Orkn* 2E 64
Southtown. *Orkn* 5D 64
South View. *Shet* 2C 66
Southwaite. *Cumb* 4H 7
Soval Lodge. *W Isl* 2E 62
Sowerby Row. *Cumb* 4G 7
Soyal. *High* 4C 54
Sparket. *Cumb* 5H 7
Spean Bridge. *High* 5D 38
Speybank. *High* 3B 40
Spey Bay. *Mor* 2G 49
Speybridge. *High* 1D 40
Speyview. *Mor* 4F 49
Spinningdale. *High* 5D 54
Spittal. *Dum* 3E 5
Spittal. *E Lot* 1B 20
Spittal. *High* 3E 59
Spittal. *Nmbd* 3H 21
Spittalfield. *Per* 4G 33
Spittal of Glenmuick. *Abers* 5G 41
Spittal of Glenshee. *Per* 1G 33
Spittal-on-Rule. *Bord* 1E 13
Spott. *E Lot* 1D 20
Springburn. *Glas* 2B 18
Springfield. *Dum* 2G 7
Springfield. *Fife* 2E 27
Springfield. *High* 2H 47
Springholm. *Dum* 1B 6
Springside. *N Ayr* 5G 17
Sprouston. *Bord* 5E 21
Sprunston. *Cumb* 4G 7
Sraid Ruadh. *Arg* 4A 28
Srannda. *W Isl* 6B 62
Sron an t-Sithein. *High* 2B 30
Sronphadruig Lodge. *Per* 1C 32
Sruth Mor. *W Isl* 4K 61
Stadhlaigearraidh. *W Isl* 1C 60
Stafainn. *High* 2D 44
Staffin. *High* 2D 44
Stainburn. *Cumb* 5D 6
Stainton. *Cumb* 3G 7
(nr. Carlisle)
Stainton. *Cumb* 5H 7
(nr. Penrith)
Stair. *E Ayr* 1B 10
Stairhaven. *Dum* 3D 4
Stamperland. *E Ren* 3A 18
Stand. *N Lan* 2C 18
Standburn. *Falk* 1E 19
Standingstone. *Cumb* 4F 7
Stane. *N Lan* 3D 18
Stanecastle. *N Ayr* 5G 17
Stanhope. *Bord* 5G 19
Stanley. *Per* 5G 33
Stannersburn. *Nmbd* 5G 13
Stanydale. *Shet* 1B 66
Staoinebrig. *W Isl* 1C 60
Stapleton. *Cumb* 1H 7
Star. *Fife* 3E 27
Staxigoe. *High* 3G 59
Steelend. *Fife* 4B 26
Steele Road. *Bord* 4E 13
Stein. *High* 3B 44
Steinmanhill. *Abers* 4C 50
Stemster. *High* 2E 59
(nr. Halkirk)
Stemster. *High* 2D 58
(nr. Westfield)
Stenhouse. *Edin* 1H 19
Stenhousemuir. *Falk* 5H 25
Stenscholl. *High* 2D 44
Stenso. *Orkn* 2C 64
Stenton. *E Lot* 1D 20
Steòrnabhagh. *W Isl* 4J 63
Stepford. *Dum* 5F 11
Stepps. *N Lan* 2B 18
Stevenston. *N Ayr* 4F 17
Stewarton. *Arg* 2B 8
Stewarton. *E Ayr* 4H 17
Stichill. *Bord* 5E 21
Stirling. *Abers* 4G 51
Stirling. *Stir* 4G 25 & 87
Stittenham. *High* 1H 47
Stobo. *Bord* 5G 19
Stobo Castle. *Bord* 5G 19
Stobs Castle. *Bord* 3E 13
Stockdalewath. *Cumb* 4G 7
Stoer. *High* 1F 53
Stonebyres. *S Lan* 4D 18
Stonefield. *Arg* 5C 30
Stonefield. *S Lan* 3B 18
Stonehaugh. *Nmbd* 5G 13
Stonehaven. *Abers* 5D 42
Stonehouse. *S Lan* 4C 18
Stoneyburn. *W Lot* 2E 19
Stoneykirk. *Dum* 3B 4
Stoneywood. *Aber* 2D 42
Stonybreck. *Shet* 1J 65
Stormontfield. *Per* 1C 26
Stornoway. *W Isl* 4J 63
Stornoway Airport. *W Isl* 4J 63
Stotfield. *Mor* 1F 49
Stoul. *High* 4G 37
Stove. *Orkn* 4J 65
Stove. *Shet* 4D 66
Stow. *Bord* 4B 20
Straad. *Arg* 2D 16
Strachan. *Abers* 4B 42
Straid. *S Ayr* 4G 9
Straiton. *Edin* 2H 19
Straiton. *S Ayr* 3A 10
Straloch. *Per* 2F 33
Stranraer. *Dum* 2B 4
Strath. *High* 1G 45
(nr. Gairloch)
Strath. *High* 3F 59
(nr. Wick)
Strathan. *High* 4A 38
(nr. Fort William)
Strathan. *High* 1F 53
(nr. Lochinver)
Strathan. *High* 2G 57
(nr. Tongue)
Strathan Skerray. *High* 2H 57
Strathaven. *S Lan* 4C 18
Strathblane. *Stir* 1A 18
Strathcanaird. *High* 3G 53
Strathcarron. *High* 4A 46
Strathcoil. *Arg* 5H 29
Strathdon. *Abers* 2G 41
Strathkinness. *Fife* 2F 27
Strathmashie House. *High* 4G 39
Strathmiglo. *Fife* 2D 26
Strathmore Lodge. *High* 4E 59
Strathpeffer. *High* 3F 47
Strathrannoch. *High* 1E 47
Strathtay. *Per* 3E 33
Strathvaich Lodge. *High* 1E 47
Strathwhillan. *N Ayr* 5D 16
Strathy. *High* 1H 47
(nr. Invergordon)
Strathy. *High* 2B 58
(nr. Melvich)
Strathyre. *Stir* 2E 25
Stravithie. *Fife* 2G 27
Strichen. *Abers* 3E 51
Stroanfreggan. *Dum* 4D 10
Stromeferry. *High* 5H 45
Stromemore. *High* 5H 45
Stromness. *Orkn* 4B 64
Stronachie. *Per* 3B 26
Stronachlachar. *Stir* 2D 24
Stronchreggan. *High* 1D 30
Strone. *Arg* 5A 24
Strone. *High* 1G 39
(nr. Drumnadrochit)
Strone. *High* 3A 40
(nr. Kingussie)
Stronenaba. *High* 5D 38
Stronganess. *Shet* 2J 67
Stronmilchan. *Arg* 1A 24
Stronsay Airport. *Orkn* 5J 65
Strontian. *High* 2B 30
Struan. *High* 5C 44
Struan. *Per* 2D 32
Struanmore. *High* 5C 44
Strutherhill. *S Lan* 3C 18
Struy. *High* 5E 47
Stuartfield. *Abers* 4E 51
Suainebost. *W Isl* 1K 63
Suardail. *W Isl* 4J 63
Succoth. *Abers* 5H 49
Succoth. *Arg* 3B 24
Suisnish. *High* 5E 45
Sulaisiadar. *W Isl* 4K 63
Sùlaisiadar Mòr. *High* 4D 44
Sullom. *Shet* 5G 67
Sumburgh. *Shet* 6D 66
Sumburgh Airport. *Shet* 6C 66
Summerhill. *Aber* 3E 43
Sunderland. *Cumb* 5E 7
Sunnylaw. *Stir* 4G 25
Sutors of Cromarty. *High* 2B 48
Swanbister. *Orkn* 4C 64
Swarister. *Shet* 4J 67
Swiney. *High* 5F 59
Swinhill. *S Lan* 4C 18
Swinister. *Shet* 4G 67
Swinside Hall. *Bord* 2G 13
Swinton. *Bord* 4F 21
Swordale. *High* 2G 47
Swordly. *High* 2A 58
Symbister. *Shet* 6J 67
Symington. *S Ayr* 5G 17
Symington. *S Lan* 5E 19
Syre. *High* 4H 57

T

Tabost. *W Isl* 3E 62
(nr. Cearsiadar)
Tabost. *W Isl* 1K 63
(nr. Suainebost)
Tacleit. *W Isl* 1C 62
Taigh a Ghearraidh. *W Isl* 3H 61
Taigh Bhuirgh. *W Isl* 5B 62
Tain. *High* 5E 55
(nr. Invergordon)
Tain. *High* 2F 59
(nr. Thurso)
Tairbeart. *W Isl* 5C 62
Talisker. *High* 5C 44
Talladale. *High* 1A 46
Talla Linnfoots. *Bord* 1A 12
Tallaminnock. *S Ayr* 4B 10
Tallentire. *Cumb* 5E 7
Talmine. *High* 2G 57
Tandlehill. *Ren* 2H 17
Tangasdale. *W Isl* 4B 60
Tangwick. *Shet* 5F 67
Tankerness. *Orkn* 4E 64
Tannach. *High* 4G 59
Tannadice. *Ang* 3B 34
Tannochside. *N Lan* 2C 18
Taobh a Chaolais. *W Isl* 3C 60
Taobh a Deas Loch Aineort.
W Isl 2C 60
Taobh a Ghlinne. *W Isl* 3E 62
Taobh a Tuath Loch Aineort.
W Isl 2C 60
Tarbert. *Arg* 5D 22
(on Jura)
Tarbert. *Arg* 2B 16
(on Kintyre)
Tarbert. *W Isl* 5C 62
Tarbet. *Arg* 3C 24
Tarbet. *High* 4G 37
(nr. Mallaig)
Tarbet. *High* 4C 56
(nr. Scourie)
Tarbolton. *S Ayr* 1B 10
Tarbrax. *S Lan* 3F 19

Tarfside—Ythanwells

Tarfside. Ang 1B 34
Tarland. Abers 3H 41
Tarlogie. High 5E 55
Tarns. Cumb 4E 7
Tarrel. High 5F 55
Tarsappie. Per 1C 26
Tarscabhaig. High 3E 37
Tarskavaig. High 3E 37
Tarves. Abers 5D 50
Tarvie. High 3F 47
Tavool House. Arg 1B 22
Tayinloan. Arg 4H 15
Taynish. Arg 5E 23
Taynuilt. Arg 5D 30
Tayport. Fife 1F 27
Tay Road Bridge. Fife 1F 27
Tayvallich. Arg 5E 23
Tealing. Ang 5B 34
Teangue. High 3F 37
Teanna Machair. W Isl 4H 61
Tempar. Per 3B 32
Templand. Dum 5H 11
Temple. Glas 2A 18
Temple. Midl 3A 20
Templehall. Fife 4D 26
Tenandry. Per 2E 33
Tenga. Arg 4G 29
Terregles. Dum 1C 6
Teviothead. Bord 3D 12
Tewel. Abers 5D 42
Thackthwaite. Cumb 5H 7
Thankerton. S Lan 5E 19
Thethwaite. Cumb 4G 7
Thirlestane. Bord 4C 20
Thomas Close. Cumb 4H 7
Thomastown. Abers 4C 50
Thomshill. Mor 3F 49
Thornby. Cumb 3F 7
Thornhill. Dum 4F 11
Thornhill. Stir 4F 25
Thornington. Nmbd 5F 21
Thornliebank. E Ren 3A 18
Thornroan. Abers 5D 50
Thornthwaite. Cumb 5F 7
Thornton. Ang 4A 34
Thornton. Fife 4D 26
Thornton. Nmbd 4G 21
Thorntonhall. S Lan 3A 18
Thorntonloch. E Lot 1E 21
Thrashbush. N Lan 2C 18
Threapland. Cumb 5E 7
Threlkeld. Cumb 5G 7
Throsk. Stir 4H 25
Throughgate. Dum 5F 11
Thrumster. High 4G 59
Thundergay. N Ayr 4B 16
Thursby. Cumb 3G 7
Thurso. High 2E 59
Thurso East. High 2E 59
Thurstonfield. Cumb 3G 7
Tibbermore. Per 1B 26
Tifty. Abers 4C 50
Tigerton. Ang 2C 34
Tighnabruaich. Arg 1C 16
Tillathrowie. Abers 5H 49
Tillery. Abers 1E 43
Tillicoultry. Clac 4A 26
Tillybirloch. Abers 3B 42
Tillyfourie. Abers 2B 42
Timsgearraidh. W Isl 1B 62
Tingwall. Orkn 2D 64
Tinwald. Dum 5H 11
Tipperty. Abers 1E 43
Tiree Airport. Arg 4B 28
Tirinie. Per 2D 32
Tiroran. Arg 1B 22
Tirril. Cumb 5H 7
Tirryside. High 2C 54
Toab. Orkn 4E 64
Toab. Shet 5C 66
Tobermory. Arg 3G 29
Toberonochy. Arg 3E 23
Tobha-Beag. W Isl 3K 61
(on North Uist)
Tobha Beag. W Isl 1C 60
(on South Uist)
Tobha Mor. W Isl 1C 60
Tobhtarol. W Isl 1C 62
Tobson. W Isl 1C 62
Tocabhaig. High 2F 37
Tocher. Abers 5B 50
Todhills. Cumb 2G 7
Tofts. High 2G 59
Tokavaig. High 2F 37
Tolastadh a Chaolais. W Isl 1C 62
Tollie. High 3G 47
Tollie Farm. High 1H 45
Tolm. W Isl 4J 63
Tolstadh bho Thuath. W Isl 3K 63
Tomachlaggan. Mor 1E 41
Tomaknock. Per 1H 25
Tomatin. High 1B 40
Tombuidhe. Arg 3H 23
Tomdoun. High 3C 38
Tomich. High 1E 39
(nr. Cannich)
Tomich. High 1A 48
(nr. Invergordon)
Tomich. High 3D 54
(nr. Lairg)
Tomintoul. Mor 2E 41
Tomnavoulin. Mor 1F 41
Tomsleibhe. Arg 5H 29
Tongland. Dum 3H 5
Tongue. High 3G 57
Torbeg. N Ayr 1D 8
Torbothie. N Lan 2D 18
Tore. High 3H 47
Torgyle. High 2E 39
Torinturk. Arg 2B 16
Torlum. W Isl 5H 61
Torlundy. High 1E 31
Tormitchell. S Ayr 4H 9
Tormore. High 3F 37
Tormore. N Ayr 5B 16
Tornagrain. High 4A 48
Tornaveen. Abers 3B 42
Torness. High 1G 39
Torpenhow. Cumb 5F 7
Torphichen. W Lot 1E 19
Torphins. Abers 3B 42
Torra. Arg 3E 15
Torran. High 4E 45
Torrance. E Dun 1B 18
Torrans. Arg 1B 22
Torranyard. E Ayr 4G 17
Torridon. High 3A 46
Torrin. High 1E 37
Torrisdale. Arg 5A 16
Torrisdale. High 2H 57
Torrish. High 2G 55
Torroble. High 3C 54
Torroy. High 4C 54
Torry. Aber 3E 43
Torryburn. Fife 5B 26
Torthorwald. Dum 1D 6
Torvaig. High 4D 44
Torwood. Falk 5H 25
Toscaig. High 5G 45
Totaig. High 3B 44
Totardor. High 5C 44
Tote. High 4D 44
Totegan. High 2B 58
Totronald. Arg 3C 28
Totscore. High 2C 44
Toulvaddie. High 5F 55
Toward. Arg 2E 17
Towie. Abers 2H 41
Towiemore. Mor 4G 49
Townend. W Dun 1H 17
Townhead. Cumb 5D 6
Townhead. Dum 4H 5
Townhead of Greenlaw. Dum 2A 6
Townhill. Fife 5C 26
Town Yetholm. Bord 1H 13
Trabboch. E Ayr 1B 10
Tradespark. High 3B 48
Tradespark. Orkn 4D 64
Tranent. E Lot 1B 20
Trantlebeg. High 3B 58
Trantlemore. High 3B 58
Traquair. Bord 5A 20
Treaslane. High 3C 44
Tressady. High 3D 54
Tressait. Per 2D 32
Tresta. Shet 3K 67
(on Fetlar)
Tresta. Shet 1C 66
(on Mainland)
Trinafour. Per 2C 32
Trinity. Ang 2D 34
Trinity. Edin 1H 19
Trislaig. High 1D 30
Trochry. Per 4E 33
Trondavoe. Shet 5G 67
Troon. S Ayr 5G 17
Troqueer. Dum 1C 6
Troutbeck. Cumb 5G 7
Trumaisgearraidh. W Isl 3J 61
Trumpan. High 2B 44
Tulchan. Per 1A 26
Tullibardine. Per 2A 26
Tullibody. Clac 4H 25
Tullich. Arg 2H 23
Tullich. High 4A 46
(nr. Lochcarron)
Tullich. High 1B 48
(nr. Tain)
Tullich. Mor 4G 49
Tullich Muir. High 1A 48
Tulliemet. Per 3E 33
Tulloch. Abers 5D 50
Tulloch. High 4D 54
(nr. Bonar Bridge)
Tulloch. High 5E 39
(nr. Fort William)
Tulloch. High 2C 40
(nr. Grantown-on-Spey)
Tulloch. Per 1B 26
Tullochgorm. Arg 4G 23
Tullybeagles Lodge. Per 5F 33
Tullymurdoch. Per 3G 33
Tullynessle. Abers 2A 42
Tummel Bridge. Per 3C 32
Tunga. W Isl 4J 63
Turfholm. S Lan 5D 18
Turnberry. S Ayr 3H 9
Turnhouse. Edin 1G 19
Turriff. Abers 4C 50
Turtory. Mor 4A 50
Tushielaw. Bord 2C 12
Twatt. Orkn 2B 64
Twatt. Shet 1C 66
Twechar. E Dun 1C 18
Tweedmouth. Nmbd 3G 21
Tweedsmuir. Bord 1H 11
Twynholm. Dum 3H 5
Tyndrum. Stir 5G 31
Tynehead. Midl 3A 20
Tyninghame. E Lot 1D 20
Tynron. Dum 4F 11
Tyrie. Abers 2E 51

U

Uachdar. W Isl 5J 61
Uags. High 5G 45
Uddingston. S Lan 2B 18
Uddington. S Lan 5D 18
Udny Green. Abers 1D 42
Udny Station. Abers 1E 43
Udston. S Lan 3C 18
Udstonhead. S Lan 4C 18
Ugadale. Arg 1C 8
Uidh. W Isl 5B 60
Uig. Arg 3C 28
Uig. High 2C 44
(nr. Balgown)
Uig. High 3A 44
(nr. Dunvegan)
Uigshader. High 4D 44
Uisken. Arg 2A 22
Ulbster. High 4G 59
Uldale. Cumb 5F 7
Ullapool. High 4G 53
Ullinish. High 5C 44
Ulsta. Shet 4H 67
Ulva House. Arg 5F 29
Unapool. High 5D 56
Underhoull. Shet 2J 67
Unthank. Cumb 4G 7
(nr. Carlisle)
Unthank. Cumb 5H 7
(nr. Penrith)
Unthank End. Cumb 5H 7
Uphall. W Lot 1F 19
Uphall Station. W Lot 1F 19
Uplawmoor. E Ren 3H 17
Uppat. High 3F 55
Upper Badcall. High 4C 56
Upper Bighouse. High 3B 58
Upper Boddam. Abers 5B 50
Upper Bogside. Mor 3F 49
Upper Boyndlie. Abers 2E 51
Upper Cuttlehill. Abers 4H 49
Upper Dallachy. Mor 2G 49
Upper Derraid. High 5D 48
Upper Diabaig. High 2H 45
Upper Dochcarty. High 2G 47
Upper Dounreay. High 2C 58
Upper Gills. High 1G 59
Upper Glenfintaig. High 5D 38
Upper Hindhope. Bord 3G 13
Upper Kirkton. Abers 5C 50
Upper Kirkton. N Ayr 3E 17
Upper Knockando. Mor 4E 49
Upper Knockchoilum. High 2F 39
Upper Largo. Fife 3F 27
Upper Latheron. High 5E 59
Upper Lenie. High 1G 39
Upper Lochton. Abers 4C 42
Upper Lybster. High 5F 59
Upper Milovaig. High 4A 44
Upper Neepaback. Shet 4J 67
Upper Ollach. High 5E 45
Upper Rusko. Dum 2G 5
Upper Sandaig. High 2G 37
Upper Sanday. Orkn 4E 64
Upper Skelmorlie. N Ayr 2E 17
Upper Sonachan. Arg 1H 23
Upper Tillyrie. Per 3C 26
Uppertown. High 1G 59
Uppertown. Orkn 5D 64
Upper Urquhart. Fife 3C 26
Upsettlington. Bord 4F 21
Upton. Cumb 5G 7
Urafirth. Shet 5G 67
Uragaig. Arg 4A 22
Urchany. High 4B 48
Ure. Shet 5F 67
Urgha. W Isl 5C 62
Urquhart. Mor 2F 49
Urray. High 3G 47
Usan. Ang 3E 35
Uyeasound. Shet 2J 67

V

Valsgarth. Shet 1K 67
Valtos. High 2E 45
Vatsetter. Shet 4J 67
Vatten. High 4B 44
Vaul. Arg 4B 28
Veensgarth. Shet 2D 66
Veness. Orkn 2E 64
Vidlin. Shet 6H 67
Viewpark. N Lan 2C 18
Village Bay. High 3B 44
Voe. Shet 6H 67
(nr. Hillside)
Voe. Shet 4G 67
(nr. Swinister)
Voxter. Shet 5G 67
Voy. Orkn 3B 64

W

Wadbister. Shet 2D 66
Wag. High 1H 55
Walby. Cumb 2H 7
Walkerburn. Bord 5A 20
Walkerton. Fife 3D 26
Wallaceton. Dum 5F 11
Wallacetown. Shet 1C 66
Wallacetown. S Ayr 1A 10
(nr. Ayr)
Wallacetown. S Ayr 3H 9
(nr. Dailly)
Walls. Shet 2B 66
Wallyford. E Lot 1A 20
Walnut Grove. Per 1C 26
Walston. S Lan 4F 19
Walton. Cumb 2H 7
Wampool. Cumb 3F 7
Wandel. S Lan 1G 11
Wanlockhead. Dum 2F 11
Wardhouse. Abers 5A 50
Warenton. Nmbd 5H 21
Wark. Nmbd 5F 21
(nr. Coldstream)
Wark. Nmbd 5H 13
(nr. Hexham)
Warmanbie. Dum 2E 7
Warse. High 1G 59
Warwick Bridge. Cumb 3H 7
Warwick-on-Eden. Cumb 3H 7
Wasbister. Orkn 1C 64
Watchhill. Cumb 4E 7
Waterbeck. Dum 1F 7
Waterfoot. E Ren 3A 18
Waterhead. E Ayr 2C 10
Waterhead. S Ayr 4A 10
Waterheads. Bord 3H 19
Waterloo. High 1F 37
Waterloo. N Lan 3D 18
Waterloo. Per 5F 33
Waterside. Cumb 4F 7
Waterside. E Ayr 3B 10
(nr. Ayr)
Waterside. E Ayr 4H 17
(nr. Kilmarnock)
Waterside. E Dun 1B 18
Waterstein. High 4A 44
Watten. High 3F 59
Wattston. N Lan 1C 18
Waulkmill. Abers 4B 42
Waverbridge. Cumb 4F 7
Waverton. Cumb 4F 7
Wedderlairs. Abers 5D 50
Weem. Per 4D 32
Weetwood Hall. Nmbd 5H 21
Wellbank. Ang 5B 34
Welldale. Dum 2E 7
Wells of Ythan. Abers 5B 50
Wellwood. Fife 5B 26
Welton. Cumb 4G 7
Wemyss Bay. Inv 1E 17
West Allerdean. Nmbd 4G 21
West Arthurlie. E Ren 3H 17
West Barns. E Lot 1D 20
West Bennan. N Ayr 1E 9
West Burnside. Abers 1E 35
West Burrafirth. Shet 1B 66
West Calder. W Lot 2F 19
West Clyne. High 3F 55
West Croftmore. High 2C 40
West Cullerlie. Abers 3C 42
West Culvennan. Dum 2D 4
West Curthwaite. Cumb 4G 7
West Dunnet. High 1F 59
West End. S Lan 4E 19
Wester Aberchalder.
High 2G 39
Wester Balgedie. Per 3C 26
Wester Brae. High 2H 47
Wester Culbeuchly. Abers 2B 50
Westerdale. High 3E 59
Wester Dechmont. W Lot 1F 19
Wester Fearn. High 5D 54
Wester Galcantray. High 4B 48
Wester Gruinards. High 4C 54
Westerloch. High 3G 59
Wester Mandally. High 3D 38
Wester Quarff. Shet 3D 66
Wester Rarichie. High 1B 48
Wester Shian. Per 5D 32
Wester Skeld. Shet 2B 66
Westerton. Ang 3D 34
Westerwick. Shet 2B 66
Westfield. Cumb 5C 6
Westfield. High 2D 58
Westfield. N Lan 1C 18
Westfield. W Lot 1E 19
Westfields of Rattray.
Per 4G 33
Westhall Terrace. Ang 5B 34
West Helmsdale. High 2H 55
West Heogaland. Shet 5F 67
Westhill. Abers 3D 42
Westhill. High 4A 48
West Horton. Nmbd 5H 21
West Houlland. Shet 1B 66
West Hynish. Arg 5A 28
Westing. Shet 2J 67
West Kilbride. N Ayr 4F 17
West Kyloe. Nmbd 4H 21
West Langwell. High 3D 54
West Learmouth. Nmbd 5F 21
West Lingo. Fife 3F 27
Westlinton. Cumb 2G 7
West Linton. Bord 3G 19
West Mains. Per 2A 26
Westmoor End. Cumb 5D 6
West Muir. Ang 2C 34
(nr. Brechin)
Westmuir. Ang 3A 34
(nr. Forfar)
West Murkle. High 2E 59
Westness. Orkn 2C 64
Westnewton. Cumb 4E 7
Westnewton. Nmbd 5G 21
Weston. S Lan 4F 19
Westown. Per 1D 26
West Pitcorthie. Fife 3G 27
West Plean. Stir 5H 25
Westray Airport. Orkn 2G 65
Westrigg. W Lot 2E 19
Westruther. Bord 3D 20
West Saltoun. E Lot 2B 20
West Sandwick. Shet 4H 67
Westside. Orkn 2C 64
West Strathan. High 2G 57
West Tarbert. Arg 2B 16
Westward. Cumb 4F 7
West Wemyss. Fife 4E 27
Westwood. S Lan 3B 18
West Woodburn. Nmbd 5H 13
West Woodside. Cumb 4G 7
West Yell. Shet 4H 67
Wetheral. Cumb 3H 7
Wethersta. Shet 6G 67
Weydale. High 2E 59
Whauphill. Dum 4F 5
Whelpo. Cumb 5G 7
Whigstreet. Ang 4B 34
Whinnyfold. Abers 5E 51
Whitburn. W Lot 2E 19
Whitchester. Bord 3E 21
Whitebog. High 2A 48
Whitebridge. High 2F 39
Whitecairns. Abers 2E 43
White Corries. High 3F 31
Whitecraig. E Lot 1A 20
Whitecross. Falk 1E 19
Whiteface. High 5E 55
Whitefarland. N Ayr 4B 16
Whitefaulds. S Ayr 3H 9
Whiteford. Abers 1C 42
Whitehall. Orkn 5J 65
Whitehill. N Ayr 3F 17
Whitehills. Abers 2B 50
Whitehills. Ang 3B 34
Whitehouse. Abers 2B 42
Whitehouse. Arg 2B 16
Whiteinch. Glas 2A 18
Whitekirk. E Lot 5G 27
Whitemire. Mor 3C 48
Whiteness. Shet 2D 66
Whiterashes. Abers 1D 42
Whiterow. High 4G 59
Whiterow. Mor 3D 48
Whiteside. W Lot 2E 19
Whitestone. Abers 4B 42
Whitestones. Abers 3D 50
Whitewreath. Mor 3F 49
Whitfield. D'dee 5B 34
Whithorn. Dum 4F 5
Whiting Bay. N Ayr 1F 9
Whitletts. S Ayr 1A 10
Whitrigg. Cumb 5F 7
(nr. Kirkbride)
Whitrigg. Cumb 5F 7
(nr. Torpenhow)
Whitsome. Bord 3F 21
Whitton. Bord 1G 13
Whygate. Nmbd 5G 13
Wick. High 3G 59
Wick. Shet 3D 66
(on Mainland)
Wick. Shet 2J 67
(on Unst)
Wick Airport. High 3G 59
Widewall. Orkn 5D 64
Wiggonby. Cumb 3F 7
Wigton. Cumb 4F 7
Wigtown. Dum 3F 5
Wildmanbridge. S Lan 3D 18
Wilkhaven. High 5G 55
Wilkieston. W Lot 2G 19
Williamsetter. Shet 4C 66
Wilsontown. S Lan 3E 19
Wilton. Bord 2E 13
Winchburgh. W Lot 1F 19
Windhill. High 4G 47
Windyedge. Abers 4E 43
Windygates. Fife 3E 27
Windyknowe. W Lot 2E 19
Winless. High 3G 59
Winscales. Cumb 5D 6
Wishaw. N Lan 3D 18
Wiston. S Lan 5E 19
Wolfhill. Per 5G 33
Wolsty. Cumb 3E 7
Woodhall. Inv 1G 17
Woodhaven. Fife 1F 27
Woodhead. Abers 2E 51
(nr. Fraserburgh)
Woodhead. Abers 5C 50
(nr. Fyvie)
Woodlands. Abers 4C 42
Woodrow. Cumb 4F 7
Woodside. Aber 3E 43
Woodside. Dum 1D 6
Woodside. Fife 3F 27
Woodside. Per 5H 33
Woodwick. Orkn 2C 64
Wooler. Nmbd 5G 21
Woolfords. S Lan 3F 19
Work. Orkn 3D 64
Workington. Cumb 5C 6
Wormit. Fife 1E 27
Wreay. Cumb 4H 7
Wyng. Orkn 5C 64
Wythop Mill. Cumb 5E 7
Wyvis Lodge. High 1F 47

Y

Yanwath. Cumb 5H 7
Yarrow. Nmbd 5G 13
Yarrow. Bord 1C 12
Yarrow Feus. Bord 1C 12
Yarrow Ford. Bord 5B 20
Yearngill. Cumb 4E 7
Yeavering. Nmbd 5G 21
Yesnaby. Orkn 3B 64
Yett. N Lan 3C 18
Yett. S Ayr 1B 10
Yetts o' Muckhart. Clac 3B 26
Yieldshields. S Lan 3D 18
Yinstay. Orkn 3E 64
Yoker. Glas 2A 18
Yonder Bognie. Abers 4A 50
Yonderton. Abers 5E 51
Ythanbank. Abers 5E 51
Ythanwells. Abers 5B 50

HOW TO USE THE PLACES OF INTEREST INDEX

This is an index to selected features shown on the map pages in Scotland only.
The index reference is to the square in which the symbol (or its pointer) appears; the text may be in a different square; e.g. Carscreugh Castle . . .3D 4 is to be found in square 3D on page 4.

Entries shown without an index reference have the name of the appropriate town plan on which they appear. For reasons of clarity, these places of interest do not appear on the main map pages. The extent of these town plans are indicated on the main pages by a blue box.
Terms such as 'museum' etc. are omitted from the text on the map; a key to the various map symbols used can be found on page 2 in the reference.
Any category in the index that does not have its own symbol in the reference will be depicted by a dot.

Entries in italics are not named on the map but are shown with a symbol.
For this type of entry, the nearest village or town name is given, where that name is not already included in the name of the place of interest.

Opening times for places of interest vary considerably depending on the season, day of week or the ownership of the property.
Please check with the nearest Tourist or Visit Scotland Information Centre listed below before starting your journey.

NTS, National Trust for Scotland Property - Always open.   NTS, National Trust for Scotland Property - Restricted opening.   HS, Historic Scotland - Always open.
NP, National Park Property - Always open.   NP, National Park Property - Restricted opening.

Loch View

D

Linlithgow

E

F

G

Lighthouse at Sunset

H

The Grid on this map is the National Grid taken from Ordnance Survey® mapping with the permission of the Controller of Her Majesty's Stationery Office.

Photo credits: © Barnabys Picture Library — St Monance, Aberdeen, Crathes Castle, Devorgilla Bridge, Loch Ken, Dundee Museum, Arbroath Cliffs, Forth Bridge, Loch Lomond, Edinburgh Tatoo, George Square, Oban Bay (Back Cover), St Andrews, St Andrews 18th Green, View from Stirling Castle.

© BigStock.com — Eilean Donan Castle (Front Cover), Glenfinnan Monument, View from Edinburgh Castle.

© PhotoDisc — Autumn Loch Ness, Mountain Landscape (Page 2), Loch in Scottish Highlands, Glasgow University, Stirling Castle, Loch View, Linlithgow, Lighthouse at Sunset, Reflection in Loch.

SAFETY CAMERA INFORMATION

PocketGPSWorld.com's CamerAlert is a self-contained speed and red light camera warning system for SatNavs and Android or Apple iOS smartphones/tablets. Visit www.cameralert.co.uk to download.

Safety camera locations are publicised by the Safer Roads Partnership which operates them in order to encourage drivers to comply with speed limits at these sites. It is the driver's absolute responsibility to be aware of and to adhere to speed limits at all times.

By showing this safety camera information it is the intention of Geographers' A-Z Map Company Ltd., to encourage safe driving and greater awareness of speed limits and vehicle speed. Data accurate at time of printing.